Ninety-Nine Windows

Reflections of a Reporter from Arabia to Africa
and Other Roads Less Travelled

Karim Ben Khelifa photo

News. Travel. Life. This is all inside *Ninety-Nine Windows*, a humane and engaging look behind the headlines with newspaper columnist Thomas Froese.

It is shortly after the historic 9/11 attacks on the United States when Froese begins his reflections from the airport cargo office in Sana'a, Yemen. Ninety-nine columns later, he concludes from the intrigue of Uganda, Africa. In between, he skillfully navigates some of the world's bumpier roads to explore themes ranging from culture to politics to spirituality.

Whether he is commenting on the Iraq War or the terrorist murder of his friends, or on lighter issues like the taste of Mecca Cola or the beauty of the African bicycle, Froese writes with his signature personal style. His captivating photos and biographical addendums complete this exceptional collection.

An educator and storyteller, a provocateur and wry humourist, Froese invites us onto his proverbial bus to discover these less-travelled places...and to stir the traveller in each of us.

Thank you for purchasing *Ninety-Nine Windows*. Net proceeds from the sale of this book are donated to the international charity Save the Mothers (www.savethemothers.org). Thank you for your donation.

ninety-nine WINDOWS

thomas froese

Epic Press
Belleville, Ontario, Canada

NINETY-NINE WINDOWS

Library and Archives Canada Cataloguing in Publication

Froese, Thomas, 1965-
Ninety-nine windows : reflections of a reporter from Arabia to Africa and other roads less travelled / Thomas Froese.

ISBN 978-1-55452-293-4.--ISBN 978-1-55452-349-8 (Hardcover ed.)
--ISBN 978-1-55452-309-2 (LSI ed.)

1. Froese, Thomas, 1965-. 2. Journalists--Canada--Biography. 3. Foreign
correspondents--Canada--Biography. 4. Journalists--Biography. 5. Foreign correspondents--Biography. I. Title.

PN4913.F76A2 2008 070.4'332092 C2008-904856-3

To order additional copies:

Contact the author at thomasfroese@thomasfroese.com
or through his website at www.thomasfroese.com
or call toll free in North America, 1-866-786-2350, at Save the Mothers

For more information from *Essence Publishing*, contact:
20 Hanna Court, Belleville, Ontario, Canada K8P 5J2.
Phone: 1-800-238-6376. Fax: (613) 962-3055.
E-mail: info@essence-publishing.com
Web site: www.essence-publishing.com

For Elizabeth and Jonathan,
my Two Young Royal Travellers

The world is a book, and those who do not travel read only one page.

Saint Augustine

Table of Contents

Addendums

Acknowledgments

Some years ago at the Savoy Theatre, in London, I saw *Letter of Resignation*, a stage drama which had one of those offbeat lines that lasts a lifetime.

As it goes, it's 1963 and Britain's Prime Minister Harold Macmillan is dealing with the call-girl sex scandal involving Secretary of War John Profumo. It's a political crisis which, in this stage version, evokes Macmillan's memories of some decades earlier when his wife, Lady Dorothy, had a lengthy affair with Macmillan's friend and political ally Robert Boothby. He recalls Dorothy even telling him of her '*plans*' to leave him for her lover Boothby.

To which the young Macmillan says, "Do you want to know what makes God laugh?"

"Tell me, Harold," Dorothy dryly responds. "What makes God laugh?"

"People making plans."

And so I have found this truism: it's good not to over-script our lives, fragile and brief and beautiful as they are, but rather to open them to possible currents and directions outside of our own devices, knowing a surprise or two will surely come along.

For me, this book is one of those surprises. Or, more accurately, it's the culmination of a series of surprises. Nevertheless, its eventual production did take planning. And it's a house of words that stands on a foundation that was laid with purpose and intention long ago.

For this, I give thanks to my friends and family: my personal mentors. You know who you are. I also thank my various scholastic and writing mentors, including columnists I've enjoyed: Herman Gooden, Michael Coren, Allan Fotheringham, Dave Barry, Rex Murphy and, in particular, the late Rich Mullins.

For initially publishing my work, thank you to editors Casey Korstanje, Rob Howard and Kevin Cavanagh of the *Hamilton Spectator*, and Larry Cornies, formerly of the *London Free Press*. Without you, this collection would not exist.

Doug Koop and editors of *Christian Week*, editors of the *New Vision* in Uganda, and editors of the *Waterloo Region Record*, thanks also for putting my views on your pages. Walid al-Saqaaf, thank you for making my *Yemen Times* experience so rich. Doug Wicken, thank you for showing me how to hold a camera so long ago. And thank you to Sherrill Brunton and Essence

Publishing for both your book design and your patience as this project evolved.

Finally, a special thank you to My Royal Babe, that is Darling Doctor Wife, and our Two Younglings for giving me so much.

Oh ... and Harold and Dorothy? Her plans eventually changed. And the couple lived a happy life together for many, many years.

Preface

In the brilliant movie *Amistad*, there's a scene with John Quincy Adams, an aging former U.S. president played by Anthony Hopkins, and Theodore Joadson, a lawyer and freed slave played by Morgan Freeman.

Joadson is at Adams' home asking for advice on the 20-some-odd African slaves who are at the centre of this true story, set in 1839, about the politics and impending trial that involves their rights after they were transported on the Spanish ship La Amistad.

The sage Adams, known by his political colleagues as Old Man Eloquent, is mumbling and pacing in front of his fireplace, appearing rather uninterested.

"What is their story?" he finally asks.

Joadson, who has a rather remarkable story of escape and survival himself, rattles off some details like facts on a curriculum vitae.

"No!" interrupts Adams. "What is their STORY? "You have proved *what* the slaves are, Mr. Joadson. They're Africans! Congratulations! But what you don't know and haven't bothered in the least to discover is *who* they are."

Adams continues to drive home the point that, like nothing else, a person's story reveals their deepest value.

He asks Joadson if he would like to be known as just a Georgian. "No! Mr. Joadson, you're an ex-slave who has devoted his life to the abolitionist movement, with many trials and hardships along the way I imagine. Now THAT is your story, isn't it?"

Narrative is that close to our hearts, that enmeshed in our souls. We are hardwired for it, told long ago in the Great Book of Old that in the very beginning there was ... the Word ... the beginning of His-Story.

At its best, this is what journalism is about.

True, this old trade might also be prone to a few flaws. The same John Quincy Adams reportedly once said that "Journalists are sort of assassins who sit with loaded blunderbusses at the corners of streets and fire them off for sport at any passenger they select."

Another politician of the era, Otto van Bismark, quipped that "A journalist is someone who has missed his calling."

Or consider G.K. Chesterton's astute assessment that "Journalism largely consists of saying 'Lord Jones Dead' to people who never knew Lord Jones was alive." Today more than ever it seems we live in this, a world with information but no context: Coleridge's proverbial water, water everywhere with nothing to drink.

Yet in our broken and sceptical times, it seems to me that journalism is still among the better of public services to bring a measure of healing and truth to our various communities.

And if it's true that story is largely humanity's purpose, then to write stories, even seemingly inconsequential scribbles on dead trees or on other mediums that still end up in history's trash heap, becomes a task that is both noble and humbling: one of those vocations in which you can lose yourself, to find who you really are.

So I'm profoundly thankful (and a little surprised) to introduce myself as the storyteller in this collection, the scribe, the one who is opening windows into some unknown places. Indeed, two decades on, I easily recall my modest first journalism job at a dairy magazine, reporting on milkmen and cows and the finer merits of round bales of hay. (A few months later – as it turns out, 20 years to the day before this book's formal release on January 1, 2009 – I found my way to my first newspaper job at St. Thomas' daily *Times-Journal.*)

Now these new roads.

Travelling them together, I think that we will become friends, you and I. My only regret is that our conversation will be so one-way, with you looking into my world, but I not having the same chance to see into yours.

However, like *Amistad's* Joadson, I am reminded anew that we all have a story. And while we aren't allowed to choose much of the frame of our destiny, the things that we put inside will always be fully ours: our life to squander or our life to grow.

So we risk. We reflect. And we leave something behind. This, I believe, is the substance of any of our stories.

Through these 99 selections, you are about to hear some of mine.

And someday, when all the stories are told, I will hear yours.

I look forward to that.

Thomas Froese
Kampala, Uganda
September 2008

W

Introduction

Memories of Dispatch One: A foreigner arrives

Before we start we need to go to the beginning, to Day One of Week Two of my life as a foreigner in Yemen.

I sit in a dilapidated cargo office at the international airport in the ancient city of Sana'a, on a mountain plateau some 2,000 metres above the sea, without a clue of what might await.

Some one million souls live in Sana'a, among the oldest inhabited cities on earth: according to legend the city of one of Noah's sons, a time-warped capital known as the Pearl of Arabia Felix, a place that for centuries was closed to foreigners.

The only things I'm reasonably certain about on this warm morning is that both the Queen of Sheba and Osama bin Laden hail from around here, and I'm likely the only person in the country wearing a Team Canada cap.

On a wall is an already-dated poster advertising a regional airline. Pictured, as if looking through an airliner cockpit, are popular global destinations like New York's Statue of Liberty and the World Trade Center's Twin Towers.

"Fly with us and see the world," says the ad, innocuously. Nobody has bothered to replace it by this day, some six months after September 11, 2001, that fateful day when a generation's defining moment crashed into our memories.

I'm waiting to collect my family's cargo sent from Canada. Over his shoulder a clerk wears a dirty *mushadda*, a red-and-white checkered shawl. He's pleasant and proudly asks if he should write my form in English or Arabic.

"English," I say.

"Are you American?" he then asks.

"Canadian," I say.

He smiles and nods. "Canadian okay. Better than American."

The airline poster looms large again, and my mind wanders to a meaningful and memorable visit once had over an Easter weekend with a friend in New York City.

Before long a cargo manager tells me that I need to return to the office "tomorrow" as it's now closing. It's just 11:30 in the morning.

A stranger comes to help, and after some hours of paper shuffling, a dozen signatures and several dips into my pockets for dirty, worn Yemeni currency (Riyals), my bins of personal belongings are released.

"I am the computer," is the parting comment from another clerk, at a last stop near the exit and loading bay, while he prints in a large ledger.

A Korean doctor friend, John, helps load my bins onto the rooftop of a beaten Toyota 4x4. John is still learning to navigate the English language, but he skillfully drives the load through the dusty and exhaust-filled streets of Sana'a.

Our vehicle meanders through strange scenes. There are goats, and women in head-to-toe black baltos looking like walking bowling pins, and men walking bowlegged, wearing dirty white robes, those checkered *mushaddas* on their heads and *jambias*, ceremonial daggers, around their waists. Some faces are worn as old maps, looking older than the average lifespan of a Yemeni man, which, so they say, is now 56 years.

It's obvious why this country has among the world's highest traffic death rates. There are apparently 14 streetlights in the capital. Looks like half don't work. Hundreds of other intersections operate on a kind of first-honk, first-drive basis. Vehicles, almost all old white Toyotas, funnel through: wobbly cars; battered *dubabs*, or taxi vans, with cracked windshields and sliding doors left open; plus undersized and overloaded motorcycles with everyone aboard wearing dusty flip-flops, but no helmets.

We reach home safely to My Royal Babe (Darling Doctor Wife). Jean is a Canadian obstetrician whose ever-growing heartbeat is to help save some of the many women in the developing world who die in childbirth, starting here in this *Felix*, or "Happy," Arabia.

We live on a typical side street. It's paved coarsely but, like many roads, has no name. Sana'a also has no phone directory. Osama could be around the corner on another street with no name, for all we know. Our apartment-flat is not posh, the ground level of a typical multi-storey Yemeni home. But it has a Western-style flush toilet, and we're thankful.

Please, come in.

Here in the front hall is where we'll later put our big Canadian flag. And there, a rather striking photo of a shepherd girl holding a lamb from the nearby countryside. Around the corner, our office will have posters of Martin Luther King and his thoughts on freedom. They'll be hung near our huge world map.

Over there are the stairs up to the landlord's, "Doctor" Ali, a pharmacist with one wife and four kids.

This is the beginning of my life as a somewhat bewildered Canadian in Arabia. Soon, the Iraq war will break out. Soon, terrorism and death will also pound on our door in a much more personal way. Joys will also come. This little flat will become the first home of our First Royal Youngling.

Flash forward six years. I have had opportunity to write columns from not just the Middle East but also Africa, and extra travels in Europe, South

America and several provinces across Canada. Many are collected into what you hold in your hands.

Darling Doctor Wife and I now have Two Royal Younglings. And while our world map still takes a wall in our study, it's now located some 10 degrees west and 15 degrees south of Sana'a in our current overseas home, in Africa, in the Kampala capital region of Uganda.

What has remained constant is something that my New York City friend told me during that past Easter visit when he showed me the slums of Brooklyn where he grew up. "You have to look past what you see to know what it's really like here."

And so I'm learning. Whether you're in the slums of New York or in developing world corners like Sana'a or Kampala, or in the rich mansions of Beverly Hills, people are people. In this sense we're all travellers, at times meeting each other when our paths are fated to cross, but often not, often just looking, observing, maybe fearing each other.

In his autobiography *Up from Slavery,* American activist Booker T. Washington says this is our challenge, "to bring the strong, wealthy and learned into helpful touch with the poorest, most ignorant and humblest, and at the same time make one appreciate the vitalizing, strengthening influence of the other."

My own cultural baggage and natural flaws, some critical journalistic inclinations and imperfect interpretive eye have kept me from doing this in its fullness. But I hope that I can still put you in meaningful touch with important issues and themes and, more so, with people, fellow sojourners whom you would otherwise never see very closely: people who are different, but who are also like you and I, seeking purpose and value, maybe even joy, even while knowing life has trouble along the way.

It was all not supposed to be this way. When I left home as a rather unripe 20-year-old, I had planned to go to theological college. My Mennonite forefathers would have smiled. Instead I fell into journalism, a world of pictures and words, the so-called black art: spilling ink to paper – becoming a different kind of scribe, becoming "This Scribe" – baptized into the ways of the newspaper, an old and venerable but very earthy type of organ.

So it was on this type of road less travelled that I discovered this rich calling, and discovered it has married well with my heritage. If you want a better look into this part of my background, jump to Window 27 – "The road to hell" and Window 51 – "Dirty feet" and their following addendums.

Many of the 99 columns that make up the bulk of this book first appeared on the opinion pages of the *Hamilton Spectator,* among Canada's more decorated newspapers, while most of the others ran in another regional newspaper, the *London Free Press.*

The addendums attached to some of these 99 windows weave a second journey. Some give more observations about Arabia and Africa, but most give some behind-the-scenes views and a biographical sketch: my family heritage and spiritual journey, some highlights from reporting in St. Thomas, Canada, (an incarnation that preceded life as a foreign correspondent), and some notes about the Royal Younglings and Darling Doctor Wife.

These 99 commentaries are also organized by theme, starting with a section on my beginnings with Jean, and ending with an important section on the world's neediest mothers. If you want to get straight to the humour, jump to Section 7 - The Lighter Side of Arabia Felix, and Section 17 - A Few More Light Ones.

With a home on either side of the ocean, I am richly blessed. I get what I call "two lives for the price of one." Your invitation, then, is to travel with me (and my family) through these pages, in order or out of order, in any direction you may find yourself wandering.

But please do travel with expectation. Because it's my hope that this is more than just a pragmatic exercise in reading the ruminations of some Canadian journalist, but that it's all entertaining and relaxing – like you're sitting on a proverbial bus, or maybe in a quieter place, in front of an open window with a fresh breeze blowing gently, able to pause every now and then, look out on your horizon and muse, "I enjoyed that. I really enjoyed that."

The prize doesn't always go to the swiftest horse; just the one that keeps running in the right direction. And success in journalism can come from a strange mix that involves, as much as anything else, unexplained chance.

I first learned this as a young graduate when I couldn't even get hired to report for the Lindsay Post, a publication in Central Ontario that I was told was "Canada's worst daily newspaper."

I had a friend in Lindsay and saw his father the day I was interviewed. "Just remember, if you don't get this job, there's a reason," he told me. He was right. Doors close. Windows open. And this collection of commentaries from the far side of the world is largely the result of my great fortune in marriage.

When Jean and I met many years after that Lindsay Post experience, she was already concerned about the horrific rate of women dying in childbirth in developing countries and was already packing to go to, of all strange places, Yemen.

One day while driving near my home, New Doctor Friend asked, "Would you ever consider moving overseas?"

I pictured myself as a water carrier in a dusty Yemeni village. "No," I said, content to continue life as a journalist in St. Thomas, Ontario, an unpretentious but homey-enough place, an old railway city just north of Lake Erie. Canada may be cold, I reasoned, but with a parka it's still comfortable.

Not long after, New Doctor Friend went off alone to Sana'a, Yemen's capital. I hopped a plane to visit. She hopped a plane to come back. Then, barely a year after meeting me, this exceptional woman became My Royal Babe, that is Darling Doctor Wife.

The words of "Dream Come True" and "Seize the Day" – our wedding songs – remain as vivid today as on that midsummer day, which was soon followed by 9/11. After our families and the world recovered from mass nervousness, we moved together to that Sana'a apartment-flat on a street with no name.

With a dozen years of journalism experience now behind me, I transitioned to foreign correspondent with little fuss. And so this has been another marriage, one of our vocations.

Darling Doctor Wife's vision to save some of the globe's 525,000 women who now die needlessly every year in childbirth is also a unique calling, one that I've referred to from the beginning as a vision of a princess for the poor. My own mother died in my early boyhood, so I understand what such a loss means. This then ties us at another level.

So we feel not only called, but called as a team in a unique and divine way, one that goes beyond simple chance. These introductory pieces share more of our beginnings.

Opposite page photo: *The front page of the author's limited-run edition of the St. Thomas Times-Journal, Feb. 14, 2001.*

First, My Lady

St. Thomas
Times-Journal
75¢ (incl. GST)
Warm, bright, clear +10 Wednesday, February 14, 2001
Special Edition

Royal wedding

• Tomorrow: All eyes turn to St. Thomas
• Friday: 'Save the Mothers?' A princess for the poor
• Our view: These kids will last - Page 6

By
Oswald J. Smith Chambers
in London
and
Martin Luther von Goethe
in Berlin

A pauper in paradise - 1

LONDON, CANADA
July 28, 2001

1

"I am a pauper in paradise. Better this than a king in chains."
Lyric by Frozen Ghost

So, the infamous marriage of Charles and Di wasn't so loveless, at least not at first. Such is the latest from the information peddlers of the royal *unio mystica*, the mysterious union that lives in perpetuity since launched via satellite to 750 million people, 20 years ago tomorrow.

It was July 29, 1981, when the world watched the liftoff of what eventually became the mother of all marital disasters. The Hindenburg fared better.

Charles has since manicured his public image, but, for better or worse, he'll be remembered as the leading man in the sad tale of a dead princess. And I, for one, am left asking how to do better.

As a man who has lived many years without matching socks, I am hardly an expert on this type of thing. I know the art – and it is an art – of living single. Marriage, I've observed only from shore.

Tomorrow, however, I say goodbye. Tomorrow, Sunday, July 29, is my wedding day, a coincidence that's strikingly humorous because I was informed of it weeks after whipping up a little engagement soufflé. It included the town crier and a run of mock newspapers. Complete with "Royal Wedding" header and smiling photos of two royal children, the Valentine's news circulated at the Grand Theatre and over London radio.

I may be a pauper, but I've dreamed of more. And, quite frankly, I've had help by studying at a royal academy of sorts.

Among the things there is the marshmallow test. I refer to experiments at Stanford University, where Professor Walter Mischel found certain four-year-olds could resist the lure of a marshmallow when promised they'd get two for waiting. He also discovered that the tykes who delayed gratification had more successes in their lives than those who grabbed without thinking.

We're talking sex, and most of us have failed rather miserably here.

The walking wounded, we've enjoyed the lie of Oscar Wilde, who said celibacy is the only known sexual perversion. In the UK, for instance, one per cent of men and four per cent of women are virgins when they first walk the aisle. How telling.

My bride, an obstetrician-gynecologist, can tell about the disease factor.

Respect and trust also enter this picture. She and I have plenty of both.

Amazingly, virgins in our mid-thirties, neither of us have had any body parts fall off. The way we see it, you can't get your body in shape without work, and getting fit for marriage is no different.

If nothing else, then, a prince does the right thing to the right person at the right time. He verbalizes the same.

Anne Morrow Lindberg refers to this in *A Gift from the Sea*. She writes of finding herself loved, the rather unbelievable feeling that changed her world, how she was given confidence, strength and new character. The man she was to marry believed in her and what she could do, and consequently she found she could do more than she realized. Harvard professor Robert Rosenthal coined this the Pygmalion Effect, the phenomena we achieve to the level of expectations of significant others.

Royal bulimia, it seems, is one of the results of failing this particular test. Scoring well, on the other hand, boosts commitment, appreciation and communication. And aren't they basic ingredients of good friendship?

My princess and I are among more than 600 souls who will marry in St. Thomas this year. Ten times as many will marry in London. Storms will inevitably arise. And, as it is now, roughly half of our ships will go down after, on average, 13 years. Innocent children will drown in the process. Is this not tragic?

I wonder if things would be different if, as singles, we gave as much attention to sailing as to our vocations. How many of us, though, will take the time to study ship construction before heading out? Blueprints happen to be in the language of the other gender. Do we bother to learn it? How many of us are relaxing and enjoying the beach while walking it alone?

Poor Charles isn't that bad a role model. We're actually helpless victims of an unstoppable divorce culture. And it's impossible to prepare for the unknowns of marriage.

If you buy such societal nonsense, good luck.

If I did, I wouldn't give my life away. I wouldn't believe in the power of faith. And I certainly would not look to the goodness of tomorrow.

Bon voyage.

Leaving it all behind 2

Sana'a, Yemen
October 5, 2002

Folks who lined up to throw pies at the prime minister for his candid suggestion that 9/11 was linked with growing global disparities and Western greed may want to stop reading this. The rest of you may meet my wife Jean, a woman I thank God for every day.

Say hello while she's back in Hamilton for McMaster University's fourth annual International Women's Health Symposium. Circle November 8 if you're interested in knowing more of the terrible global tragedy of women dying during childbirth.

Worldwide, almost 600,000 women now die annually while giving birth. That's the same as three jumbo jets filled with pregnant women crashing daily. Today, if your mom or wife or sister or daughter were on such a plane, would it matter?

In Hamilton, one mom dies about every two years during childbirth. For every maternal death in Hamilton, however, 115 women die in university hospitals here in Sana'a. Across Yemen, a staggering one in nine women won't survive delivery. It's not commonly known, but the rate of maternal death is actually the largest discrepancy in public health care between rich and poor countries.

Jean, a McMaster University obstetrician-gynecologist, is making the issue her life's work. The symposium she organizes at the Royal Botanical Gardens in Burlington is part of that.

Journalist Sally Armstrong, author of *Veiled Threat: The Hidden Power of the Women of Afghanistan,* is among the speakers who will talk of the challenges women face in the Third World, that is, the majority of the world. Others will share how organizations such as governments and universities, not to mention participants, can help.

Note, Jean's current work in impoverished Yemen is possible thanks to private sponsors and a unique relationship with McMaster. It's a template I imagine others would also desire, to bring their own skills to an area where they're needed most.

"Global tensions are giving people exposure to things outside their borders," Jean says. "That doesn't mean they know more about women's health, but they know more about the inequity of resources."

Jean's vision, though, goes beyond what she can accomplish herself. She's now spearheading the birth of a Canadian-based international program to see professionals in the Third World care for their people by linking with experts and resources in rich countries such as Canada. It involves creating training centres in as many developing countries as possible over the decades.

Known as Save the Mothers, the program will outlive Jean if it becomes what we hope. And it will need support from many organizations.

Jean also has written a manuscript, *Where Have All the Mothers Gone?* Based on previous experience in Africa, the work is now seeking a publisher. But I thank God for Jean, not because of what she does but because of who she is.

My wife is the only person I've seen literally shed tears for people she's never met. Her parents tell me she was just a little girl when she first announced her desire to be a doctor for poor people far away. That would have been near the time my own mother died, the summer before I started kindergarten.

It's been said that we need to be willing to leave the life we've planned to get the life waiting for us. If this is true – and I've found it is – then the West is facing a significant crossroads. September 11, 2001, for all its horror, is the mother of all wake-up calls, especially for a new generation tired of hollow definitions of success. Didn't this summer's visit by Pope John Paul show what many yearn for? Lose yourself; gain life.

That's why I don't accept the nonsense of the PM's attackers. They hoard things they don't own. I'm not saying the West should feel false guilt for being rich or for the evil terrorist acts of others. Our tremendous institutions have historically helped bring various freedoms to many people.

But have you heard of the Rich Young Ruler? Eventually his wealth defined who he was. And at the end of the day he lost his soul because he couldn't walk away from it all.

How sad.

A pauper in paradise - 2 3

LONDON, ENGLAND
MAY 21, 2005

It's been said that if you find a good friend in life, you're fortunate. Find two, and you're exceptionally blessed. And if you have three, then you're surely mistaken.

The thought comes to mind while Jean and I are across the pond, in London, promoting Jean's brainchild, Save the Mothers International.

It's a fitting place to be, because five years ago today we met in Ontario's London. A planned group event at a Victoria Day fireworks became our first date when nobody else showed up. Jean's been unable to get rid of me ever since.

Here in the original London, the big yawn these days is the Camilla Effect. Think of the Diana Effect, tornado that it was, and turn it inside out. Yes, the Camilla Effect has been England's biggest non-story for months. "Old Gits to Wed" was one headline about Charles and Camilla's scruffy walk to the altar.

It's precious little for British media that normally feed off royal fare such as illicit trysts, bulimia and Nazi armbands. The attention paid to the Charles and Camilla nuptials was a far cry from the 750 million people who tuned in to watch Charles and Diana's fairy-tale wedding at St. Paul's Cathedral in the summer of 1981. It's light-years from Di's funeral.

Jean, who was in London during both of those events, says about the first, "All I remember is that dress and its train that went on for three miles." And the second, "The flowers seemed to never end."

That's the Diana Effect.

Which begs the question: Rather than doing the mistress thing and all but destroy a princess, not to mention their own spirits, why didn't Charles and Camilla simply marry decades ago, before Di even came along?

Apparently because Camilla, who we know is no oil painting, didn't have enough majestic appeal for the palace. And the prince, who reportedly gets his toothpaste squeezed for him by a valet, wasn't man enough to either leave her altogether or put his overbearing family in its royal place.

That really would have saved an ocean of grief. But we live in strange times, where pollsters say 98 per cent of Brits disapprove of drunk driving but half believe adultery is fine "under certain circumstances."

With that said, it seems to me that this new, rather dull face of England's monarchy is not a bad thing. Because unlike the dreamy Diana Effect, Camilla and Charles are now displaying a marriage that's closer to, for lack of better words, normal.

That's not to dismiss the value of a good fairy tale. In fact, on the day I proposed to Jean in Canada's London, I published a special Royal Wedding edition of the *St. Thomas Times-Journal,* my employer at the time, complete with full-front-page story and our childhood photos.

I took Jean to London's Grand Theatre, where, on our entrance, dozens of folks were reading copies of said newspaper. And I had London radio announce the engagement of the "prince and princess." With all that set-up, it's a good thing she said yes.

Later, incredibly, in one of those truth-is-stranger-than-fiction scenarios, I discovered our wedding day of July 29, 2001 – witnessed by 400 of our closest friends – was 20 years to the day after Charles and Di's.

Clearly the marriage gods were telling me something. And not that our union was destined to explode like the Hindenburg. Rather, the message was simply, "Your marriage is something very noble. Don't blow it. Because, yes, it also has the potential to burst into flames."

It's a reminder, I suspect, every thinking couple since Eden has received in one way or another. But even in our era of lonely hearts and broken homes, there are ways to beat the rotten odds.

One is to do what Charles should have done long ago. Show courage while choosing your relationships. Walk away from what you believe isn't best. Use both your heart and your head. Know yourself. Pray hard.

In the end, don't settle for anyone who can't be both your lover and your best friend. I didn't. And you know, now I really do feel like a prince.

W

It's an interesting holiday, Victoria Day, the day I met Unknown Doctor, Jean, a day taken off with fireworks by Canadians every third weekend in May to honour the former long-time British monarch Queen Victoria, something even the Brits don't bother with.

Jean and I were to see such fireworks in London, Ontario, with a larger

social network known informally as "The Over-30 Unclaimed Precious Jewels Club." But when nobody from the group showed up, we saw the fireworks by ourselves and went to dinner.

Then I brought my date one city south to St. Thomas to what I figured every young lady must enjoy, a late-night tour of the St. Thomas Times-Journal, my employer, a paper that my New Doctor Friend had seen often over the years while visiting family in her native St. Thomas.

By this time I understood that journalists can have certain leverage in their dating lives, and in this case pleasant lines again fell to me. Jean, who grew up in Toronto and now practiced in Hamilton, was to speak about her overseas work to a local high school. Froese happened to be the education reporter for St. Thomas and Elgin County.

"Are you dating this girl?" Sensible City Editor asked when I pitched the story idea.

"Not yet," I responded.

"Thom has to start dating someone from Hamilton because he's dated everyone from St. Thomas," quipped another office colleague.

My reportage on the good doctor's work, a full page worth, then rolled off the presses. Sometime later I sang, impromptu, to a hall of wedding guests to impress her, my date for the evening. And sometime later, after she spoke publicly, I wrote perfect tens on her evaluation form, adding, "I want to marry the speaker."

Later I leaned on my vocation again, getting permission to use those rumbling presses of the Times-Journal to print a special edition run for Valentine's Day 2001, with a Royal Wedding front page to impress now New-Bride-To-Be.

Excerpts: "To be announced is a July 29 wedding, ending speculation that has swirled around the royal pair in recent months. It heightened when they were photographed together swimming in the Red Sea, off the coast of Yemen, three weeks ago ... At almost a foot shorter than the prince, the attractive brunette was named by the medical journal Babes Today in 2000 as one of the 10 prettiest doctors ever. She is known to have boundless energy and a pleasant nature with people of all lots ... The imperial motto of the Chamberlain's, the royal house of the princess, is 'spec et fi des' or 'faith and hope.' Prince Thomas was reportedly quite inspired when he learned of this."

There's a quip that if you're in journalism and you want to get married, that's great, because when you're a journalist you can get married lots of times. Such can be the profession's cost.

My experience was different. I found this certain audacious spirit, one that's either natured or nurtured in many a journalist, very much buoyed my early relationship with the woman who became Darling Doctor Wife.

Now some years later at the Standard, the young campus paper I helped birth in Uganda, I see the same phenomena with reporters' dating lives. And as I've seen a steady stream of female "sources" visiting the newsroom, I've joked with these budding African scribes, "There's no reason why you should be unattached by the time your internship ends." They laugh wildly.

"There's a saying in Africa," one told me, "that the baby learns from the mother bird. We know how you got Jean. So we're learning from you."

When I was a boy, Dad Froese tells me, I would say I wanted to be two things: a farmer and a father. Deathly shy, I suppose I believed that farming is a private affair.

Journalism also attracts shy folks. It's just that many are shy egomaniacs. How else could This Scribe rise to sing impromptu to a wedding hall full of guests?

While I wasn't on the evening's roster, I went to the podium and told the crowd that one day the groom, a financial planner with a farm background, came to me for advice on how to win the heart of the bride, a doctor with a farm background.

Wondering what was going to come out of my mouth next, I concluded this totally fabricated story by noting that I instructed the groom to sing to his love what's affectionately known as "The Moo Moo Song," which I somehow recalled as a tune sung by a cow on an old TV ad about its love for a certain steak sauce.

The entire dangerous venture – just to impress my New Doctor Friend sitting a few feet away – was a story I assumed everyone would see was just a big fish tale. And it went off remarkably well: so well that Jean started seriously noticing me, and so well that, besides several compliments from guests, the groom approached me later and said, "Thom, I recall we had a conversation, but I just recall it a little different."

"My friend, there was no conversation."

My own boy, Royal Youngling 2, is apparently heading for even bolder things. Still two years old, he often looks up at me and says, "You Thom Froese." Then he smiles and exclaims loudly, "Me Jon Froese!"

(By the way, since you're wondering, you say it "Froze.")

Now, a farm lesson learned while often walking alone along an old railway line through some fields under the night stars, near my former St. Thomas home.

It's been said that when we ask for that proverbial piece of bread from the Divine, He doesn't give it. Instead He takes the field of our life and begins to work it. He removes the stumps and rocks. He tills the hard ground. He then sows wheat and grows it with the right touch of sunshine and rain. He then harvests it. He thrashes it. He grinds it into flour.

Finally, a good length of time after the entire process began, the flour is baked into bread. And then, just when we've all but forgotten the original request, our piece of bread is served – for good measure, sometimes, with butter that's been churned from our most sacred of cows.

This, in fact, was my relational journey before my good fortune in marriage to My Royal Babe, a road that was worthwhile in itself, but one that I knew was coming to an end when, one day, looking into The Good Book, I came across the 81st chapter of the ancient Hebrew Psalms, which ends with this: "But you would be fed with the finest of wheat; with honey from the rock I would satisfy you."

And so it happened.

Finally, the best marital story I've ever had the pleasure to report involved Wilf Brown and Sophie Czyse, a couple who had met in 1943 on Goat Island, on the Niagra River. Wilf and Sophie were engaged by Christmas 1944, just before he went to Germany for a year.

Their future together, however, came crashing down due to family problems (Sophie's meddling mother). And Wilf recalled for me the tearful post-war breakup on the American side of the Peace Bridge, in Buffalo, NY. "All she kept saying was 'Please Wilf, just go.' My pillow was soaked with tears that night."

At the time, Wilf didn't even know what went wrong.

Fifty-four years later (both married other spouses who eventually died), Wilf went on a wild and elaborate hunt for Sophie with details too lengthy to share here. And in a page from a Harlequin Romance novel, he found her.

I watched the two – he at 80, she at 75 – finally wed in St. Thomas, and occasionally visited them at their home on Sunset Drive, a stone's throw from my own residence while working at the Times-Journal.

And their honeymoon? In Oberammergua, Germany, to see the world-famous Passion play of Christ.

"I've always believed in fate," Sophie told me. "That life is like a book that's written someplace, and our history is written in there."

And it's from this book that, I believe, we get our royalty.

(For more on Dr. Jean's work, see Window 64, Windows 96 through 99 and their addendums.)

Within days of arriving in the Arabian Peninsula, my tenure as an editor at the Yemen Times began. A simple handshake and smile struck a deal that lasted 40 months.

While artillery light shows erupted over Afghanistan and Iraq, a few countries over, I was the only native English speaker on staff at this fiercely independent English newspaper, the first English paper in a country of then 20 million.

It has about 50,000 readers (with shared copies, newspaper readership in developing countries is many times circulation), many who are educated Yemenis in government and business, or Western expatriates, plus the Internet crowd overseas.

"The job of a good journalist is to afflict the comfortable and comfort the afflicted." That's the motto – originally penned by Chicago-based writer Finley Peter Dunne – that I saw posted on the Times' newsroom wall on my first day. And I was home.

I discovered that Yemenis show deep warmth to Western expatriates, even if we are all believed to be "American." And I found my writing was shaped less by the region's great history and culture and more by differences between East and West.

Too easy to see were the needs: for political freedoms and gender equalities and a better life in general, often manifested in the common person's desire to escape to Europe or "America." Where's the longest lineup in Sana'a? In front of the American embassy.

Some Yemenis love their country enough to touch these various wounds. One is Walid al-Saqqaf, the Times' (former) publisher and editor-in-chief, a consummate professional with whom I quickly developed a meaningful and lasting friendship.

Here is Walid, some of the region's afflictions and, I hope, at least some comforts.

Opposite page photo: *The Yemen Times in a sea of Arab language publications.*

My Yemen Times Launch. Let's Roll.

WINDOWS

The tools of freedom

4

SANA'A, YEMEN
June 1, 2002

"There comes a time in the life of every person and nation to decide, in the struggle between truth and lies, if they will choose to stand on the side of good or evil." You'd think James Russell Lowell, an Englishman who wrote this 150 years ago, was writing about contemporary Yemen.

Newspapers here include *al-Ayyam, al-Gumhuryah* and *al-Thawra,* known in English as the *Days,* the *Republic* and the *Revolution.* At least a dozen other newspapers are read in this capital city. None, however, carry the Western banner the *Free Press.* "Free" and "press" are yet to be forged together in this part of the world.

Consider *al-Shomu'a,* or the *Candle,* a daily paper known for exposing corruption and the inadequacies of some officials. It was recently shut down. Indeed, Yemeni journalists can be harassed, jailed or banned from their writing careers.

Not long ago things were brighter. It was the spring of 1991 when North and South Yemen unified and this country undertook an exceptional experiment in the Arab world. It's called democracy.

While its theocratic neighbours watched in horror, Yemen birthed 40 political parties in anticipation of the first free elections ever held in the Arabian Peninsula. In 1993 they took place.

Yemen then introduced relative freedom of the press. The government could no longer close newspapers without court approval. Overnight, publications doubled to more than 100, half of them newspapers.

The wheels of Yemen's promising change, however, soon wobbled off. Because it opposed the 1991 Gulf War, Yemen was punished by neighbouring Saudi Arabia, which kicked out as many as two million Yemenis working there. Dependant families back in Yemen lost their income, and the country had to absorb the newly returned unemployed.

Then in 1994 this fledgling democracy fell into civil war when the oil-producing South pushed to secede. The three-month war cost 7,000 lives and sucked an estimated US$5.5 billion from an already impoverished economy. It killed the political opposition and many newspapers.

Laws protecting a free press remain intact, on paper. But the Ministry of Information can still control newspapers by issuing, and revoking, licences. Criticizing Islam, in particular, can result in jail or fines or, if a mild case, just a beating.

Enter the *Yemen Times.*

Launched just before unification by University of Sana'a professor Abdulazia al-Saqqaf, Yemen's first English paper garnered a reputation for hard-nosed attacks against the government. After he was arrested for certain coverage of the civil war, in 1995 al-Saqqaf became the first Arab to receive the International Freedom of the Press Award from the U.S. National Press Club.

Later his independent paper was charged again for accusing officials of siphoning foreign aid into their bank accounts. Prosecution was dropped after al-Saqqaf died in a traffic accident. The accident appeared true; still he's heralded as a martyr for freedom.

"We need help," acknowledges his 29-year-old son, Walid, who now publishes the paper.

Large illiterate populations such as those in Yemen remain ignorant of the larger world because they rely on state-controlled broadcasters. Internet use does not yet balance that out. Less than one per cent of the population of 20 million has Internet access, and just one-quarter of that number have their own computers.

Indeed, more than half of Yemen's 20 million people can't read Arabic, let alone English. And the *Times* has limited resources.

But there are an estimated 50,000 English readers among Sana'a's million souls. So, with photos of the late al-Saqqaf hanging in rooms throughout the *Times'* building alongside appeals for God's strength, the paper now runs up to 15,000 copies a week for a significant readership base that includes many of Yemen's reputable decision-makers.

It's the type of thing one can't help but cheer, especially as one discovers more about this proverbial underdog country that, despite its slide, clings to freedoms that are unique to this part of the world.

Native English speakers who teach ESL are particularly valued, like gold, here. Too bad, then, that while the West is now preoccupied with American politics and hunting al-Qaida, Yemen is seen as a one-dimensional place harbouring everyone's worst terrorist fears.

In truth, this country has pursued promising ideals against tough odds and, quite frankly, could use that help.

5 *Tolerance, anyone?*

SANA'A, YEMEN
February 8, 2003

Chalk up a victory for misguided tolerance in the recent flap with Lebanon's ambassador to Canada, Raymond Baaklini.

The ambassador shared various wonky views with a Montreal-based

Arab newspaper, including that Canada's "Zionist party" controls 90 per cent of Canada's media.

He says he regrets the furor that followed and his remarks were for Arab audiences. Still, he reiterated in a subsequent *National Post* interview that "Jews or Zionists" control Canada's media.

Rather than request a more suitable representative from Lebanon, Foreign Affairs Minister Bill Graham says Baaklini's regrets are good enough and it's case closed. So tolerant.

Then again, Arab audiences would understand completely. That's because, as I've discovered in Yemen, folks here are also incredibly tolerant. Especially about Jews. Really.

In fact, if Ottawa wants to make it to the tolerance big leagues, I suggest it closely observe Yemen. With practice, there's no reason it can't become as open-minded as this country's government.

For instance, the following is preaching from a mosque on Yemeni television: "O God, destroy the United States and its allies and let them suffer, particularly tyrant and arrogant Americans. Destroy the Jews, for they are within your power."

Tolerated.

Then there's anti-Semitic school curriculum.

Tolerated.

Graffiti on a main drag here in Sana'a, in English no less, states, "Get the #@!%& [Jews] out of Jerusalem."

Tolerated.

But it's the media that can really set the tone. Here's what has come across my own desk. You be the editor.

This report will prove to you beyond a reasonable doubt that the American government is the biggest and most murderous terrorist organization, along with the United Nations and their Hidden Masters of the Jews Masonic Illuminati Super Government.

And,

The biggest Israeli ring ever existing in the United States has been detained in connection with the September 11 attacks. But, instead of trying them and making them known to the public, they've been sent back to Israel amid the silence of the Jews-controlled American media.

There it is. The truth is out. But Jews don't control Yemen. No sir. That's because none are left. There were thousands here at one time. But most fled after a killing campaign 50 years ago. The remaining few hundred aren't allowed into Yemen's government.

It's all tolerated.

There are some not-so-tolerant people here also. My boss, Walid al-Saqqaf, publisher of the newspaper that employs me, is one. That's why, unlike Yemen's Arab-language press, the *Times* won't print the big story on the Jewish world conspiracy.

Walid, in fact, calls Israel a scapegoat. "We say the Zionists are putting hurdles in our way, even though it's our own corruption and mismanagement," he notes. "People may have a point regarding Palestine's strife and so on, but we don't have enough bread to eat and we still want to destroy Israel."

Walid represents a new wave that's growing in pockets across the Arab world. Particularly since 9/11, some level-headed Arabs are leaving the conspiracy blame game. Globalization is also revealing what they're missing.

Dignity, a voice and other practical tools for economic and political change are what they really want. The tiny Arab island nation of Bahrain, for example, just held its first free elections. Change may spread.

Which is why Ottawa needs to stay focused on Yemen. A country that didn't even have a bank until the 1960s, this place is so backward even Houdini wouldn't quickly escape its ways.

"This is a culture of fear. If you don't go along, you're not a good Muslim," Walid explains. "People are used to it."

Walid, who lived in Washington briefly as a youth, credits his late journalist father for his progressive thinking. Still, he predicts it might be 100 years before Yemen can move on. Cultural change can be painfully slow.

That's the good news for Ottawa. There's time for Foreign Affairs to learn how to let larger gobs of tolerance creep into Canada's national psyche. That will attract more men like Baaklini. And then we'll all be that much more Canadian.

Sure, it may kill us. But we won't offend anyone. And that, after all, seems to be what it's all about.

6 *Hungry?*

"We're all starving beggars in need of the same piece of Bread."

SANA'A, YEMEN
February 21, 2004

One of the more startling things to see here is how dogs come out at night. Yes, in this capital city, the dogs rule. Especially the bony-ribbed ones at the neighbourhood dump, around the corner from where Jean and I live.

They look for food scraps, as do the goats and cats that also visit the smelly depot. What really hits, though, are the people who patiently wait for our – or anyone else's – garbage and then scrounge through it for anything to ease their own gnawing hunger.

It's something to think about when the price of your gasoline rises. Oil-rich OPEC countries will soon trim production, which will raise gas prices worldwide, to various degrees, so the barons don't lose profit.

Yemen, which produces little oil, has bigger worries. Consumers here are about to see major hikes in commodity prices, part of an ongoing economic recovery program led by its government and the World Bank.

Some Yemenis fear the price of their gas, diesel produced domestically, will rise 50 per cent. It will boost government coffers. But business costs will rise, and higher prices will then trickle down to many goods and services. More people at dumps. No wonder the Yanks are doubling their yearly food aid to $15 million.

Remember, unlike in Canada, the only social safety net here is begging. I can't tell how often the poor, usually women and children, ask for handouts on the street or at our door. Several million Yemenis are also migrant workers, mostly in Asia, sending money home to their needy families.

It's something to watch, because while politics in Palestine and Iraq is predictably upsetting, nothing boils Yemeni blood like what they believe – rightly or not – is the bombing of their economy by policies that aren't working. Yemen's last major price hikes, seven years ago, led to plenty of demonstrators being killed on the streets.

And the Middle East can't afford this quasi-democracy to come undone. Yemen, poor orphan that it is, may have a few terrorist insurgents. But it's also a bellwether. In fact, 800 delegates from dozens of countries, including UN chief Kofi Annan, recently met in Sana'a to explore democracy and human rights in the region.

Sana'a, interestingly, is also the Arab cultural capital for 2004. Tourists who haven't been scared off by largely unfounded fears know the value of Old Sana'a, a UN World Heritage Site. This historic quarter – with ancient mud-brick buildings and bustling traditional *souks* (markets) – is a live open-air museum.

But back to hunger. It kills 24,000 people worldwide. Every day. It's increasing in the poorest countries. But, incredibly, in some developing countries, obesity is also a problem. For example, world health officials say one in four kids in African countries like Morocco, Zambia and Egypt are significantly overweight.

Getting fat, while the hungry beg, and die, beside your table. What a loss, since there's plenty to go around for everyone if distributed fairly.

What does this say to the rich West, where obesity is now very much in front of us, all over the news, not to mention our mirrors? How then shall we live?

A slim build, I personally don't consider myself immune from the gluttony in our time. I've put on 50 pounds in the past 20 years. (In my late teens, I had just 140 pounds on my 6-foot-1 frame.) But this is about more than body weight.

It's a reminder that we're all poor: if not materially, then spiritually or emotionally or intellectually, or in ways we each know privately. So in my family we make a point of skipping a meal or two regularly, because there's nothing like a hunger pang to remind us of these truths.

It doesn't put food on anyone's plate. But it helps us to identify in a small way with the hungry and to remember "There, but for the grace of God, go I."

And it helps shine the light on this other poverty of spirit: the one that knows no racial or cultural or geographic borders, the one that says that, as humans, we're all starving beggars in need of the same piece of Bread.

What do you think about that? Care to join us sometime?

The real war 7

SANA'A, YEMEN
December 11, 2004

We're at Khalid School, which, with 8,000 students, is one of Yemen's larger public schools. This morning, about half are lined up outside. It's exercise time. Hands up. Down. In front. Straighten up or get a swat from a teacher brandishing a stick.

From a rooftop, I watch. After the drill, the younger kids, in green uniforms, go inside. The older ones, in tan, sit in the courtyard. The sun beats onto this, their classroom.

A teacher tells me there are 75 teachers. "Most are the other kind." He means women. Khalid, though huge, is among Yemen's better schools. Teachers call some others "slums."

Until the 1960s, when Yemen's imam, the clerical ruler, was thrown from power, most students attended madrassas and Koranic schools. Studying the Koran was seen as the best education.

Now about 950 of the Islamic schools face reform – or closure. Yemen's cabinet says this will help "modernize Islam" and remove the schools from "extremism, militancy and certain curricula promoting deviant ideologies."

Globally, there are about six million madrassas plus 12 million of the more elementary Koranic schools. Dating back centuries, many are now in the world's poorest countries, funded by groups, sometimes militant, from places like Saudi Arabia. Impoverished kids often attend without choice. It's a cheap, often free, social service.

Will converting them into secular schools make the world safer, as proponents suggest? That's debatable. And it may be simplistic. Most madrassas are backward, but not militant. And while it's great to teach math to kids who might otherwise only hear that any unbearded man is going to hell, the bigger challenge, in my observation, is to reform some broader thinking.

For example, rote learning is common here. It comes from religious teaching emphasizing memorization of the Koran. Memorization – not necessarily understanding.

The result? As an Aussie teacher told me, students can't put information into different forms. "So a girl in Pakistan told me she memorized the order of the planets but didn't know which one was beside Earth."

Things then get built on shaky ideas like "Al-Wala'a, la al-Kafa'a," ("Loyalty, not qualifications.") Ask Jean, my wife and a doctor. Helping officiate medical exams here, she notes, to her dismay, how Iraqi and Palestinian students get marks for their nationality, not skills. One recently passed without initially knowing he had a basic birth-control device in his hands.

Yes, even educated people believe things like eating pork, which is unclean in Islam, removes one's "jealousy capacity." This is why Western couples, who presumably eat bacon and ham without shame, cheat on each other. And recently a top government official said Israel is poisoning Yemen's populace through exported pesticides.

You get the idea. Critical thinking isn't encouraged. New, secular curriculum, in itself, won't teach that.

What's needed is what one writer to a Pakistani newspaper said after 9/11: "a [broader] reformation in the practice of Islam that moves it forward, not backward. Or there is no hope for Muslims anywhere. Oxford and Cambridge were the 'madrassas' of Christendom of the 13th century. Look where they are today, among the leading institutions of education in the world. Where are our institutions of learning?"

It's sad, considering that 1,000 years ago, when the first madrassa was created in Baghdad to train leaders of the Islamic empire, Islam led the world in science, math and literature. That was when *ijtihad*, the concept of independent reasoning, flourished. Muslims looked at the world with clarity.

What would it take to return to that? Besides some deep soul-searching, I'm not sure. But I do know many young people here are on the street, uneducated, jobless, hopeless, angry and susceptible to extremists who play on their fears. Unlike in North America and Europe, the number of Arab youth is exploding.

And it seems to me that if we are in a so-called war of civilizations, the biggest battlefields may not be in places like Iraq as much as in the classroom. It would help if more thoughtful Muslims from places like the West, having all kinds of advantages given to them, came to help.

When I arrived in Africa with Darling Doctor Wife to help launch her program, Save the Mothers, the keen folks who run the host university noticed I was a journalist. Figuring I had nothing else to do, they asked if I could birth a newspaper for them. So, with considerable financial help, I did. And the Standard remains the only regularly published campus paper in Uganda.

You might think this would be my biggest accomplishment here. You would be wrong. While creating the newsroom, I felt best about having the nearby stairs fixed, stairs that for decades were giant, Goliath-like, uneven concrete steps leading halfway into a wall at their bottom.

"They were made by a Ugandan," said Astute Contractor, a Ugandan himself, laughing, when I commissioned him for the job.

Weeks later, when the work was largely, but not really, finished, this was our conversation.

Me: "Great, you're almost finished. Just a couple of more to even out."

Astute Contractor: "Mr. Thom, If I get nine out of eleven on a test, isn't that good enough?"

Me: "No, it's not the same. All of the stairs need to be the same height."

Astute Contractor: "Mr. Thom, I know that even in Canada, the stairs are not all even."

Me: "Well, actually they are."

Which is to say that East Africa has challenges like those in the Arab world. Africans love their certificates. They have the highest percentage of degree holders among immigrant groups in Canada. And here in Uganda, students sacrifice greatly, begging and borrowing school fees. From a young age, many are up at dawn for school days as long as 12 hours. The brightest kids get splashed over the papers like athletic stars.

Like in Yemen, however, rote learning is killing these poor, "educated" kids. Facts are drilled into young brains until they leak from the boreholes. Creative problem solving skills, meanwhile, are terribly neglected. And due to the heavy pressure to perform, cheating at all levels is rampant.

The result? Uneven stairs. Uneven lives.

Add to this a dearth of resources. I know of a Uganda photography program that for years taught scores of students every term with just one outdated camera. Students memorized the course text, got tested on it and then passed – without ever gaining the skill, or joy, of shooting their own photos.

Another time, seeing huge stones that needed to be crushed for a house foundation, This Scribe asked how workers would do it, with equipment or manually. "Oh, no," said the site manager. "We don't need to do it manually. We have a sledgehammer."

Some beat the system because they have opportunities for higher learning elsewhere. So the burden of change in their homeland largely rests on their shoulders. That is, if they don't leave – like, for example, plenty of Ugandan doctors who go to Canada and the UK.

These are today's development issues in Africa. So don't send money. Send money and other things, including people who can bring new ways of thinking to build new indigenous leaders for a new, self-sustaining future, new stairs to tomorrow that Africans can climb with pride.

8 Put out a paper, carry a gun

Sana'a, Yemen
November 27, 2004

Ever wonder why you don't live in a George Orwell novel, a place where up is down if the right person says it's so; a place that sooner or later, like a rotten empire, will always implode under the weight of its own self-deceit?

One reason is because of the newspaper you're reading. American writer Walt Lippman put it aptly: "The newspaper is the Bible of democracy." This is what good journalists believe, even here in Yemen.

Yes, on my first visit to the *Yemen Times* I saw this creed on a newsroom wall: "The job of a good journalist is to comfort the afflicted and afflict the comfortable." How sacred. And costly.

Take Abdulkareen al-Khaiwani, editor-in-chief of the Yemeni newspaper *Al*

Shoura. It's now closed and al-Khaiwani is in jail, serving a one-year sentence. He made the mistake of sharply criticizing certain government officials. He's now also had his skull cracked open by an inmate who tried to kill him.

Reminds me of Zahra Kazemi, the Canadian-Iranian photojournalist who died last year after her head somehow got crushed while she was interrogated by prison officials in Tehran. Meanwhile, reform-minded papers in Iran continue to be closed hand over fist.

Yemen's press actually has more freedom. Reporters Without Borders' recently-released annual *Press Freedom Report* notes that Yemen has more media liberty than most Gulf countries do. Canada, by the way, ranks 18th out of 167 nations. And North Korea now holds the notorious bottom spot.

Officially, the big rules here are to never slam the president or the Islamic faith. And never report news that jeopardizes national security, whatever that means. Regardless, after a string of government crackdowns, this country has slid to 135th on the global list. That's below Somalia and Afghanistan.

So if journalists here aren't carrying a mobile in one hand and a handgun in the other (which an editor at one troublemaking weekly reportedly does), then they're simply trying to deal with tightening government control through a media-license system that England outgrew centuries ago.

Of course media are kicked around in most places. Only about 1.4 billion of Earth's 6.4 billion people have access to a free press. Some 2.5 billion people don't, and the other 2.5 billion live in countries where media is only partially free. Not surprisingly, most of these people live in the developing world.

Which begs the question of whether building strong media is integral to Third World aid and development. Certainly it is.

So why does the international aid community respond easily to needs like water projects or health clinics yet ignore the key role that a free press has in sustainable development? Without a free press, societal institutions and civil liberties that support other advances simply can't be built.

This thinking has been slow in coming. Maybe the press in the developing world hasn't told its own story well enough. The reality is that it survives hand to mouth. Equipment is outdated, and staff are poorly trained and poorly paid. Imagine having to choose between telling the truth or getting extra cash under the table to feed your family.

Some still manage to be a force. *Yemen Times'* editor-in-chief Walid al-Saqqaf, who recently asked Western embassies to write Yemen's government about al-Khaiwani's jail experience, is trying to get European donors to fund Yemen's first national newspaper association. That could build an entirely new infrastructure here.

And not all groups have ignored the plight of Third World media. A Yemeni editor once thanked the New York based Committee to Protect Journalists by writing "If it hadn't been for the CPJ, we would be writing from our graves right now."

Nonetheless, to bring lasting transformation, international donors really do need to wake up to media in the planet's neediest places. And more well-trained Western journalists need to move alongside the Walids of the world.

It's the type of work that gives satisfaction like few things can. It helps teach folks to fish, rather than just giving them a fish. And, maybe, just maybe, it helps tear down systems that in the end are destructive for everyone.

W

With my family, including the Two Royal Younglings, I return to Canada each summer. And inevitably the question (often from a typical store clerk) is asked, with a wide-eyed look of disbelief: "You live where? Is that safe?"

"No, not really," I often reply. "But then again, life isn't safe."

Westerners tend to miss this, often living like a cocky teen who thinks he's invincible. Our days are filled with sporty distractions and video amusements and medical marvels that further keep us from thinking much about our mortality.

In the developing world, life's brevity is clearer.

Global politics and the so-called threat of terrorism has some bearing on this. Start a war or two nearby, and the neighbours will have an opinion on it. But larger day-to-day dangers lurk in more-unexpected places.

The driving in many developing nations, for example, is a lethal mix of white-knuckle boldness and shoddy vehicles doing wobbly things like in the photo to the right. (By the way, it was taken by This Scribe hanging out of our own vehicle's passenger window while My Royal Babe drove.)

Or take simple kitchen appliances. One day, brand new to Yemen and its ways, I accidentally blew the glass cover of our kitchen stove somewhere into space, in a million pieces, almost taking myself with it.

So no, Yemen is not safe. Neither is leaving bed. It's not meant to be.

Opposite page photo: *Two packed vehicles on a dangerous mountain-pass near Hadramount, Yemen. The left vehicle, along the outside curve, is in an opposite traffic lane.*

Is It Safe? Are You Kidding?

WINDOWS

Ah yes, peace and quiet 9

SANA'A, YEMEN
May 24, 2002

Thank you for your wishes for "peace and quiet" and "safety and peace." It seems one can't keep anything secret any more. The Internet shows that newspapers from China to Switzerland to Australia have reported the recent racket in Yemen.

Specifically, there were four blasts here in Sana'a in a month: two near the United States embassy, one at the home of a Yemeni intelligence official and another at Yemen's civil aviation building. Nobody's hurt, and police have arrested two suspects from a group calling itself Sympathizers of al-Qaeda.

It seems a suitable name, since it must hurt to be in Osama bin Laden's camp these days. And these folks truly do appear sympathetic. After one bombing here, they apologized for collateral damage and promised to reimburse neighbours.

Extremists here are sore that a few dozen American military are training Yemeni security to fight terrorism. The Friends of Osama are also demanding release of 173 mujahedeen held for several months without formal charges. The group has given the Yemeni government 30 days to release the militants or it will begin suicide bombings.

You may think it's all enough to keep one in bed. But one does learn to take these things in stride. Consider that after the September 11 attacks on the United States, a Canadian embassy official in the region sent a no-nonsense e-mail telling Canadians to leave Yemen without delay. Within 24 hours that changed to "Please disregard the previous warning."

Alerts from other embassies are also clear as mud, usually suggesting to be on guard for "strange things." Is there anything not strange to a Canadian in Yemen?

Most Yemenis realize Westerners among them are here to help. And life is uncertain regardless of where one lives. You or I might get hit by a truck while crossing the street. Indeed, in Yemen, with 1,300 traffic deaths a year, an accident is a far more likely way to go than terrorism.

Of 13 countries in the Middle East and North Africa, Yemen's death rate per 10,000 vehicles is only behind Syria's. According to the Transportation Research Laboratory, that's a rate 16 times higher than Canada's, which runs in the middle of the world's 24 most motorized countries.

In the last 15 years traffic deaths in Western countries are down while in the developing world they're up: 40 per cent in Asia, 36 per cent in the Middle

East, 26 per cent in Africa and 16 per cent in Latin America. Outside Yemen, some of the places it's particularly dangerous are India, Kenya, Uganda and Ethiopia.

If these places are anything like Yemen, it's no wonder. Consider this warning from a consulate office:

"Yemen should be considered risky. Within cities, minivans and small buses pick up and drop off passengers with little regard for other vehicles. Despite traffic lights and traffic police, each intersection requires an act of negotiation. Yemen has no traffic laws governing turns on red lights, maintaining lanes, merging or right-of-way. Drivers commonly drive on the wrong side of the road.

"Many underage drivers are on the roads. Many vehicles are in poor repair and lack functional turn signals, headlights, taillights, and brake lights. Pedestrians, especially children, and animals constitute hazards. Major intercity roads are paved and maintained in fair condition, but rural roads generally require four-wheel drives or vehicles with high clearance."

They forgot to mention folks hanging from backs and sides of trucks, even on narrow mountain roads. Overloaded motorcycles with drivers and passengers wearing flip-flops are a precious sight. Windshields on cabs are cracked like topographical maps. Fumes are deadly. And don't forget the mines from the 1994 civil war.

The good news is that since alcohol is banned in Yemen, you'll never get hit by a drunk driver. Also, kidnappings on rural roads are down. Tribes who detain motorists want human leverage to get government funding for services such as hydro. Thankfully, they do have a reputation for treating their guests very well.

The reality is that life has inherent risks. When we try to play it safe, it seems to me we only create more insecurity. And that's too bad, considering the need for more Westerners to link with the developing world.

10 I'm safer in Yemen

"And getting stuff over to Saudi? Forget the mail. Try donkeys."

Sana'a, Yemen
March 6, 2004

Hey, what's going on over there?

First, a Stoney Creek 15-year-old gets an AK-47 in the mail, past customs, from an American Internet-game buddy. Then some American cruisers scream over the border in a movie-like scene, chasing a suspicious truck, only for it to kill some poor lady moments later in Niagara Falls, Canada.

Having grown up in that region, I guess things have changed since the evening I strolled across the Rainbow Bridge to see the sights, gripping as they are, on the U.S. side of the falls.

But if you want real border action, come to Yemen. Visit Sadda, a town just south of the border of big, oil-rich cousin Saudi Arabia. In Sadda, you can get weapons at an arms souk like you get fruits and vegetables.

Thousands shop in the open-air market for arms that come from places like China, Russia, Belgium and, heck, even Israel. Guns of all shapes and sizes are everywhere. A larger item, like an 85-mm surface-to-surface missile, goes for US$2,500. Anti-aircraft missiles, while not on display anymore, can also be had if the price is right.

And getting stuff over to Saudi? Forget the mail. Try donkeys. You bet. Donkeys easily carry illicit goods past unsuspecting border guards. One good swat to its backside and a trained mule can go through rugged mountains and cross at some unknown point of the 1,350-kilometre-wide border and then return on its own to Yemen.

The Saudis – who export their own weapons, namely militant religious ideology and terror money – blame the porous border for things like the terror bombings in Riyadh last May. Since then, border patrols have managed to seize at least 90,000 rounds of ammunition, 2,000 sticks of dynamite and hundreds of guns and bazookas.

Thus, the wall. It was going up in 20 kilometres of neutral territory. Established after decades of border disputes, the land was reserved for local tribes and vital grazing pasture. Yemenis got so livid over the treaty-breaking intrusion that they compared it to Israel's West Bank barrier, a blow as low as any Arab could ever dish another.

Thankfully, the whole thing blew over after Yemen's president, Ali Abdullah Saleh, flew to Saudi's royal princes in Riyadh. They smiled and hugged and kissed like good men in this part of the world do. Wall construction stopped and everyone agreed to do a better job harnessing things like those out-of-control donkeys.

It won't be easy. Even here in the capital, where there are far fewer guns than in the countryside, it's not uncommon to see semi-automatic Kalashnikovs, the Russian version of AK-47s, bandied about. Once I saw a pistol fired aimlessly in the air in front of a restaurant. The guy was obviously upset over his food.

Nonetheless, despite its Wild-West reputation, Yemen is not the most heavily armed country on the planet. It's second. Believe it or not, the country 90 minutes down the road from you packs significantly more heat.

For years, authorities believed Yemen had 60 million guns, or three per person. But unlike in Michigan, you can't get a gun here when opening a bank account. (And that's not because most Yemenis don't use banks.)

And now the Geneva-based Small Arms Survey, the authoritative voice on what's happening with weaponry worldwide, confirms that of 639 million firearms on earth, Yemen, in fact, has 10 million at most, one gun for every two Yemenis. Meanwhile, the Yanks have about 250 million. That's almost one per person. Finland (Finland?) takes third, and South Africa has, by far, the most gun murders.

The good news is that there are slightly fewer small arms on the world's streets these days. New government laws and a decline in wars in the 1990s have helped. The bad news is that a couple of people have been shot dead somewhere during the time it's taken you to read this.

Such things will always be terribly troubling. But, despite appearances, at least things over here aren't as dangerous as they seem. In fact, it may be safer here than it is where you are. Imagine that. And Yemen's guns aren't even registered.

Jihad with some soul

11

"Remember, a few guys with box-cutters wrought 9/11."

SANA'A, YEMEN
April 11, 2003

Trying to galvanize sagging troops, one of Saddam Hussein's recent public pronouncements was to formally call for Muslims everywhere to join his ranks and fight Islamic jihad, or holy war. Should we care?

No, we shouldn't. Yes, we should. Compelling arguments go both ways.

Starting with no, we shouldn't care, consider that Saddam is a secularist not recognized by Muslims as an authority on jihad. If some Muslims are running in the fields of holy war, it's because others opened the door for them.

Six months ago, for example, 450 Iraqi and Sunni and Shiite religious leaders met in Baghdad and proclaimed that if "this century's pharaoh" – that's U.S. president George Bush – attacked Iraq, jihad would become the "duty" of all Muslims.

Leading clerics in Pakistan also recently called for jihad, noting that the war actually started years ago and simply intensified after Bush's declaration of a "crusade" in the wake of 9/11.

Note also that *jihad* can mean various things. It literally means "holy struggle." That's either one's struggle for self-improvement through humility and self-control, or the "lesser" jihad of military action, to be waged only if first attacked.

But any call for jihad is not a government conscription of troops. In Yemen, for example, religious scholars also recently formally condoned jihad. But with a moderate government here, *jihad* doesn't mean military service.

Moderate Muslims make practices of jihad broad enough that everyone feels they're taking part. For example, something as benign as donating blood to the Red Crescent Society can be an acceptable way of fulfilling jihad.

So no, Saddam's call shouldn't keep us from going out for groceries today. With that said, by attacking Iraq Uncle Sam may have opened a Pandora's box of ugly things we may not yet fully understand. Rightly or not, the perception among many Muslims is that Gulf War II is part of a new Christian-Jewish crusade.

Iraq today. Yemen or another Muslim country tomorrow. If the war is protracted, that thinking will become even more mainstream, and jihad may take more threatening forms in the broader region here. *Yemen Times* publisher Walid al-Saqqaf puts it plainly: "The Yemenis are very emotional people."

In protests in Yemen, continuing here regularly but peacefully these days, even women have demanded that Yemen's government open its borders to let them fight.

"I am prepared to go and perform martyrdom and defend my brothers in Iraq. I am prepared for death," one woman told the *Yemen Times*.

Yemen's government won't open its borders. Still, it's believed hundreds of Yemeni men, those with means and money, have managed to join their Iraqi brothers by crossing through countries with less stringent travel rules.

For them jihad is a powerful concept. Holding the belief that your enemies can take your body but can't touch your soul makes one fight with uncommon fierceness.

Muslim tradition also says martyrs get extra rewards in heaven, such as eternally youthful wives. It's said that nobody in Allah's heaven wants to leave except a martyr who, seeing his prize, wants to return to Earth and get killed again in Allah's cause.

So even if these fighters don't win militarily, Saddam's call for jihad may only bolster the longer term breeding of a Muslim coalition of the willing: fighters using things other than military might. Remember, a few guys with box cutters wrought 9/11.

Their type of jihad could become a terrible psychological nightmare. Even after Saddam is gone, there may be no closing it, nor keeping it from creeping to your own quiet neighbourhood. To beat this type of jihad, we need to recognize that desperate people do desperate things.

Some Muslims in this region do seem desperate. Millions of youth in particular feel lost. Their system of schooling doesn't prepare them for the world's new marketplace.

And in my observation, their system of religion, especially when controlled by radicals, doesn't satisfy all the deeper longings of their spirits.

The longer these core issues burn, the more a certain jihad of the soul will fester. Nobody needs to call for it.

It arrived here long ago.

When a child screams in Baghdad ... 12

SANA'A, YEMEN
February 28, 2003

Fear is a funny thing. Along with other Commonwealth citizens, Jean and I were recently informed that most staff members of the British Embassy here are leaving and that we should consider doing the same.

Getting out of Yemen is not a new message. But concerns now are that commercial airlines might unexpectedly halt services if Iraq is bombed.

Fair enough.

There are more than 400 Commonwealth citizens in Yemen and at least that many Americans, 300 Germans and various other nationalities. If you're not an aid worker, usually in health care or education, you're likely in Yemen's relatively small oil fields.

Unlike expatriates in some other parts of the Middle East, it appears that many, especially those with smaller companies, will stay for now. We plan to return to Canada in April for the birth of our first child.

That's a hard wait for loved ones.

"Come home," is what my worried dad told us – a dozen times or so – during a recent phone call.

Still, issues such as domestic poverty and the plight of Palestinians in the occupied territories inflame the Yemeni more than the Iraq crisis does. While millions just marched worldwide against war on Iraq, the Arab world has been, as one Arab paper put it, "in a coma."

In fact, it is illegal to protest in Yemen without state approval. You demonstrate when you're told. You're given a placard with a mug of the president to hold high. And everything, in theory, stays under control.

The bigger threat to foreigners here comes from radicals who, as a German official recently said to me, have an "individual neurosis." If they need to be a hero, and if they dislike a community, the threat is incalculable.

The recent murders of three Western aid workers at Jibla Mission Hospital? You can't protect yourself from that. Besides, where is it safe? The space station?

And when people get fixated on personal safety, they develop the wonky idea that tranquillity and happiness, whatever that means, is some human birthright. Which is probably why our generation has been described as lost, "huffing and puffing down the fast track to nowhere, always looking to the dollar sign for direction."

But, you know, security is a strange thing too. We spend our lives searching for it and then hate it when we get it.

So when Jean and I do hunker down in the refuge of Canada, albeit briefly, my bigger fear is that we'll forget important questions like, when a child screams in Baghdad will anybody hear?

Iraq's 13 million children are already dependent on state rationing. Now, war. One international report suggests it could result in over one million refugees, many trapped in Iraq without enough food or water. Add the dead.

To the most ignorant of people these folks are different anyway, not Canadian, not American. They have a different colour of skin, language and dress. They might as well live on Pluto. But don't the best of us also grade human suffering? The 3,000 deaths on September 11, 2001, were horrible. So were those recently of NASA's astronauts. How will we rank their lives against Iraqi Brownshirts controlled by an evil mustachioed madman?

Will we really worry about blood and brains and charred babies on someone else's kitchen floor any more than we'll fret over our dying RRSPs? Will it all be more than a TV special?

Remember what the Nazis told the Nuremberg trials? Their war was somewhere out there, not in their own neighbourhood.

Times have changed. But don't feel too guilty if, in all honesty, you're not much different. Indifference is, after all, part of our shared human nature. And that's what we should fear.

Buffing Arabia's image 13

Sana'a, Yemen
March 2, 2004

The Middle East.

Quick, what do you think of? Oil? Terrorism? Women wearing head-to-toe burqas? Islam? Script with funny squiggles? Can you honestly think of much good? If you had a free ticket to holiday anywhere, would this region even make your short list?

Of course, it has good things. People here are, well, pretty much like anywhere. Parents raise families. Kids go to school. Folks marry, dance, cook, write poetry, fight, reconcile and so on.

I've yet to meet anyone in Yemen, for example, who's burned a U.S. flag or shouted "Death to America." Just as London isn't full of tweed-clad MBA students or white-collared insurance agents, the Middle East – Morocco in the west to Pakistan in the east, Turkey in the north to Somalia in the south – has more variety than any silly monolithic stereotypes we believe.

It's something to keep in mind the next time you hear some yahoo has blown up a bus or shop in Israel. It simply has nothing to do with the experience of millions here, just like, say, SARS will never be experienced by millions of Canadians.

But then, we live in a world of perceptions. Consider that while terrorism kills thousands yearly, most victims live in Africa, Nepal and Columbia. We don't hear that, because they have nothing to do with the few hundred Western victims. In truth, more people die of traffic accidents and falling off ladders than from any global terror threat.

But that's not politically important.

The whole thing comes to mind because if there's one thing I've discovered during my two-year tenure in Yemen, it's that most acquaintances back home have no appreciation for tourism here.

Sure, Yemen has some black eyes from incidents such as the bombings of the American warship USS Cole in 2000 (now back in service after a $250 million repair) and the French oil tanker Limburg in 2002. That Yemen is a tribal nation with a weak central government and, in parts, a Wild-West mentality doesn't help.

But its capital, Sana'a, with its historic quarter designated a UNESCO World Heritage Site, is among the oldest inhabited places on Earth. And for anyone living in this giant outdoor museum, it's no surprise that Sana'a is named the Arab cultural capital for 2004.

To help celebrate, the Germans recently came to town for Yemen's first-ever open-air concert. Believe it or not, the 70-member Europa Philharmonie Orchestra, among Europe's best, played Mozart and Brahms, Beethoven and Strauss under the stars, against a stunning backdrop of ancient mud-brick buildings that look like giant gingerbread houses.

A thousand VIPs from across the region listened. Hundreds of locals lined the area, some peering out from area windows and rooftops. Your best billing at Roy Thomson Hall wouldn't compare. And this was free. The only glitch was that the crowd, which gave a ten-minute standing ovation, couldn't control its applause throughout the show.

It shows what exposure can do for an unknown product. Some feel Yemen has antiquities on par with Egypt's pyramids. But due to incidents such as the ship blasts, Aden, a port city with the most picturesque beaches in the region, is all but blowing away. Its free-zone shipping terminal, which normally handles goods from around the world, is now bankrupt, bought out for $200 million by Yemen's government.

The irony is that rather than hurting any Western commerce, which they like to gloat about, the few bomb-happy extremists are actually hurting their own kin. And, unlike in Canada, Conan or the Rolling Stones won't bale these folks out. Poor orphan Yemen couldn't afford their cleanup crew.

The saving grace is that while the number of European tourists – who normally make up more than half of Yemen's tourists – has fallen, visitors from other Middle Eastern countries are up. Total visitors, about 100,000 a year now, are slowly rising to pre-Cole-blast days.

There are no easy solutions to it all, especially when the truth gets mired in the mud of fear and politics. But, in this town, 2004 promises to bring some pretty good times. If only a few more North Americans would put down the so-called news and come take a look.

Like caged birds. That's how some expatriates, like foreign oil workers confined to residential compounds in Sana'a, lived. At the time, Yemen pumped about 500,000 barrels of oil a day, a small percentage of the output of Saudi Arabia. Now even that is dwindling.

Free to move at will, Darling Doctor Wife and I never lived with such restrictions. And so my original Yemen Times column, "A Canadian in Yemen," had a relaxed approach, complete with my mug shot from above the Sana'a cityscape, wearing a Team Canada hat.

Things changed one early morning when we were greeted with the news that three American friends – Bill Koehn, Dr. Martha Myers and Kathy Gariety – had just been shot dead by an Islamic extremist in the southern town of Jibla.

I instinctively began working. Word spread quickly around the globe. CNN wanted information from us and our friends. The Hamilton Spectator, the main newspaper for which I was freelancing, put the drama on its front page. Canada's largest paper, the Toronto Star, referred to Jean and me in its coverage. In their own shock, my Yemen Times colleagues got busy with their own reports.

While death came knocking, more disturbing was that it almost took my dear Jean, who was originally scheduled to be at the hospital that morning. She and Dr. Martha were the only two Western obstetricians in Yemen and often consulted each other.

The tears flowed throughout our close-knit community, aid workers from the United States, the UK, Germany, Holland, Australia and South Korea. Somebody played 'Your Faithfulness,' a heart-wrenching song by Brian Doerksen about the frailty of life, and it became a theme. At the Times, publisher Walid al-Saqqaf confirmed there were likely more targets, a hit list including journalists.

But we wouldn't leave. We wouldn't run. Not yet. Not like this. And so for weeks, every time I left the house or the security of the Times, every time I turned the key of our vehicle, I thought about it. Every time – sometimes stopping, sometimes looking, always wondering.

The "Canadian in Yemen" then disappeared, and the new name "Jamil Abdul Karim" began appearing in a new Times column called "East and West."

"We really like your new name," my Times colleagues said of the pen name, which translates "Beautiful Servant of the Most Gracious One." Most didn't know that I chose it as a tribute to our slain friends.

These dispatches open with a report on the murders written by the Associated Press, then continue with my own thoughts about the costs any one of us may be called to consider.

Opposite page photo: *A merchant in Sana'a with a handful of Yemeni Riyals.*

Consider the Cost

WINDOWS

Three Americans slain in Yemen

December 31, 2002
By Associated Press

A gunman slipped past guards at a mission hospital and opened fire yesterday, killing three American missionaries with shots to the head and wounding another.

Officials said the gunman may be part of an Islamic militant cell targeting foreigners and secular minded politicians in Yemen.

U.S. investigators joined Yemeni authorities in the search for clues in the attack in this Arabian peninsula nation, the ancestral home of Osama bin Laden's family and a front line in the U.S. war on terrorism.

The White House said it was too soon to tell if the attack was connected to terror organizations. Many militants, some trained by bin Laden's al-Qaeda network, have taken refuge in Yemen, where government control is weak in tribal areas and guns are plentiful.

Anti-American sentiments are running high in the Middle East because of perceived U.S. support for Israel and the standoff with Iraq. Many of the region's predominantly Muslim population also believe the U.S. war on terror is part of a campaign against Islam.

The gunman, identified by Yemeni officials as Abed Abdul Razak Kamel, was arrested after the attack at the 35-year-old Jibla Baptist Hospital, a compound of several one-storey tin-roofed buildings on a hilltop in Jibla, a small town of richly ornamented stone towers, known as the 12th-century home of Yemen's Queen Arwa.

The gunman entered the compound hiding a semiautomatic rifle under his white robes and black leather jacket to make it resemble a child. He was therefore able to pass a security checkpoint where visitors are supposed to leave their weapons.

He then entered a room where hospital director William E. Koehn was holding a meeting and opened fire, shooting Koehn and two others in the head and killing them instantly, officials said.

Next, he headed to the pharmacy and shot pharmacist Donald W. Caswell in the abdomen. Hospital officials said Caswell was in critical condition.

The International Mission Board of the Southern Baptist Convention identified the two other victims as purchasing agent Kathleen A. Gariety, 53, of Wauwatosa, Wisconsin, who arrived in Yemen 10 years ago, and Dr. Martha

C. Myers, 57, of Montgomery, Alabama. Koehn, 60, of Arlington, Texas, had planned to retire next October after 28 years at the hospital.

Caswell, 49, of Levelland, Texas, has been in Yemen for 18 months and was recovering after surgery, his father, 71-year-old D. C. Caswell, said.

Myers had been in Yemen for 24 years, said her father, Ira Myers. He said his daughter "had the opportunity to talk to the native women. That would not have been possible for a male doctor in that culture. She delivered lots of babies."

"People in the community really loved her," Dr. Jean Chamberlain-Froese said of her friend and colleague, Myers. "She knew the language and she was really out in the community. She was just a really caring individual."

"Everyone [on the hospital compound] wants to leave now. Everyone's in shock," Julie Toma, an administrative assistant, told freelance journalist Thomas Froese in Sana'a, the Yemeni capital.

Yemeni authorities said Kamel, the 30-year-old alleged attacker, told interrogators after his arrest that he planned the attack in collaboration with Ali al-Jarallah, who was arrested for allegedly shooting to death a senior Yemeni leftist politician on Saturday, Yemen's official news agency, Saba, said.

"The killers knew each other and wanted to make a statement at the same time," said Walid al-Saqqaf, editor-in-chief of the Yemen Times. "They agreed—one would take Sana'a, the other, Jibla."

The slayings were the first in Yemen of Western aid workers. Years ago, several Indian Sisters of Charity from Mother Teresa's organization were killed in the Yemeni port city of Hodeidah, also by Islamic extremists.

Officials said Kamel belonged to a militant cell that may be targeting foreigners and Yemeni public figures who have strayed from the path of Islam in the extremists' eyes. A security official said up to eight others in the cell were being sought.

Abdul Salam Mohammed, a Jibla resident, said Kamel had rented a house near the hospital a month before yesterday's attack. "We didn't see much of him...as he didn't go out much. I remember he had a long beard and a moustache," Mohammed said. "On Monday morning I saw him without both."

The White House said investigators were trying to determine whether the attack was linked to terrorism. "We strongly condemn and deplore the murder of three American citizens," spokesperson Scott McClellan said.

The shooting was the second recent attack on American missionaries in the region. On November 21, a gunman killed an American missionary nurse in the Lebanese city of Sidon. Lebanese authorities have yet to determine who was behind that shooting.

In a country where quality health care is impossible to find, Jibla hospital had gained the trust of the Yemeni and had a country-wide reputation. It is staffed by a multinational team of over 100. Even so, due to decisions at its American-based head office, it was to close if new administrators could not be found soon.

A woman from Jibla who identified herself only as Fatima said yesterday's attack was "a crime unacceptable in any religion. This contradicts Islam."

"They cared for us and looked after us. I can't even count the number of children they treated and saved," she said.

Yemeni president Ali Abdullah Saleh – whose government has co-operated with Washington in the war on terror – sent a message to U.S. president George W. Bush condemning the shooting, which he said would "strengthen our determination to eradicate terrorism," Saba reported.

After the attack, a Yemeni military jeep was posted outside the hospital, with a soldier manning a machinegun mounted on the back. The Southern Baptist missionary board said its 80-bed hospital in Jibla treats more than 40,000 patients a year and its missionaries also teach English to Yemenis.

Many people from Ibb, a city of 100,000 eight kilometres from Jibla, rely on its services. The hospital provides free care and medicine to those who cannot afford it.

Six months ago, the Southern Baptists announced they would have to pull out of managing the 100-bed operation. Uncertainty was compounded two weeks ago when a local Yemeni non-governmental organization retracted its commitment to take it over.

As a result, Yemen's Ministry of Health was to take over the hospital yesterday, the day of the slayings. It's believed the gunman timed the murders, wanting to kill the Americans before they left.

Jack Graham, president of the Southern Baptist Convention, called the three victims "martyrs" who were "killed in the line of duty."

About 30,000 U.S. citizens, most of Yemeni origin, live in the Arab country, the U.S. Embassy said. Ambassador Edmund J. Hull said an evacuation was not planned but that the embassy would help Americans in Jibla leave if they wish.

The embassy urged Americans in Yemen to enhance their security, saying it was requesting additional protection for them.

The U.S. State Department has frequently urged Americans to exercise caution in Yemen, an impoverished and factionalized nation that has seen a number of recent attacks thought linked to al-Qaeda. "Everyone wants to leave now."

Something beautiful

14

"In the end, of course, every one of us will die. What will you leave behind?"

SANA'A, YEMEN
January 17, 2003

Jarring images of how an Islamic extremist burst into, of all places, a hospital in the last days of 2002 to fire bullets from his Kalishnikov into the heads of our friends will linger for a while.

My wife, Jean, and I and some colleagues are still laying to rest what has become known across Yemen as "The Jibla Tragedy."

At Jibla's mission hospital, we lost loved ones. Violently. Life will never be the same. Indeed, as we discovered later, victim Dr. Martha Myers was just about to phone Jean for a consultation on a patient when the crazed gunman burst into her world to kill her.

Some thoughts:

It's tempting to think that as Christian aid workers, that is, Christian "missionary" aid workers, the three slain Americans – Myers, widely known as "Dr. Martha," administrator Bill Koehn and purchasing agent Kathy Gariety – had no business bringing their faith to the Muslim world.

"With Missionaries Spreading, Muslim Anger Is Following" was the headline on a *New York Times* analysis after Jibla. It's a popular view among those who would never consider putting a toe of their own into the waters of foreign aid work. And it's wrong.

Consider this. Hundreds of Yemenis lined the gates of Jibla hospital on the day Bill and Martha were buried on its grounds. Why? Because these three mission workers – Kathy's body was flown back to the United States for burial – were loved deeply by the Yemenis. The day after, when most American and foreign staff left the hospital, hundreds of locals lined the gates again to say farewell.

But isn't Yemen the reported new home of big, bad Osama, with gun-toting wide-eyed crazies running amok? Unfortunately, yes. Then again, have you been to downtown Toronto lately? What is its murder rate?

Several Yemenis have actually approached Jean and me with more collective embarrassment over Jibla than anything else. They know their country is backward and impoverished, and they're thankful aid workers are raising standards in all kinds of ways.

It's true that aid workers may be targeted more these days. The United Nations says about 200 were killed worldwide in a 30-month period up to January 2001. That's a rising rate.

But while such workers, especially from the West, are increasingly in the crosshairs of religion and politics, missionary activity per se is hardly the main cause.

Here it's more that Arabs feel like 90-pound weaklings on Mr. America's beach. Western policy on Palestine is one kick of sand in the face. Another is the looming war with Iraq.

As far as the activities of Bill or Kathy or Dr. Martha go, judge for yourself. Dr. Martha's reputation in particular was legendary among locals. If a Yemeni needed food, she'd give it. If he needed money, okay. Children? Bring them over. By example, she showed how we are all, in fact, starving beggars in need of the same piece of Bread.

Further, if the blood of martyrs is the seed of something new, how much more precious is the blood of those who give up their lives while working in the lands of their foreign friends?

So while murder is a terrible thing, these three aid workers were very much honoured in their deaths. They died how they lived, sacrificially. And they died doing what they loved. As one friend put it, "They died happy and joyful."

In the end, of course, every one of us will die. What will you leave behind? That's perspective. This is what these three souls have given Yemen and now much of the world. They're not the first. They won't be the last.

But if love is stronger than death, and I believe it is, then something very powerful happened in Jibla. It's called leaving something beautiful for God.

Bill, Kathy, Martha: Jean and I and many others look forward to seeing you again sometime. Until then, thank you. May you rest in peace.

A foolish and pure love 15

SANA'A, YEMEN
January 4, 2003

It didn't take long for what started out like a normal day in our household to turn into the day from hell.

My wife, Jean, was still in her pyjamas when the phone call came early Monday morning. Three American aid workers in a missionary hospital in Jibla were slain. We knew two of them, one very well.

Silence.

The jarring news of how an Islamic extremist burst into a hospital room to shoot these three felt like getting brushed by a truck. It was only the night before that my wife changed plans to be at the hospital for a morning meeting. Indeed, if life is a game of inches and seconds, we escaped personal tragedy by the thinnest of margins.

The victims were, by all accounts, remarkable people.

Hospital administrator Bill Koehn, 60, at Jibla for 28 years, was on the verge of retirement. He maintained he would rather stop work than be reassigned by his employer to America or England. His hobbies included carving little wooden figurines of the Yemeni people.

Victim Kathy Gariety, Jibla's purchasing agent, also loved the Yemeni community. "I've been so blessed by this hospital and I just want to bless this place" is what she told co-workers at a recent Christmas party.

It was Dr. Martha Myers, 57, whom we knew best as a friend and colleague. Martha would call regularly to consult with Jean about complicated obstetrical cases. We last saw her a few weeks ago with friends here in Sana'a, three hours north of Jibla.

"People in the community really loved her. She knew the language well, and she was really out there," notes Jean. Martha's community involvement included helping the Yemenis with disease prevention and clean water projects.

For such uncommon commitment – to their faith and to the people they served – these three were thanked by bullets to the head from a Kalishnikov. Their killer reportedly targeted them because of their key posts and good reputations in the community.

A couple of thoughts. First, it's tempting to judge aid workers in dangerous spots around the globe as a bit wonky. You know – masochists or martyrs or just a bit dense for standing under bombs and bullets falling like rain.

Indeed, foreign embassies here issue advisories all the time. Westerners in Yemen – and there are a few thousand of us – are told to be alert, vary travel routes and keep clear from common Western hangouts. So, in London, take the long way home and avoid the city's centre because people have been knifed downtown. How useless.

Yemen, despite its Wild-West reputation, has far fewer murders than Toronto has. The bigger danger around here is white-knuckle driving.

Another tendency is to think Islamic extremists run amok here like wide-eyed yahoos shooting their guns into the air. When Americans are killed, there must be dancing in the streets, no?

Actually, the number of Islamic extremists in Yemen, a country of 20 million, is likely closer to dozens than hundreds.

Several Yemenis have approached Jean and I personally with more collective embarrassment than anything over the Jibla slayings. They know their homeland is impoverished and backward. So they're thankful aid workers are improving standards in all kinds of ways.

"Who is go to heaven?" [*sic*] was the touching e-mail we received after the murders from a local businessman, a virtual stranger. Yes, the Yemenis also easily discuss questions of eternal life, because, unlike in Canada, where bringing religion into the public square is an embarrassment, matters of faith, albeit in an Islamic context, are what people anguish about over here.

Yes, certain evils lurk in this part of the world, as they do in Canada. But it's the folks who keep their doors locked and curtains drawn who are truly menacing, is it not? That's the thinking that made Bill and Kathy and Martha tick.

They may have been killed for such foolish notions. But if love is stronger than death – and I believe it is – then their deaths, as is often true with martyrs, are actually the seeds of something new for many people. Something new from under the snow.

It's not a bad thought at New Year's. It's not a bad thought, really, for any time.

I quit 16

Like Snoopy says, "Never put off to tomorrow what you can avoid altogether."

SANA'A, YEMEN
January 6, 2003

The Yanks. We love 'em. We hate 'em.

Indeed, Jean and I are still recovering from the news of the brutal slaying of three U.S. aid workers, including a doctor friend, at Jibla's missionary hospital.

The killer, apparently an Islamic extremist, reportedly said he killed "to get closer to God." Right. And who better to kill than American Christians? It's killing two birds, innocent as they may be, with one stone.

Indeed, U.S. foreign policy really has folks in a huff these days. In fact, many of us would bend over backward to disassociate ourselves from the Yanks. No?

I would. Why? Not because of the United States's insistence to take down Saddam. No sir. Rather, consider this. Those Americans simply work too hard.

Certainly if our friends in Jibla weren't doing such a noticeably fine job, they wouldn't have been mowed down.

Also consider a recent global survey that shows the average working American gives his or her job more hours a year than workers in any other industrialized nation. According to the International Labour Organization, Americans give 12 days more than average working Canadians, Mexicans and Japanese and a full three months more than holiday-happy Brits and Germans.

They're just showing us all up.

Now come to Yemen. It's a fantasyland of time off. That is why my New Year's resolution is to quit work altogether. Yeah, if there's one thing I need to avoid here, it's being mistaken for an American.

I actually enjoy work. When working in the privacy of home, some journalists get to wear pyjamas regularly. And at the Yemeni newspaper that employs me, I'm the lone Pale-Skin and the only native English speaker. Considering the *Times* is an English paper (Yemen's best, at that), my colleagues like me.

Still, I have good reasons to quit. First, there's family. Jean and I will be new parents of a little bambino, our first, this year. Cigars later.

No work also means more friendships, hobbies and sports. Moreover, I can better promote the Yemeni Way, a lifestyle that really puts the Americans in their place. Crazy as it sounds, try this at home.

Throw out your watch and every clock in sight. Really.

The Gregorian calendar also has to go. The Islamic calendar, started in AD 622 when Mohammed emigrated from Mecca to Medina, is a superior option.

For conservative Muslims, it's now actually the year 1481. That means Columbus hasn't discovered America yet, so Americans don't exist!

The Islamic year is also shorter. Time spent doing nothing goes faster and holidays come quicker. Great. Islamic holidays are long. I just experienced my first Ramadan, a full month when Muslim folks, here anyway, sleep all day. That's when they fast. The nights? Party on!

Also, get a new business week. Yemen's weekend is Thursday and Friday. Brilliant.

To avoid more excessive business, divide the workday. In Sana'a, businesses close for three hours every afternoon. What an escape. Most guys chew qat-leaf, an amphetamine that really can jettison you back to the 15th century.

The system has a few hiccups. Like efficiency. Stock candles. The lights do go out. Jean can tell of oxygen suddenly running out halfway through surgeries.

Then there are Yemen's "emergency" workers. I see last year they had problems rescuing a pedestrian who fell into a Sana'a road pit. So they left a shovel on site for the public to dig him out. Three days later, still trapped, the guy died.

What's really funny is that this dirt-poor country relies so much on major foreign aid, much of it from the United States. Without it, piles of beggars would die in the streets.

Yeah, life without a good sense of time is rather cheap. Most Yemenis aged 30 and up don't even know their own birthdays.

But are these not small quibbles if we're to escape America's driven ways?

Yes sir, join the Yemeni Way. Don't be a slave to time. Like Snoopy says, "Never put off to tomorrow what you can avoid altogether."

And really, unlike those dead U.S. missionaries, what better deadline can one put off than thinking half-straight about eternity?

The following was written in response to the Hamilton-Wentworth District School Board, in Canada, after this Astute School Board banned a group I'll call Praying Student from holding certain lunch-hour prayers and religious clubs.

When originally published, this column garnered more newspaper reader response than any other in this book. A couple of folks even noted that I might be interested to know about famed writer C. S. (Jack to his friends) Lewis and his satirical little book 'The Screwtape Letters,' which features a little devil writing his minion thoughts, just like in my column.

Jack, my apologies. Really, I never knew.

A little devil speaks 17

Sana'a, Yemen
February 7, 2004

Dear Hamilton school board trustees:

Since you've sought input in the unfortunate situation of students wanting nauseous faith-based activities in certain schools, here's some devilish advice.

First, deal with this letter and its sensitivities behind closed doors. Nobody needs to tell you how to run your schools. Asking for guidance from the province was prudent for your image, but the decisions, my friends, are all yours.

Naturally, I suggest you quickly destroy any remnant, small as it may be, of any religious or spiritual thought or expression in all your schools. This includes Christian and Muslim prayers, discussions, clubs or you name it at Westmount Secondary School. Who knows what could eventually come of it?

For example, late last year I was observing the University of Illinois, in Urbana, where 20,000 university students from North America and beyond gathered for several days to learn how to be so-called salt and light on this dirty little ball you call Earth.

Missing Boxing Week sales, these fools took trains, planes and buses there to learn how they might help fix our messed-up planet by – get a load of this – going to the poor and oppressed. These suckers even gave $1 million from

their own pockets for lost causes like victims of Iran's earthquake. (A real beaut, I may add.)

Initial damage in Hamilton appears minimal. Just a couple of dozen McMaster University students attended. But 1,500 Canadians were at Urbana.

And the whole thing is a concern, because while their hopes are foolish, they're also very dangerous. At least some youth might eventually take them who knows where.

Needless to say, I personally find that salt stings like hell and light is terribly blinding.

So, besides extinguishing any flicker of God-talk in your schools, I suggest the following:

Emphasize that truth doesn't exist. This gives little reason to leave bed in the mornings, but it's foundational. Students need to know they're the centre of their universe, a chance collection of atoms without purpose. You know, Evolution 101.

Focus on power, money and prestige of future jobs. Keep students dissatisfied. Preoccupied.

Don't mention that while North Americans spend $10 billion annually on video games, 300,000 kids die in armed conflicts worldwide; or that while there are 100 million orphans on earth, last year your continent spent $30 billion on pets.

Don't forget, sexuality is a wonderful distraction. Give plenty of room for everyone to roam aimlessly, like scattered sheep in the hills and valleys of free choice. Choice, as you know, is good, as long as students don't choose abstinence until marriage.

Remember, offensive strategies are also needed. Continue the myth that Christianity is an oppressive white ethnocentric religion. Don't mention that Latin America, Asia and Africa have more Christians than North America and Europe.

And certainly, never, ever allow Jesus Christ's name to be uttered in any school. Unless it's cursed.

Some students will question these things. Be on your guard. They're like dynamite and can upset the equilibrium of everything.

One tactic is to remind them that if they want to bring hope to the slums and garbage communities of the world, or even their own schools, there is a price to pay. But be careful, because this can backfire.

At Urbana, for example, the 20,000 heard about Hans and Sophie Scholl, a couple of university students in Germany who defied Hitler and distributed anti-Nazi leaflets on campus. They were arrested and, within hours, tried and beheaded. Strange thing, but this type of thing can empower certain students even more.

This is why some are so dangerous. These countercultural types have led revolutions and even transformed societies. They have a certain something, deep within their young spirits, a certain radical courage that is very unpredictable.

And this, in the end, is what you absolutely must completely destroy. It's cautious, well-paid conformists that you want to mould, students that have something I affectionately call a passion deficit. That, really, is best for everyone.

So at all costs, do not allow anyone to rock any boat: not their own, and certainly not yours.

Trusting this all helps and that, of course, you sleep well.

Affectionately yours,
An Anonymous Little Devil.

Having worked as St. Thomas and Elgin County's education reporter for some years, I knew the backstory to this, that in the latter 1980s the Elgin school board was taken to court by the Ontario Ministry of Education because it allowed Bible stories in its school days.

For some decades, these stories were told by frightening old ladies from the Elgin Area Bible Club, using things like flannelette cut-outs of sheep or that shepherd boy David, who killed a lion and giant with just his bare hands and a slingshot.

I know, because years earlier the same kind of club told me those stories in the Niagara regional city of St. Catharines, at a public school called Maple Crest,

a fine school with a flooded rink and as free and Canadian a name as anyone could imagine.

Of course the old ladies over in Elgin were not so menacing, and I say this not just because I dated daughters of two of them and married into the family of a third. Still, as the years rolled on and the stories continued, one little girl got the shakes and ran to the arms of her parents, telling all, especially about her nightmares of hell.

So Esteemed Court in Ontario strapped the Elgin board with a heavy fine and banned those old ladies. Years later, Astute School Board in Hamilton understood. Rather than allow any expression – be it Christian, Muslim, Hindu or Snoopy Worshipper – the board preferred instead to leave just one voice, that of Postmodern Secular Zealot, worshipping at the altar of self.

The whole thing gives me shakes of my own, as it reminds me of the principal's strap at Maple Crest. The first time I got it was in Grade 2, after I couldn't stop laughing in the classroom of Mrs. Clark, whom I recall as a rather attractive brunette, at least as far as a seven-year-old thinks about his teacher.

I can't remember why I was laughing uncontrollably, nor why a chum named Paul Pittiwanika joined me in celebrating the hilarity of it all. Poor Mrs. Clark thought we were laughing at her, which I know I never would, and so we were sent to the office for our due punishment.

You might think such natural boyhood expressions are innocent enough, but there at the office we faced our reward: either the floppy black strap, a light and thin piece of rubber that produced a very quick and sharp pain, or the heavier red strap, which stood straight out and gave a duller but longer-lasting pain.

The palm of the hand was always the choice place of contact. And school authorities not only checked your hand to make sure they wouldn't open any cuts, but also sometimes asked which strap you preferred, which I always thought was quite democratic and decent of them.

The count and force, however, was up to them. Just like it was sometime later during another special visit to the office, this time with Best Boyhood Friend Paul Blakely after the two of us had a little fist-fight on Maple Crest's front lawn, a poor choice of location. (Fights were normally off school property with eager kids forming a circle around the combatants, which in those years often included Enzo Coplin, a kid built like a military tank (his mom would apparently hit him over the head with an iron frying pan), and Robin Meeshod, the insecure challenger who got flattened bloody every time.)

Anyway, the morning after such a thing as the strap, everything would be fine again, and we would all sing the national anthem and "God Save the Queen" while looking up at the red-and-white flag and a fine picture of

Elizabeth, who I actually thought, like Mrs. Clark, was quite attractive also.

This was followed by the Lord's Prayer, which, like the Yank's Pledge of Allegiance, hasn't been publicly spoken for some time now because, as old rock 'n roller Larry Norman put it, "Our money says 'In God We Trust,' but it's against the law to pray in school."

More than 50 years after launching, the old ladies of the Elgin Area Bible Club are still telling those stories, just after school hours to avoid that legal strap. And Praying Student in Hamilton is still at it, just quiet though, with eyes open.

Shortly after laughing all the way to the office, Paul Pittiwanika left Maple Crest, and I never saw him again. Best Boyhood Friend Paul Blakely and I later stood in each other's wedding parties, and he's now a good cop in the Niagara region, a family man who's left, like myself, with just memories from our wonder years, when our skinny arms held some fat trophies for being so smart and hip and sporty in our final year at that school, now torn down because the neighbours weren't having enough kids to fill it.

And now to make kids everywhere better and braver, there's zero tolerance, which is another crying shame in a Brave New World playground that's so very afraid of its own shadow.

The Rich Young Ruler 18

EDMONTON, CANADA
July 5, 2004

I don't generally get reverse-culture shock. That's the phenomenon where, after spending time in the developing world, some people return to their rich homelands to scream and pull their hair out while walking in long supermarket aisles filled with every pet food imaginable.

But I did feel a kind of reverse-culture poke when Jean and I recently spoke about our Third World work to folks in this rich oil town that's also known for having one of the world's largest malls. The West Edmonton Mall probably has more flush toilets than some of the planet's poorest countries have.

And I did feel at least a mild reverse-culture something from being in embittered Western Canada on election night when Ontario saved multimillionaire Paul Martin, a politician who has let Canada slide into an embarrassing foreign aid abyss despite his past promise to give "substantial flows of foreign aid to the world's poorest countries."

I find Ottawa's concern for the world's poor not unlike what I just read in the *Edmonton Street News*, a scrappy little tabloid sold to me on the street by an aboriginal. A voice for the homeless, it hounds Alberta's MPPs for things like feeding on steak and wine at the price of one homeless person's rent, "after a day of snoozing in the legislature."

It was 35 years ago when former Liberal prime minister Lester Pearson first said Canada would give 0.7 per cent of its national income to impoverished countries. Several Liberal governments have since repeated that pledge. But the best any has ever managed is 0.5 per cent, which Martin virtually halved when he was finance minister.

Interestingly, 0.7 per cent is the goal set for rich countries at the latest World Summit for Sustainable Development in Johannesburg, South Africa. If all donors reached it by 2005, $200 billion more would be freed for clean water, health care and basic schooling in Third World countries. Five donor countries have hit the target. Eight more probably will do so by 2010. At its current rate, Canada will get there by 2040.

The journal *Foreign Policy* ranks Canada way down at 18th out of the world's 21 richest countries in how its aid, trade, immigration, investments, peacekeeping and environmental protection help poor countries. Embarrassing indeed.

Taxes aside, even everyday Canadians are not as generous as we might think. According to the Fraser Institute, of all of the provinces, Albertans give the most per capita to charities, at $1,294, slightly more than Ontarians. That's less than the least generous U.S. state, Rhode Island, whose residents give double that amount.

How much greater is the need abroad? A Simon Fraser Public Research Group report explains that if the world population numbered 100 people, six would own half the wealth, 70 wouldn't read, 50 would be malnourished and 80 would have substandard housing. One would have a college degree.

These things become clearer for me in the summer when, back in Canada, I give personal thanks on my wedding anniversary, on my daughter's birthday, on Canada Day and even on my birthday, which falls on Bastille Day, France's national holiday celebrating its revolution, which gave birth to freedoms that still shape democracies like ours.

I can slow down to reflect as well on the privilege it is to live for much of the year among some of the world's more needy people in places like Yemen, among the impoverished and the runts and black sheep of today's global family. If only a few high-ranking politicos, of any Canadian party, would take similar opportunities.

Until they do, I doubt our understanding of the outside world and foreign aid needs will improve much. Not with a minority government. Even if they develop a conscience about their old aid promises, Liberals will still be more concerned about survival than anything. And that's too bad.

Not because we'll leave much of the world in want. Global poverty, to some extent, will always exist. But, because, it seems to me, Ottawa has become like the Rich Young Ruler: the young man who had it all but who allowed wealth and power to define all that he was and who, at the end of the day, lost his soul.

Looking south of the Snowy 49th Parallel, we see in recent years the Mighty Yanks have been fingered for being less than generous. Remember the criticism for their so-called lax response after the 2004 tsunami? Is it fair?

Maybe not, says civic researcher Arthur Brooks, who writes that the Excited States is in fact exceptional for generosity, largely because it's such a darn religious place.

Brooks cites evidence that America's religious – those in church regularly – are way more likely to give to charity (91 per cent compared to 66 per cent) and way more likely to volunteer (67 per cent to 44 per cent). Compared to secular folks, the religious are also, he says, 10 per cent more likely to give to secular charities, like a United Way, and 21 per cent more likely to volunteer for one.

And just how religious are Americans? Among 32 countries surveyed by the International Social Survey Programme, results from the United States show 23.4 per cent of the population attend church at least two or three times a month, compared to 11.4 per cent up here in Canada. (It was 18.7 per cent in Italy, 11.7 per cent in Australia, 7.8 per cent in Britain, 6.6 per cent in Sweden and 5.6 per cent in France.)

So there you have it. Many folks in the pews apparently do put their money where their mouths are.

Lies, shame and fear - 1 19

"Adam blamed Eve. Eve blamed the serpent. The serpent blamed God. Nobody likes to fess up."

LONDON, CANADA
July 31, 2003

Let's hope someone, somewhere, learns something from the murky death of Zahra Kazemi, the Canadian-Iranian photojournalist whose brains somehow got bashed in while she was in police custody for photographing student protesters outside a Tehran jail.

"If you mess with Canadians, face the consequences" seems a suitable lesson for Iran, a fossilized Islamic state that's like a tired Mick Jagger routine.

Entertaining in a strange way, intriguing for its longevity, but, like short-legged lies, able to run only so long.

Unfortunately, we know that without basic reform, Iran won't learn much today.

By the way, in my other home, Yemen, a poorer but more progressive Islamic state, you can scoop a "get-out-of-jail-free" pass if connected with the right tribe. For example, a few months ago, 10 jailbirds, including a couple of key suspects in the bombing of the USS Cole in 2000, reportedly dug through a rock-hard washroom floor in Aden with, yes, their bare hands.

Three confused guards were suspended and the Yemeni government offered US$10,000 for the recapture of the motley crew. Meanwhile, reports abound of plenty of other Yemenis jailed without charges over questionable circumstances.

And Yemen's local precinct houses aren't the Hilton. Want food? Ask your family. Your bed? Try the floor. Sorry, no sheets. Yes, you're crammed with dozens into a space the size of an average Canadian living room. You need the toilet? Pay the guard. It's all enough to make you cry.

But back to telling lies. It's human nature. Adam blamed Eve. Eve blamed the serpent. The serpent blamed God. Nobody likes to fess up. Yet in the Middle East, denial can be a fine art. If on the receiving end, don't take it personally. It's just a tradition practised to preserve honour.

Remember how Westerners laughed at Mohammed Saeed Sahaf, the outrageously comical Misinformation Minister of Iraq who insisted that Iraqis were routing coalition troops when Iraqi troops were in fact running away, at times literally in their underwear? Arabs didn't laugh. But most didn't believe Sahaf either. They knew he was simply trying to save Iraqi face.

In fact, in my experience, Arabs will take Westerners at face value, but they'll look to the subtle meanings behind the words of fellow Arabs. So we shouldn't be surprised that Iran initially claimed Kazemi died of a stroke and then threw in a red herring, blasting Canada for the police killing of a young machete-wielding Iranian in Vancouver, self-defence or not. It's classic deflection.

Ottawa needs to recognize such cultural nuances while holding Iran's feet to the fire. In doing so, Ottawa can also learn its own lesson, namely that it needs to take seriously Canadians overseas, particularly those in volatile areas.

For example, Nova Scotian William Sampson, a businessperson in Saudi Arabia, waits in jail there more than two years after arrest, facing execution over questionable charges.

Gar Knutson (Liberal MP for Elgin-Middlesex-London), Canada's secretary of state for Central and Eastern Europe and the Middle East, tells me Ottawa can try to put diplomatic pressure on rogue countries mistreating Canadians. "But at the end of the day, we don't have any great power. Every country is sovereign, and people have to play by the rules of that country."

Fair enough. Those who travel to unstable areas know the risks. But if a passport from a world-class nation such as Canada is essentially useless when it really counts, why not just travel with a hockey card in your back pocket?

Surely Canadian citizenship offers more. My physician wife and I believe it does. And since our desire is to see people live healthfully and free, things rather Canadian, we work in Yemen.

In the fall we return there, now with our infant daughter. It's called giving to others some of what you've been blessed with yourself. I suggest Kazemi had similar thoughts. That's why she was in Iran.

Her death should leave behind more than a trail of deceit and political justification. It should shine the light on, if nothing else, the need to protect the many other Canadians now living abroad.

20 *Lies, shame and fear - 2*

LONDON, CANADA
August 4, 2004

A handful of lessons are buried in the sorry state of Iran's recent investigation and trial involving the death of Canadian photojournalist Zahra Kazemi. They're buried in the pile of lies and nonsense that's often engrained in the not-so-free world, where, in my experience, up is certainly down if the right person says it's so.

Kazemi died at the hands of Iranian interrogators last summer after photographing students demonstrating at a Tehran jail. So Lesson #1 seems to be, if you want to be a journalist in a place such as Iran, realize authorities may exact equal parts of blood for any ink you spill to reveal something as nebulous as the truth.

Canadians may find this quite infuriating, since Kazemi held Canadian citizenship. But in the past four years, Iran's fundamentalist judiciary has all but destroyed that country's independent press, closing scores of newspapers and jailing dozens of journalists who support Iran's more reform-minded parliamentarians.

Further, truth in the Middle East, strange as this seems, often doesn't matter. This is because while the West has inherited a Greco-Roman worldview of guilt or innocence, the Middle East spins on an honour-shame axis.

There's not a right or wrong way of doing things as much as an honourable or dishonourable way. So lying, if it preserves group honour, is morally acceptable.

Lesson #2, then, is that we need to understand how hugely important a culture's mores are to its actions.

Let's also remember the planet's general lack of freedom. About 1.4 billion of Earth's 6.4 billion people now have access to a free press. Some 2.5 billion people live without a free press, and the other 2.5 billion live in countries where the media is only partially free. Not surprisingly, most of these unfortunate folks live in the developing world.

So, Lesson #3 might be, as terrible as the Kazemi murder is, if anything good is to come of it the international community needs to place it in the light of broader needs and respond accordingly.

For example, with outside help, my newspaper employer, the independent *Yemen Times,* is spearheading Yemen's first association of newspapers to help face pressures in that impoverished Muslim country. Pressures like a government bill, now defeated, that told Yemen's press to forfeit profits and donate to a fund that would protect journalists harassed by government officials. Follow the logic here. Pay me, so when I slap you around, there's money available for your legal defence. Stunning.

The reality is, if international aid groups leave the world's neediest media to fend for themselves, existing hand to mouth at best, then civil liberties that produce any country's societal and economic well-being will never be created.

The last lessons are for Ottawa. Incredibly, just weeks ago, with the Kazemi affair hanging in the air like the Hindenburg, Canada's ambassador to Iran, Philip McKinnon, reportedly told Iranian government officials that he'd like to see Canadian-Iranian trade increase.

Iran already annually receives hundreds of millions of dollars of Canadian grain, pulp and paper, and equipment related to oil and telecommunications. Considering the Kazemi farce, why?

Instead of just wringing its hands and crying bloody murder, why won't Ottawa stop working with Iranian metals and crude oil? Why not ban Persian rugs until Iran's judiciary stops sweeping the truth about Kazemi's death so conveniently underneath them? Why grant easy visas to Iranians, including 1,200 post-secondary students studying in Canada, among the largest student groups from anywhere?

Goodwill in any relationship needs to flow both ways. And if Ottawa is as outraged as it says it is over the Kazemi case, Iran should feel it.

Lesson #4, then, is say what you mean. And #5, mean what you say.

It's important to understand why some other places don't approach freedom of the press, or life in general, in such a straightforward manner. But in doing so, Ottawa shouldn't think it needs to maintain any political niceties.

In the end, a place like Iran needs to start learning its own lessons about how other countries do things.

And if Canada isn't willing to play political hardball when one of its own is so carelessly tossed to the wind, one has to wonder if a Canadian passport is not rather overrated.

This means war

21

"Ever consider such a wild experience? Neither did I."

SANA'A, YEMEN
March 7, 2003

Listen to the words of a cargo handler at London's airport, spoken while he cleared freight I shipped to Yemen last year: "Those people are backwards and they don't want to change. As far as I'm concerned, I couldn't care less what happens to them."

Such compassion from someone who's living, I suggest through no doing of his own, in one of the richest countries on earth.

Of course, others share similar crusty thoughts. But they're wrong. And on the eve of war with Iraq, it's good to remember that.

Consider Dr. Marty Robinson, a retired professor of obstetrics who was at the University of Western Ontario for forty years. An amiable, bow-tied member of life's old school, he was just here, leading a team of other London doctors. Having visited here annually since 1988, Robinson was the second North American doctor to set foot on Yemeni soil.

Since then, his teams have advised on health policy. They've trained surgeons. They've brought equipment and books. Recently they helped begin work on what will be this country's first cancer centre.

"We've all benefited from a good education in Canada," he said. "The Yemenis are very appreciative."

My wife, Jean, also an obstetrician, helped get tens of thousands of dollars of medical equipment here, courtesy of Sisters of St. Joseph in Hamilton. "God bless you" was the grateful response.

Then there's Geoff Chambers, a communications student from Australia. "I went hiking and met a boy who insisted I go to his home. It was just a cave. He gave me all he had, tea and dates...Later, a total stranger on the street invited me to dinner."

Yes, Yemen is backwards. And charming. So much so, Geoff wants to live here. Some foreigners, including Jean and myself and hundreds of other expatriates, already do.

That's great, you say. Yes, it is.

Ever consider such a wild experience? Neither did I.

Of course, good reasons will anchor some folks in Canada. But honestly, is huffing and puffing down the road to so-called success, always looking to the dollar sign for direction, one of them?

You're not qualified to work in the developing world? You are if you speak English. Millions want to learn it.

Too old? Marty is over 70.

Too young? Geoff is 20.

You have kids? Nice. Jean and I return to Canada soon to deliver our first. Then we'll bring the bambino back here.

Broke? People with money love to support worthy causes. And, unlike most, Canadians have free health care to fall back on.

So visit. Or check out another needy place. It's not as difficult as it seems. Historically, millions left Europe for North America during times that were much harder. And with no return ticket.

Marty and Jean. Two people. Much good. Compare two with 200,000. That's about the number of American and British troops now in the Gulf region. Do the math. Imagine the potential of coming to the Arab world in such a big way with something other than a spiked fist. Yes, armies of aid workers.

Unrealistic? You're right. I guess it's better to watch unwieldy governments paint themselves into horrible corners.

Rather than spending tens of billions of dollars blowing up Iraq, what if, for example, some of that change helped Arabs gain decent higher education? Then youth won't be driven to Islamic extremism under the guise of cheap schooling. Isn't that a better way to make allies?

People need to see how things tick outside their own neighbourhood. Maybe a few more Canadians, lucky as we are, will slow down sometime and think about that.

If, later, you want cargo moved, show the fellow at London airport a map. Point out your destination. And remind him that any journey starts with one step.

W

Some parents have a certain knowing attitude: a mix of gentle wisdom and quiet understanding. Our Two Royal Younglings are helping me get just enough to start.

Both were born in Hamilton, by the way, so that nothing but Canada is their birthplace in their passports. But My Royal Babe and I are most thankful that they're growing up in the developing world, experiencing that wider breadth of the human family.

One thing that fatherhood has given me as a journalist is a wider soul, somehow connected on a different level to the sea of other parents out there. That news story of an injured child, or abducted child, or that street-enslaved or starving or even dead child now has an entirely new dimension.

I'm also reminded that children are children anywhere. In impoverished countries they may be shabbily clothed and dirty faced, but they're often smiling when you least expect.

In fact, many love to approach white foreigners. In Yemen, that's common in traffic at stoplights. Many times I've seen these little ones run over to beg for their families and then go wild with joy with a simple personal gift. Take a photo, a 'surrah,' of them and watch them go even wilder.

These musings touch on these things, and at times, like at Christmas, wander to the gentle Jesus who said, "Let the little children come to me".

Included are a few extra photos of the world's smaller people. This includes a couple of published shots of our Youngling 1, Elizabeth, plus her counterparts on the Arab street, and then some young faces from our current home in Uganda.

Enjoy.

Opposite page photo: *The author with his two-week-old daughter, Elizabeth.*

WINDOWS

Meet the Kids

A daughter of the world - 1

22

Hamilton, Canada
June 20, 2003

Nobody knew. Prior to the birth of our first child, two weeks ago today at St. Joseph's Hospital here in Hamilton, Jean and I kept her name, Elizabeth, top secret from absolutely everyone.

"It's from the Bible and it's not Dorcas," is all I would reveal, before adding, "If and when we have a boy, we have a biblical name for him too. And it's not Nimrod."

So imagine the confirmation we felt when, prior to our return to Canada for the delivery, some Western friends in Yemen said goodbye to us by reading the biblical story of Elizabeth.

The gospel writers tell that Elizabeth was a cousin of Mary, mother of Christ. Barren, she was surprised to conceive her son, John, later in her life.

It seems our friends wanted to remind Jean and I that while angels may not advertise it, the arrival of even common children into this world is a supernatural event. Indeed, in Hebrew, *Elizabeth* means "consecrated to God." *Katherine*, our newborn's middle name, means "pure" in its original Greek.

Dorcas, by the way, doesn't mean "buck-toothed girl with big glasses" but "gazelle." And *Nimrod* is not "he who can't tie his own shoes" but actually "hunter."

The heritage of names has been largely lost in our culture, but not in the Middle East. That's why Arab names run as long as trains.

Take the name Ali bin Ahmed bin Saleh Al-Fulani. Ali to his friends and family, his family name is Al-Fulani. The *bin Ahmed bin Saleh* means he's son of Ahmed (a common derivation of the prophet Mohammed), who is son of Saleh.

But I digress. The point is that bright-eyed Elizabeth Katherine is here, and she'll grow up in Yemen for at least for a couple of years.

True, the developing world can be unkind. Some moms don't even survive childbirth. Instead of Pampers, rural moms may have a few rags. You can imagine the infections. There's poor nutrition. And later, parents deal with the cold realization that their children will never escape their country's desperate straits.

Expatriate children, especially girls, also have challenges. How do you get them into, say, piano lessons or soccer if they're not available? And schooling? These are questions Jean and I will face as we continue our global work.

Yet cross-cultural kids are incredibly mature and aware of humanity in all of its breadth. And really, for all the resources Canada's hurry-up instant-Internet-connection culture offers, how are Canadian youth faring?

It seems they know that classic song "Cat's in the Cradle" from the 1970s all too well, where the boy becomes just like Dad in all the wrong ways. Harry Chaplin's poignant lyrics cut to our culture's soul.

> "Not today, I got a lot to do"...
> "When you coming home, Dad?"
> "I don't know when. But we'll get together then, yeah. You know we'll have a good time then."

Consciously or not, it's also easy for baby boomers – a generation that's had success at everything it's done – to make their kids feel like life is about winning and acquisitions more than stewardship.

But what's worth more than the better home or clothing or holidays or even schools is connecting with our kids and passing values from one generation to the next, so they can then build their own futures on solid ground.

Giving that kind of intelligent love takes time, thought and patience. As a father for just two weeks, I don't pretend to entirely know the way. But I suspect it has something to do with becoming childlike ourselves, without resentment, prejudices or worry for tomorrow, stripped of our veneers of sophistication that hide our true selves.

It seems that comes through the purifying influence that children can have on adults. Many children seem to carry that mysterious truth that sets us free. At least the feeling I get from Elizabeth.

I think it's something that will at least give me a chance. Now let's hope she likes flying.

23 *A daughter of the world - 2: "Daddy's home!"*

CHARLOTTETOWN, CANADA
July 12, 2003

My first big experience as a part-time stay-at-home dad unfolded here in Canada's birthplace, in a hotel, just before Canada Day.

I don't think even the Fathers of Confederation could have helped. Birthing a country is one thing. Stopping a three-week-old from crying is another.

I didn't have to say much in my SOS phone call to my wife, who was busy at a medical conference here. "Babe, come right away," I said, while little Elizabeth, wrapped in her blanket like a giant taco, wailed beside me in support.

I don't know. Was it because I accidentally tore the Velcro off her diapers? Who makes these things anyway?

Really, there's a lot to learn for new parents. Breast or bottle? Cloth or disposable? Rocking or vibrating chair? And the painkillers during childbirth – how long to wait for them?

Sometimes it seems there's a conspiracy to make new parents look extra stupid. Seriously, apparently 85 per cent of us use baby car seats incorrectly.

Still, the good news is that Elizabeth, middle name Katherine, has arrived into this world, a bright-eyed and, usually, content little girl. And despite new-father challenges, I'm fine.

As a journalist who often works from the home office, including while in the Arab world most of the year, I'll have a unique role in her life.

I'm not alone. In the minority, yes. But there are more stay-at-home dads than ever. In Canada, there are at least 70,000 of us, giving a whole new meaning to the phrase *Daddy's home*. One in four preschoolers of working moms are now cared for by dads.

And this is good because, all things considered, kids don't want designer clothes or that Disney vacation or even a bigger house. They want, quite simply, their parents. Both of them.

Think of Harry Chapin's '70s classic "Cats in the Cradle," where the boy grows up to be "just like Dad" in all the wrong ways. The pain of absent parents cuts to the soul of the baby boomer culture.

In *The Capitol of the World,* Ernest Hemingway puts it well. A father is looking for his runaway teenage son, and as a last resort, after a long journey, the lovesick father takes out a Madrid newspaper ad: "Dear Paco, Meet me in front of the newspaper office tomorrow at noon. All is forgiven. I love you." The next day, 800 men named Paco show up at the news building wanting to restore a broken relationship.

Living in our instant, hurried culture makes it all the harder to build those healthy connections with our kids. Yemen, my other home, or Uganda, where Jean and I will eventually take our global work, has less pressure in some ways.

But these places have other challenges. If stay-at-home dads feel on the fringe in Canada, imagine living in a part of the world where men won't pick up a vacuum for another 50 years? And where does one find, say, piano lessons or soccer practice for Elizabeth, if it's not available? And good schooling?

Still, as a child growing up in the developing world for at least a few years, Elizabeth will have a tremendous chance to experience humanity in all of its breadth.

And, at the end of the day, it seems to me that parents and children are in all of this together. Kids have a way of keeping us adults honest, wherever we may live.

That's why it's been said if we're ever going to understand a place like heaven, we need to become childlike: that is, without resentment, prejudices or concerns for tomorrow, stripped of our veneer of sophistication that we easily hide behind.

Such is the purifying influence that children have on adults. They're carriers of that mysterious truth that sets us free. At least that's the message I get from Elizabeth. It's something I believe will at least give me a chance.

Now let's just hope this girl likes flying.

The next column was among this book's more enjoyable commentaries to write, and now my family has a tradition where one of the Two Royal Younglings "writes" our family's Christmas newsletter. Everyone loves it, seeing life through the eyes of a child.

The idea to do so for a column came after I saw a London Free Press piece "written" by the regular columnist's cat, complete with mug shot of the prodigious feline.

So this letter to Santa from Elizabeth was published on Christmas Eve, along with her mug and our family photo in my usual slot in the Hamilton Spectator, a decorated paper that's among Canada's more progressive media outlets.

A good time was had by all. Almost. Read the postscript.

Dear Santa: Keep singing 24

SANA'A, YEMEN
December 24, 2004

Dear Santa:

Hello from Yemen. I hope you and Mrs. Claus and Rudolph are fine. I can't wait for Christmas. It's my second one. Mommy and Daddy found a Christmas tree and put it in the living room for you.

There's no snow here. It's not like the North Pole. Or Hamilton. That's where I was born. That's in Canada. Sometimes I mix it up with other places because Mommy and Daddy take me so many airplanes. I'm 18 months old now, and I've been in lots of countries.

On airplanes, Mommy cares for me. But Daddy takes my picture and calls me "pretty girl." Sometimes "silly girl," but mostly "pretty girl." He asks, "How did you get so pretty? Where you born pretty, or did you get pretty along the way?" It's hard to say, but I look like Mommy, so maybe it's both.

Do you like Christmas pictures? Daddy says every Christmas his daddy would take him and my Tante Heidi for their family picture. That was in the '70s. It was just the three of them. And their cats. Daddy says he wore goofy white turtlenecks with bright-red jackets. My Opa is in his 70s, but I've never seen a white turtle on his neck.

This is our Christmas picture for this year. It's from a place called Kokoban. That's an hour from our house. My other grandpa took it. He and Grandma visited us earlier this year. I was really little then.

People live in those rock houses. But Daddy says the hearts of people around the world are the same, whether we live in a rock house or not. Daddy knows, because he works at the newspaper. That's a factory that makes letters into words and then strings them together so people learn things.

We don't have cats. But we have another family. They own our house. It's called a flat because it's flat. They're nice to us. Mr. and Mrs. Ali have four children. One is a girl. They're *big*. Soon we'll invite them down for yummies.

They're Muslim. They believe some things about Jesus. But they don't think Jesus came to earth to die for our sins. If He didn't, I think He came an awful long way for nothing. I guess that's why nobody here sings at Christmas.

We're foreigners, so we can sing. Today is Christmas Eve. So we sang about Jesus with other foreigners at a concert. Mommy played the flute. Mostly, we sing just to ourselves, though. Not too loud to wake the neighbours. We sing that Jesus loves all the children of the world, like my crayons: red and yellow, black and white, we're all very precious in His sight.

Muslims love children too. So they have lots. In the Middle of the East, if you don't have children, some people even think something's wrong. Maybe God doesn't love you. They might look down on you. Jesus never had His own family. Did people look down on Him too?

It must be hard with no family at Christmas. It would be like you with no Mrs. Claus. Who would help you with your mail?

Mommy and Daddy said they'd help me with this letter, if my wish list was realistic. I don't know what that is, so I'll just ask for what I want. I wish everyone gets a family and a Christmas picture. And I wish they can sing as loud as they want, so everyone knows how much God loves them, even when it's raining or when their swings break. Is that okay?

When Daddy sees this letter, he'll probably call me a silly girl. But then he'll pick me up and kiss me and help me type it. And Mommy will paste in our picture, and pray that it gets to you in time and that you put it in a special place.

I guess that's all I have to say. So from my family over here to yours over there, Merry Christmas. Don't get too busy. Sing every day. And remember: don't eat too many cookies, because you still have to get around next year.

Love,
Elizabeth Katherine

Yes, this preceding selection brought smiles around. Except to a few information gatekeepers at a smaller sister paper of the Spectator down the Ontario highway.

Here a couple of thoughtful editors thought quite hard about it all and then told me that they didn't believe Royal Youngling 1 could write such a piece, and they didn't think their readers would be fooled either, so they wouldn't run my column as usual.

Now I have nothing against this publication, which will remain nameless (but it's in a fine new downtown building in an otherwise progressive burg that was once called Berlin when the German Kaiser was still a force, a really with-it spot that's now like Boston North, home of Conestoga College, Wilfrid Laurier University and the University of Waterloo, brainy places I've personally studied at).

So after I told My Royal Babe and everyone in Yemen and Santa himself, and after I stopped laughing and checked the calendar (to remind myself from where it originates), I replied to these thoughtful editors with some Christmas common sense. Still, no luck.

Scrooge was more enlightened.

Looking for Oz

25

SANA'A, YEMEN
November 2, 2002

The children. Oh, the children. The smallest hold tightly onto black tent-like baltos that drape over their mothers. Others sing in a school courtyard near our home. But the beggar kids who run to our vehicle when it's stopped at intersections really get me.

Sometimes dirty faced, always playful, they'll melt any heart. My wife, Jean, and I offer them pencils bearing Canada's flag and, in broken Arabic, tell them Jesus loves them. That always gets a big smile. If we take their photo, a *surrah*, they go wild with joy.

As beautiful as they are, the children are also a reminder that population growth here is out of control. Yemen has 20 million souls, double of 1987. Forty per cent of 280 million regional Arabs are now under 15. That's the highest youth rate in the world.

Consider also that Yemen, among Earth's poorest countries, has an annual average income of $450, 40 per cent unemployment, no social safety net and dwindling water resources.

The children.

To help them out of poverty and related problems such as terrorism, international donors meeting in Paris recently announced a $2.3-billion loan for Yemen. That came after the French oil tanker Limburg exploded off Yemen's coast.

The alleged voice of Osama bin Laden gloated on news channels that "youths of God" plan more hits on the economic lifelines of America and its allies.

But as a small oil producer, Yemen needs foreign companies to get oil out safely. You can imagine new security fears and higher insurance rates for incoming vessels. Whose lifeline is hurt?

Reaching further than grinding poverty here, however, is the heavy blanket of Islam. Next week will mark the start of Ramadan, the highlight of the Islamic year. For a month, folks rest and fast during the day and then shop, visit and feast, if they can afford to, at night. Like children clutching their mothers' baltos, they'll cling to their religion in a way most Westerners can no longer imagine.

Why? In the Muslim world, conforming to the group is more important than individual liberty. As one Syrian intellectual put it, "The role of Islamic thought is to explain, not to search and question."

Indeed, if you're called several times daily, including at 4 a.m., to recite scripted prayers, and if you're given religious messages over loudspeakers in the streets, as in Sana'a, how do you find much else?

I liken it to going to Oz. Most of us want a heart, courage and brains. But where do you turn if, at the end of the road, you discover the wizard isn't everything you expected? To corrupt authorities? To embittered clerics? Do you admit you're lost? Or, as I've found here, do you blame your problems on others, namely Jews and Americans?

If you think that's harsh, consider the first-ever Arab Human Development Report released this year by scholars who are Arabs themselves. It notes that the Middle East is "richer than it is developed," but three key needs are keeping Arabs behind much of the world.

One need is freedom from what the report calls a "patriarchal, intolerant and sometimes suffocating social environment."

Another is knowledge. Incredibly, in the last 1,000 years, say the scholars, Arabs have translated as many books as Spain translates in one year.

The third is women's rights. Into the 21st century, half of Arab women remain illiterate. Ask Jean, an obstetrician, why. Once, when a Yemeni was told about her medicine, the woman responded, "Don't tell me. Tell my husband. I'm just a cow."

Which brings us back to independent thinking. The report partly defends Islam's support of justice, peace and tolerance. But it also explains Islam's deeply ingrained teaching to never defy tradition.

One tradition is that truth is only in text, not personal experience. And that's why the reality of Islam so often doesn't mesh with the ideals of Islam. "Whom do you hate?" "America!" "Where do you want to live?" "America!"

Ramadan helps some Muslims forget such enigmas. But they won't go away.

The children here deserve more. For their sake and for the security of the global community, let's hope at least some can, by some miracle, find a brighter future. A simple pencil and a "Jesus loves you" may be small tools to give them. But it's an honest message. And that's what they need.

The bastards want our kids 26

Kampala, Uganda
December 16, 2006

One of the unexpected things I've caught since coming to Africa for the long haul is a certain disturbing feeling in the pit of my stomach. It's grown there quietly, feeding, I suspect, on the various foreign sights and sounds around here, especially those of the children.

Of course, African kids are more than stereotypical media images of bony starving waifs. There's more to African life than "Do They Know It's Christmas?" that 1980s hit song by BandAid about Africa's Christmas chimes of doom. Still, unlike in Canada this holiday season, some African children will starve to death. Many others will experience childhood as it was never meant to be.

And having my own young children here doesn't help my stomach much, not when my three-year-old asks, as she did recently, "Daddy, what's a Muzungu?" I can't really respond, "Well, Elizabeth, in an African context, *Muzungu* means 'rich white person,' and this, sweetie, is what you and I are. Just remember, if some children call you this, it's not mean-spirited; it's just rather matter-of-fact. So don't worry; Be happy."

Likewise, when visiting a Ugandan orphanage, Elizabeth's mother and I can't easily explain to her why some kids have no mommies or daddies. There's so much that little ones don't understand. So many of them here – Elizabeth and her brother, Jon, included – sing innocently and honestly about how "red and yellow, black and white, Jesus loves all the children of the world."

So then why does the UN's 2006 *State of the World's Children* report that 11 million kids under five are now dying yearly from malnutrition or disease? Why do 600 million live in abject poverty? Why can't 100 million (or more) access even primary schooling? Why do 2.5 million have AIDS, a killer that's orphaned another 15 million, with plenty more coming?

Why during this, the Mother of all Childhood Seasons, when toys spill over in so many living rooms, do so many children live in this sad and sorry and terribly true state? Why are truckloads of innocents becoming nothing but cold, dead statistics? Can't Jesus do better?

Despite some gains, disparities are stretching across the globe like some hideous alien's tentacles. Simon Fraser Public Research Group reports if today's world had 100 people, 50 would be malnourished, 70 wouldn't be able to read, and 80 would have rotten housing. Six would have half the wealth. One would have a degree.

Of course, there's a complex web of reasons for all this, and none have much to do with Jesus: poor personal choices, destructive cultural mores, wars, government corruption, unfair global trade – and the list goes on. Metaphorically, the lunatics are taking the asylum. Control is falling to the bastards among us, and children are suffering the most.

If you find this offensive, consider recent science from Paul Zak, of Claremont Graduate University's Center for Neuroeconomics Studies in California. Zak suggests human nature is basically good, that our brains are even hard-wired to co-operate. People find it natural to, for one thing, share. But, some two per cent of us, at least in Zak's lab studies, are "pure non-co-operators," always hoarding, always into themselves at all costs.

The technical term in Zak's lab for these people is moral "bastards." Their

brains apparently work differently, like those of sociopaths, who don't – or can't – care about anyone, maybe due to dysfunction of the chemical oxytocin.

So, it can be argued, there really are bastards out there. The question is, how do we save our children from them? And how do we avoid becoming bastards ourselves? It may seem strange, but when one is a Muzungu in Africa, especially at Christmas, these are the things that can fester in one's stomach.

But, then again, on one level or another, maybe we're all bastards. And maybe God loves us anyway. Maybe that's why the story of the first Christmas has been left for us to ponder.

It's something to think about the next time you hear the radio play BandAid's unnerving song about Africa's children and what we have or haven't done for them. And it's something to give thanks for when you see that wonder in a child's eyes on Christmas Day.

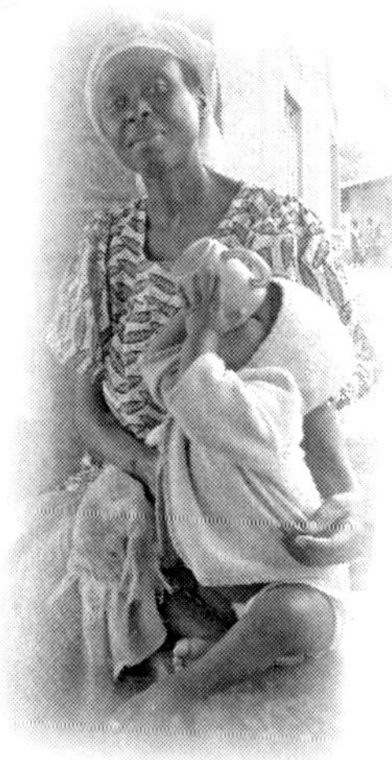

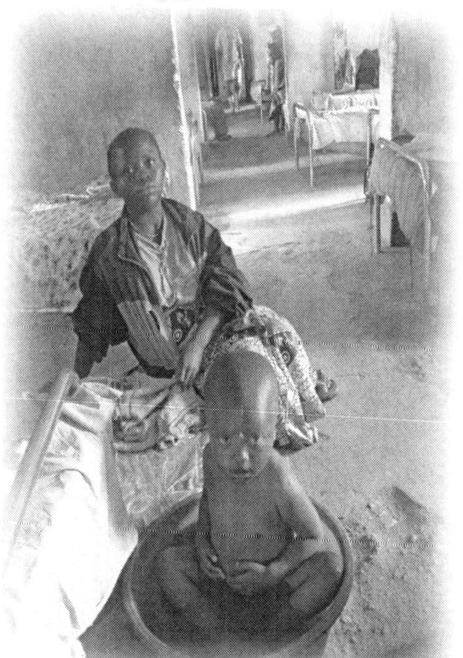

Few people liked Saddam Hussein. He was even loathed by many Arabs, including in Yemen where an estimated 30,000 Iraqis live.

But when the Americans attacked Iraq to start Gulf War II, they enflamed some deep regional undercurrents, namely a profound feeling of victimization.

Politically, many Arabs feel victimized by corrupt leaders. Economically, many feel victimized by a global system they believe favours the West.

And in a culture that hinges on a powerful "honour-shame" paradigm, this can't be overstated. The Arab psyche is one of deep humiliation, and this permeates everyday life.

So anyone who shakes a defiant fist, in particular at the wealthy West, anyone who tries to restore lost honour, like Saddam did, isn't so bad after all. The bigger picture of the Iraq War, then, is less about Iraq and more about Arabs fighting an entire host of shames, many long-standing, like in Palestine.

As my Yemeni landlord told me after I asked what should happen to the then-captured Saddam: "Like at the end of any good story, the hero should die." The hero.

Among my other observations in these selections is that anyone who lives so close to war can't help but see the players – Iraqis, Palestinians, You-Fill-in-the-Name – through a different lens.

If you don't believe me, visit and discover some unexpected friendships with folks who are more complex than any two-dimensional stereotype might suggest.

Opposite page photo: *An American soldier comforts an injured Iraqi girl.*

WAR. HONOUR. SHAME.

WINDOWS

The road to hell

27

LONDON, CANADA
September 9, 2002

> "*Perdition* (per dish en): a state of final spiritual ruin; hell; utter destruction"

I have an Arab friend who looks very much like a stereotypical Western mobster. A gentle spirit, he also reminds me of a boy named Michael, son of Mike Sr., a gangster in the recent Tom Hanks film *Road to Perdition.*

"A year after 9/11," I asked him in a Toronto coffee bar, "why do some Arabs still have a hard time admitting Arab-Muslims were involved?

Most of the hijackers were Saudis. Osama bin Laden claims to be Muslim. So why, for example, in Yemen, where I've lived most of this year, does the mainstream press report, straight-faced, that Jews were behind the attacks, that 4,000 Jews played hooky from work, knowing what would hit that day?

Closer to home, why don't Arab and Muslim groups in Canada distance themselves more from extremists linked to 9/11?

"It's too big a question," says my friend, who's been in Canada for two years and who, if he ever returns home, will be hunted because he's left the Muslim faith.

It seems the answer, in part, can be found in the ethos of Arab culture. It accentuates honour. Period. In Yemen, you can get what you need *inshallah.* That's a catchy, face-saving phrase, translated "God willing." I've discovered it means definitely *yes*, definitely *no*, or anything in between.

Anthropologists confirm that self-respect, in fact, is the largest need of Arabs as a people-group. Which is why Arab dictators, often families with concentrated power, tend to run their countries like the mob: without accountability, but with plenty of rivalries and revolutions.

Consider this string of political slayings: King Feisal II of Iraq, murdered with his family and prime minister in 1958, corpses defiled in the streets; King Abdullah of Jordan, killed in 1951; Saudi Arabian king Feisal, shot dead in 1975 by a young relation; Qassem in Iraq, shot by two brothers, one later killed; Ibrahim Hamdi of former North Yemen, murdered with his brother in 1977, their assassin later blown up by an envoy's rigged briefcase; Egypt's Anwar Sadat, shot dead publicly; generals Oufkir and Mehdi Ben Barka, political challengers in Morocco who met strange deaths; and innumerable Arab officers hurried from specially convened tribunals to the firing squad.

Of course, our culture has its own problems. I heard of the attacks on America while in a Hamilton mall last September 11. It was on a row of monster TV screens that I watched the Twin Towers crumble. Could another setting be more indicative of a self-absorbed society?

We easily feel threatened with the "terror" of Islam. But do we see that Arab-Muslims are also very afraid of us? They resent the economic and military dominance of the West, particularly the New Rome of America. They're bitter over its foreign policy, especially perceived blind support of Israel. They fear more infiltration of our pop culture. Globalization and the spread of the English language are harmless to us, but they too are insidious threats to Islamic values.

Add frustration fuelled by poverty, on top of the corruption and repression, and one gets the picture that, while most Arab-Muslims may never think of flying a jet into a skyscraper, many may feel satisfaction or at least a cool ambivalence to such acts.

Which brings us to the boy, Michael, in *Road to Perdition.* In a poignant scene, he realizes the terrible truth, that there is blood on his father's hands. Caught up in his Lone Ranger picture-paperback, tears flow down his innocent face. He faces the inevitable. *Is my father a hero or a villain? Is he a good man or a bad man?* The tears continue. It's too big a question.

The good news is that Michael finds peace by giving honour where it should be given. And eventually, as the story goes, he's given new choices and a new family. In a way, his journey is not unlike my Arab friend's.

"We're all God's kids. We're all His sons and daughters. And He has a plan for each of us," he told my wife and me in that coffee bar, while, incredibly, sharing his desire to someday return and help redeem his homeland.

In the end, those are the thoughts we need to shatter our stereotypes. Satisfactory acknowledgement or not, they're what will lead us to recovery.

Simply pushing the replay button on the terrible crimes of yesterday, I'm afraid, leads to another road.

I enjoyed 'Road to Perdition,' and its exploration of family honour and loyalty and patriarchy, because these themes run deep in The Froese History Book.

My forefathers are a strand of Mennonites who got their start in Friesland, a province in north Holland that's too small and wet to find on most maps. The Mennonites – not to be confused with their younger cousins, the black-hat Amish, who starred in the movie 'Witness' (Harrison Ford, not Tom Hanks) – were 16th century religious reformers originally known as the Anabaptists.

They were burned at the stake, drowned in rivers and starved in cages that hung in Europe's public squares, because they were too reform-minded for even the mainstream reformers of the day, Martin Luther's Protestants.

So the Friesen Mennonites wandered east to the steppes of Russia, where they eventually tilled land very expertly for Catherine the Great. In time they got so educated and established and hip that they owned a growing slice of Russia's productivity, becoming in some circles a new bourgeois.

Getting rid of them, though, was as easy as telling them to pick up a gun for their adopted country. As pacifists they'd rather take a walk, which is exactly what they did over and over, first into nearby Prussia and eventually over the ocean to Canada and other far-flung places.

W

I became a bit of a wandering Mennonite myself as a young man leaving home and looking for nebulous things like my future. I didn't wander far: just to an early-morning bus and then to relatives down the Ontario highway. But it was far enough for Dad Froese to question the state of my New World soul and for others to wonder if all this pacifism stuff would hold up among us.

In this case, add some more recent chapters from The Froese History Book. Mom and Dad Froese met in Canada as post–Second World War immigrants from Germany. After marriage and Child 1 in Canada, Mom, pregnant with me as Future Scribe (and with Child 1 in tow), returned to her family in Berlin.

This is where I was born, sometime after John F. Kennedy faced the Russians and visited to tell a million tear-filled waving Berliners "Ich bin ein Berliner," that is, that he too was a "Berliner" (which, by the way, in Berlin, is the name of a jelly donut).

To reunite his family, my father did what any Canadian might: asked Ottawa for help. Then he realized he'd have better luck with the papers. So a columnist at the Toronto Telegram wrote it all up as an intriguing international drama, and one warm day in the summer of '68 it appeared on the Telly's front page headlined "One man's fight for his two children." Following are some excerpts...

[July 3, 1968 – Page 1]: "This is a report about Gunther Froese, a St. Catharines licensed masseur now wandering somewhere in West Berlin on the verge of a nervous breakdown because the Canadian government never could seem to find the time to take a long look at the very justified complaint he had. For the last three years Mr. Froese has been buffeted from department to department, politician to politician . . . [This week] Mr. Froese went to pick up Heidi and a son he had never seen . . . Mrs. [Hannelore] Froese was under psychiatric care . . . Armed with a custody order, Mr. Froese went to visit his daughter. [Heidi] was in a children's home . . . But the superintendent of the home called police. They set up a roadblock and arrested Mr. Froese . . . Mr. Froese was beaten up . . . He has been promised help in the last 11 months from this list of prominent Canadians: Prime Minister Pierre Trudeau,

Progressive Conservative leader Robert Stanfield, NDP leader Tommy Douglas, acting Justice Minister Donald S. Macdonald, James McNulty, his area MP and at least a score of others. But there wasn't any help in Berlin this week . . . The Canadian Military Mission in West Berlin is keeping its hands off . . . Today, Mr. Froese is alone in West Berlin . . .

[July 4, 1968] "Yesterday we told of the ordeal of Gunther Froese. The [Canadian] government didn't even try to take action after our report yesterday. Today, Mr. Froese vanished. We have engaged a private detective to try to find Mr. Froese since the public authorities in Berlin have as little interest in him as Ottawa . . .

[July 12, 1968] "Today, Mr. Froese is in Copenhagen and as soon as he can get on a plane he will return to St. Catharines – victorious. He has his two children with him and that was the only victory he wanted . . . In a statement by, of all people, the lawyer for his wife, the court was urged to give Mr. Froese police protection . . . Two German police cars and a Canadian military vehicle escorted Mr. Froese and his daughter to the plane. After arriving in Copenhagen, Mr. Froese left his daughter with friends and flew to Munich to pick up the son he has never seen." [Excerpt ends.]

And this – with another German detective or two, plus international law professors, thrown in – was what led to the day before my third birthday, the day my father and I met for the first time in a small town near Munich, Germany. And with the blessing of the courts in Canada and Berlin, Dad Froese took me aboard a plane also. With Child 1, we flew from Copenhagen to New York, and then back to Canada, eventually arriving in Niagara where the three of us started our lives anew.

True to Mennonite sentiments, there Dad Froese got his hands on a historic estate property, Ye Olde Niagara Home, not far from the world-famous falls, just off of Lock 7 of the old Welland Canal. He fixed up the place and launched a business to care for the disadvantaged of the region, folks who became our extended family for many years.

Mom Froese, meanwhile, remained in Berlin, never to return. In the summer before I started kindergarten, we received the post with the wide black border around its edges. My mother was dead.

(For more on the author's personal background, see Windows 51, 62, 78 and 95 and their addendums.)

Twenty-three years later, as a young scribe, I had the chance to work in the streets of a newly-unified Berlin, with its shamed and haggard addicts. In too short a time they gave me too many memories: rushing with one to a clinic, her head on my lap, to get her stomach pumped; getting a kiss on the cheek from a prostitute seeking a way out; serving bread and wurst to others in an coffee bar with signs saying 'Keine Drogen erlaubt,' or "No drugs allowed."

While in Berlin, I also paid my respects at my mother's gravesite, which I found is a short walk from the apartment she had lived and died in.

Not long after that, back in Niagara, I was Dad's best man, publicly thanking him for teaching me to have things like farmer's perspective: a certain world-view that respects life's seasons and rhythms and the need to sometimes work hard ground, not unlike the clayish land we broke in the large plot of land that was our garden in the back of Ye Olde Niagara Home, planted with every life-sustaining vegetable imaginable. Dad's wedding gift? A golden hoe.

Along with the former family business, that garden is now gone, developed with nondescript houses. But Dad Froese, now approaching eight decades, remains in Ye Olde Niagara Home, tools in hand on any day he can, still hoping to improve it, loving the days when his grandchildren are home from Africa and visiting.

Recently, with all of us sitting around the dinner table there in Niagara, I read to Dad Froese for his birthday. In hand was 'Of This Earth,' by Canadian Rudy Wiebe, winner of the Governor General's Literary Award for writing the memoir of his Saskatchewan boyhood and Mennonite heritage.

In my nicht-so-gut Deutsch, I read aloud into a rather holy moment. Royal Youngling 2 – that is, my son, Jonathan Thomas, the third generation – sat beside me, and his Opa, the family patriarch, across from him.

"Herr Gott, du bist unsere Zuflucht fur and fur ... Lord God, you have been our refuge in all generations." And "Hier auf Erden bin ich ein Pilger. Und mine Pilgern, und my Pilgern wahrt nich lang ... Here on Earth I am a pilgrim. And my pilgrimage will not be very long."

Later, our broken voices somehow carried by phone over the ocean, Dad told me how much he enjoyed the rest of that Mennonite book. And another I had given him. And picturing his own boyhood from the Danzig region of Old Prussia so vividly again.

In Uganda I've stumbled across a group known as "Friends of Mennonites," a kind of Mennonite support group that meets monthly to eat food that really schmeckts and chat about how they wish they were Mennonite and other lofty things. After discovering I was the real deal, a bona-fide Mennonite in Uganda, members offered my young family a standing invitation to their homes.

In neighbouring Ethiopia there are now about 5,000 Mennonites, indigenous Africans who took on the Mennonite cloak, thankful for the work that Mennonite aid workers have carried out in their country in recent decades.

While I appreciate this heritage, I do hold it all loosely. I've found that the real appeal of Mennonite tradition is its pilgrim-like spirit of wanderlust and thanksgiving. And to experience this, you just need to be a human who travels light.

In fact, for the traveller in you, pick up a Mennonite Your Way, a global listing of Mennonites who open their doors for trekkers of any stripe on a budget. Stay the night, have breakfast, leave – in many cases – just what you can afford.

We've been duped 28

Sana'a, Yemen
March 31, 2003

If truth is the first casualty of war, one has to wonder what that does in the so-called battle over hearts and minds of people, not only in Iraq but also across the Arab world and beyond.

During months of diplomatic poker at the UN, we heard the Americans tell of the pressing need to disarm Saddam Hussein. We were told that another 9/11, or worse, would happen unless Saddam's weapons of mass destruction were found and destroyed.

When inspectors couldn't find such weapons quickly, the Americans tried, with flimsy evidence, to link Iraq to terrorism. Al-Qaida has actually been found in Yemen far more than in Iraq.

Washington also was willing to let Saddam take the money he's amassed during his reign of terror – reportedly US$7 billion – and disappear into exile. No luck. In the Middle East it's more important to save face than to save your skin.

Now, however, its real plan for Iraq is coming to light. It's never been to simply disarm Saddam. It's to get rid of him, one way or another, so the Americans can set up shop and reshape the Middle East into a kinder, gentler place where, for one thing, the flag of democracy flies and economies run free.

Invade a dysfunctional region of the world to fix it—that's the plan, according to reports in the media such as *TIME* magazine. Opinions may vary whether such a grand vision is worthy, let alone possible. But isn't it strange that it never even got debated before Baghdad was hit?

There are a few things to consider. First, a conquered Iraq won't turn into any post–Second World War Germany or Japan. Arab Muslims want to preserve the past more than work for some future economic miracle. Frankly, the work ethic on this side of the world is valued differently. That means resources such as Iraqi oil might always be handled by outsiders.

Second, despite Washington's hopes, a post-Saddam Iraq will not in itself bring peace to the occupied territories in the Palestinian-Israeli battleground. It's the conflict between Arabs and Jews, not Saddam's despotism, that causes Israel's strife. Of course, Saddam plays on that. Indeed, it's a wonder he didn't immediately begin to fire Scuds at Tel Aviv after attacked.

Most importantly, while some Iraqis will welcome the Americans as liberators, some won't. That's because they're xenophobic when it comes to occupation. The Middle East, remember, was under colonial rule for part of the 20th century.

Mohammed Abbas, former editor-in-chief of the *Baghdad Observer* and now a colleague of mine at the *Yemen Times*, tells me some Iraqis still don't forgive Britain for staying for two decades after "liberating" Iraq after the First World War. "They still hate them," he says.

This is where things get messy. Arabs here, I've discovered, live with a terribly profound feeling of defeat, inferiority and powerlessness. In my observation, they have fears that permeate everything they are and everything they do.

Some people in Yemen, a country with a political love-in with Washington because of Sana'a's official anti-terror stance, even fear a U.S. invasion. That's partly why several protesters, including an 11-year-old boy, were shot dead by Yemeni police when a recent demonstration moved to the U.S. embassy in this capital city.

"It seemed to me that death was nothing for them," said one eyewitness at the scene. Protesters here see Afghanistan. They see Iraq. They know the

West's colonial history in their region, and they connect the dots. Next thing you know, somebody's boy is in a pool of blood.

So my worry is that while the Americans will eventually get Saddam and win the war, they'll lose the battle for the hearts and minds of the Arab world. Suicide bombers and snipers and others who see an updated version of Western colonialism will bring their own intifada to Iraq. Bloodshed could then spread to who knows where, including North America.

Of course it's easy to think those who see Pax Americana on the doorstep of the Middle East are overreacting. But considering the wounds of this region and America's quiet plans for Iraq, can you blame them?

Disarm ... Decapitate ... Whatever 29

SANA'A, YEMEN
March 28, 2003

Washington admits that it wants to shape the entire Middle East into a kinder place. Sooner or later, that goal may take the United States to Yemen's terrorist haven.

A political cartoon of Saddam being "disarmed." Frame one, his right arm is cut off. Frame two, his left arm goes. Last frame, to quote the American objective on the first night of bombing Baghdad: decapitation.

I have yet to see anyone actually draw this. But it nicely illustrates that when Americans say they'll disarm Saddam, they mean so much more.

And I wonder, if Washington is serious about preventing future terrorism hits in brutal 9/11 style, or worse, why isn't it marching on Sana'a?

One reason is that Yemen's president, Ali Abdullah Saleh, sits squarely in the Yanks' anti-terror camp. A former military chief who has led this fledgling democracy astutely since North and South Yemen unified in 1991, Saleh has garnered U.S. president George W. Bush's friendship and at least $100 million in U.S. anti-terrorism aid.

Indeed, their political relationship seems to be a pure love-in. In November a CIA missile obliterated al-Qaeda suspects huddled in a car rolling along the soil of this sovereign nation. Barely a murmur in government halls here.

Shortly after, Washington turned a blind eye to 15 Scud missiles shipped to Yemen from, of all places, North Korea. The kicker came days later when Saleh openly revealed he spent U.S. money, apparently with CIA approval, to buy arms from Russia.

Yemen, among Earth's poorest countries and very dependent on foreign aid, reportedly spends US$540 million on arms annually. In 2002, Moscow reportedly sold it 15 Mig-29s and 80 tanks. Those deals, says Saleh, will continue.

Saleh, probably the most outspoken Arab leader against striking Iraq, has also said he isn't averse to sending Islamic warriors to protect Palestinians in the occupied territories.

None of this bothers Washington. The Yanks, after all, are busy dealing with Saddam's madness.

Yet while evidence linking Iraq to terrorism is flimsy at best, serious terrorist threats simmer in places like Pakistan, Saudi Arabia and Yemen. This is why, for example, Yemeni-Americans in locales like Buffalo are charged with laundering terrorism money.

It's why Yemenis like Muhammad Ali Hassan al-Mouyad, a prominent cleric usually in Sana'a, is being held in Germany. Yemen wants him back, but the Yanks want him extradited to the United States. They say he's used a Brooklyn mosque to help funnel millions of terrorism dollars, apparently personally delivering $20 million to Osama bin Laden.

Then there's Abu Hamza al-Masri. Wanted in Yemen for terrorist activity, this Egyptian-born imam, with one eye and a hooked hand, used to preach in London's Finsbury Park mosque. He's called British Prime Minister Tony Blair a fair target for Muslim warriors and wants Muslim youths to fight a holy war against Westerners.

There are other frightening examples linking terrorism to Yemen more than to Iraq. So does this mean the United States should hit Sana'a? Of course not. But some folks here feel that, sooner or later, it will.

That's partly why last Friday's protests in front of the U.S. embassy, which saw up to four protesters killed by Yemeni police, were so bloody. Protesters see Afghanistan, then Iraq. They connect the dots to Yemen. That makes them afraid. And angry.

Considering the current political love-in with Washington, an American attack here seems far-fetched to me. But look at the woolly things pulled over our eyes already.

After months of diplomatic poker in the UN, Washington now admits it wants to use a new Iraq to reshape the entire Middle East into a kinder place. Some may feel that goal is valiant. Others will say it's impossible. Either way, isn't it funny it wasn't mentioned before?

All we heard of was the need to disarm Saddam. In truth, the plan has always been to kill him, or at least put him in exile, so the Yanks can effectively set up shop in this region.

Take that massive agenda, combine it with Yemen's worst terror crazies, and add Europe's historical colonial presence in the Middle East. Can you really blame Yemeni masses for fearing they're next? God help them if radicals ever overthrow Saleh.

Any ideas on what assurances to offer?

30 Arabia's great Superman goes to court, naked

SANA'A, YEMEN
January 24, 2004

So, we'll soon see the mother of all trials hit the proverbial fan. Forget O.J. or Jacko or second-rate dictator Slobodan Milosevic. The trial of Saddam Hussein promises to be the courtroom event of our time.

CNN. Al Jazeera. BBC. Let's hope everyone is there. The CBC, too, for that knowing Canadian perspective. And why not? Mussolini was lynched. Hitler shot his own brains out. Mao and Pol Pot and Stalin all died old without a proper day in court. In terms of a decent despot trial, the 20th century kind of ripped us off.

But now, can you see Saddam consulting his lawyers on what to wear on that big first day? It will all be so very surreal.

And what do they think in Yemen about the Butcher of Baghdad, recently demoted from mythical evil to shabby figure in need of a razor, a haircut and a place for his stash of American cash?

"Like at the end of any good story, the hero should die" is how my Yemeni landlord sees it. Did you get that? The *hero*.

Indeed, Saddam likely will seize the global spotlight to go down as the great Arab Superman who could have saved Islam from the Bushies and the Jews. Sadly, some Arabs will buy this, while others – the odd cab driver here in Yemen for example – still can't admit it's actually Saddam in custody.

Granted, even otherwise reasonable people, like our landlord, an educated pharmacist, can believe the wildest things. After his expressed view about Saddam's fate, he told Jean and me that U.S. Security Adviser Condoleeza Rice is the world's seventh richest woman, thanks to income from the many bomb factories she owns.

Then he added, with extra zest, "And she's Jewish."

That's when Jean, who usually shows uncommon grace in the midst of strange behaviour, burst into laughter and asked him if he's noticed Rice's skin colour lately.

"Well," he relinquished, "she acts like she's Jewish."

Keep honour. Avoid shame. That's what's Saddam's trial will be about, because, quite frankly, that's what everything is about in this part of the world.

It's the axis on which certain cultures spin, the fig leaves that certain people and groups choose for cover.

Yes, some Yemenis believe Saddam attacked Kuwait in 1990 because, well, the Americans forced him to. Others claim Jews brought down the Twin Towers and that 4,000 Jews didn't go to work there on September 11, 2001, because they knew what would hit. Such dizzy theories are one result of the terrible lack of trust, even among families, that's so deeply rooted in Arab-Muslim culture.

People grow up in fear. And with a stinging poverty of dignity. As an observer here, I can't say enough how important it is for the West to grasp this. In today's war of ideas, and in international relations in general, humiliation is the most underrated force.

Yes, Saddam's trial may be a circus. It will be hard not to pull out the popcorn and grab a front row seat. But international prosecutors simply can't afford to debase Saddam to the extent that will disgrace other Arabs who already feel like their faces are in the mud.

Of course, some Iraqis themselves will want justice at the gallows. But swinging Saddam from a rope won't bring anyone lasting dignity, either. Revenge is a need of people who feel powerless, a raw emotion that tends to go when their sense of impotence goes. No, the real needs of Iraqis are much deeper.

Besides, if they were not collaborators, some Western governments were at least benefactors of the ruin that Saddam wrought during parts of his 30-year reign. If it's half-fair, Saddam's trial will also put these sins on the table.

Wherever things go, let's hope that any Saddam-like spirit of hatred isn't left to linger anywhere. Hate won't help Iraqis rebuild on new ground. And it will only entrench the dark hero status that some mixed-up folks already give Saddam.

In the end, dictators are terribly weak and cowardly monsters. To be properly exposed, they need to be tried in a court that rises above such things itself.

To give a better idea of the Arab psyche on shame, consider the sign I once saw at a Western hotel in Yemen, in its recreation centre's change room, near the showers, a fine little warning that said, "No nudity allowed."

"Hmm," I thought. "Showering here could be tricky."

Many Arabs are wired to be hypersensitive about this type of thing, which is why interrogations of undressed prisoners at places like Abu Ghraib prison in Iraq were so powerfully humiliating and destructive.

Some of the better moments of my previous life as a reporter at the Times-Journal were spent in the Elgin County Courthouse, a 155-year-old stone building with creaky stairs and wooden seats, bad acoustics and enough stories to fill a few libraries.

There on Wellington Street in St. Thomas, a short walk from my desk in the city's newsroom, is where details came out on dirty deals of biker gangs, and drunk drivers killing innocents, and the man who tried to kill his wife by blowing up their house.

He barely survived the process, which started by leaving on the gas one winter morning. It ended with the house literally disappearing from its lot. It was one of those "you have to see it to believe it" things. The thunderous blast, which I personally heard some distance away, left living room remnants hanging from trees several neighbours over and regional media capturing images from overhead choppers.

The deepest deception I ever reported, though, relates to a woman, well-dressed and professional, who, thanks to her long-time psychotherapist, discovered long-buried memories of child abuse at the hands of both her parents in ways I won't describe.

It took years for the therapist to uncover these dark secrets, hidden because of trauma and so-called repressed memory syndrome. But the woman's terrible and painful memories did come back, and her crusade to finally reveal everything to everyone unfolded there in this venerable hall of justice.

Her greying parents included a father who had supported the family, barely, for years by rising early during star-filled mornings to deliver the London Free Press along the often-snowy back roads of Elgin County.

He and his aging wife sat in the hardwood prisoner's docket, a couple of scared mice, in front of a mammoth historic painting that included Lady Justice, blindfolded, her scales suspended in one hand and double-edged sword of truth in the other.

Very expert witnesses on these things then took hours to give their very expert credentials before they uttered their very expert words.

Finally, after two weeks, it all leaked on the courtroom floor like an embarrassing puddle underneath the dress of a two-year-old. The woman, and the therapist who fell for her stories, were in fact victims of something else known as false memory syndrome. This is like finding out the dream you had about showing up at the office buck-naked is actually true. And there you stand, exposed. All the memories dredged up over the years were, in fact, no memories at all, just some primal imagination.

The relieved parents walked away, a shattered family behind and uncertain years ahead. The woman returned to her private house of confusion, the therapist (who over the years had charged hundreds of thousands of dollars to the province for his services), back to serving more people. And This Scribe, to his keyboard to tell all.

It's one more example of Eden and our great capacity to fool ourselves, not a lot different than what happened in the mind of Saddam Hussein, who was hanged while claiming innocence the whole time.

W

While I now sit at my desk in Africa, back on the other side of the ocean there are pens scribbling names on petitions and "Save our Courthouse" banners plastered around St. Thomas in defence of the stately building. It's now in danger of closing at the hand of progress, with a potential new court for Elgin-London-Middlesex at the other end of the same Wellington Street.

Whatever its fate, I'm no longer there to scheme how to get one of those precious seat cushions (the court clerk would always guard his like a lion), no longer able to observe the activity of the day's docket. Too bad. There's much to still learn.

Learning Arabic 101

31

"While the cost of killing each other is going through the roof, language lessons are a steal."

London, Canada
May 7, 2003

One of the things I've discovered as a part-time resident of the Middle East is how easily things such as cultural nuances can hide in plain view. See what I mean by counting the *f*'s in the following sentence. Note your answer before moving on. (Don't cheat.) "Files on foreign nations are the result of years of scientific study combined with the expertise of spies."

Our brains often miss the *f* in "of" or see it as a *v*. Congrats if you saw all six *f*'s. Most folks don't—it's an example of how reality isn't always as we perceive.

Looking to Iraq, this means we need to show some cultural sensitivity while helping to rebuild the country. Let's not be like the stereotypical American crossing the border to Canada with snow skis in the middle of summer.

A friendly Arabic *asalam allykum*, a common greeting meaning "peace be upon you," will go farther. Yet in all you've seen on your TV in recent weeks, have you heard a coalition soldier use that, or any Arabic phrase, even once? What does this say?

By the way, it cost about 75 cents U.S. to kill a man in Caesar's time, $3,000 in the Napoleonic war, $5,000 in the U.S. Civil War and $21,000 in the First World War. It's now taken about $50 billion to blow up Iraq, and at least another $100 billion is needed to occupy and rebuild it over several years.

So while the cost of killing each other is going through the roof, language lessons are a steal. In Yemen, my part-time home, you can get Arabic instruction for US$10 an hour. That means $100 million, the amount of aid Ottawa is offering Iraq, would pay for almost seven million hours of classes.

Of course, aid groups such as the Red Cross and CARE Canada need some of these funds. But trust me, learning Arabic takes plenty of time. Arabic script, which runs right to left, is a world of confusion in itself. Phonetics are incredibly strange. And with regional dialects, even native Arabs are constantly learning of their evolving tongue.

The language lessons I refer to, however, entail much more. They require understanding a culture's soul. We wear cowboy hats to Calgary's stampede, not a toque from Quebec's winter carnival. Likewise, Middle East society has its own garb.

Westerners value freedom, youth and individual rights, while Arabs value status, age and duty to community. Westerners underscore private wealth, are future oriented and reward individual merit, while Arabs underscore hospitality on request, are past oriented and reward you for who you know. Westerners value romantic love, while Arabs negotiate status matches.

The list goes on. And such lessons are learned best by rubbing shoulders with other cultures in the classroom of everyday relations. To some extent, our generation realizes this. Recently, 800 youth from across Canada and 15 other countries gathered in Ottawa for the first-ever Canadian International Model UN Conference. Unfortunately, there were no youth from the Middle East.

Similarly, Arabs and Muslims get short shrift in U.S. cultural programs. About 25 per cent of Earth's 6.2 billion people are Muslim, but just 10 per cent of participants in U.S. state department exchange programs are from Islamic countries. And, not surprisingly, for every four foreigners in the United States on exchanges, just one American goes abroad.

While bringing outsiders to North America is fine, we need to leave our bubble and learn the lingo of others on their turf. Cultural bridges need to run both ways. For starters, it seems to me that many Iraqis honestly would appreciate a simple *asalam allykum.*

Anything less than that, I'm afraid, is like crossing Iraq's border with skis. It's a vacation from reality. And a great way to pile Arab resentment even higher.

Searching for Jack Kennedy 32

Sana'a, Yemen
November 29, 2003

Call me a dreamer, but ever wonder how things would look if John F. Kennedy were involved in today's so-called war of civilizations?

"He was shrewd. He was clever. Iraq's intellectuals saw in Kennedy a different kind of leader" is how my Iraqi news-office colleague Mohammed Abbas views his legacy. "He wanted to avoid conflict between the West and East, that is, Russia. I think Kennedy's loss was a loss for the whole world."

This, from an Arab-Muslim.

True, Camelot was more myth than reality. Jack Kennedy had some serious dents in his armour. But, this week, 40 years after his death, he's still seen as one of the tallest torchbearers for a better world. Why is that?

For one, he was trusted. Once, after Kennedy sent his emissary to former French leader Charles DeGaulle – to show photos of Russian missiles in Cuba and ask for French support – DeGaulle even said, "You don't need to show photos. I know John Kennedy. If he says there are missiles in Cuba, I believe it."

Why aren't more upright Americans, like U.S. General William Boykin, respected by Muslims anywhere close to this? Boykin, a top intelligence official and conservative Christian, made world headlines recently. Describing his battle with a Muslim Somali warlord, he bragged, "My God was bigger than his God."

One wonders how a top officer of, uh, intelligence – that is, someone who should grasp international relations – can perform such stupid sandlot swagger. Boykin could learn from Senator Joseph Lieberman, a Jew, who near that time told an Arab-American group, "We meet here today not as Muslims or Christians or Jews, not as people of Arab or European descent or African or Asian descent. We are children of the same God and of the same father, Abraham. We are quite literally brothers and sisters."

Kennedy, a Catholic, avoided war with the Soviets and the Third World War, because he knew that whether those atheists worshiped his God or not, they loved their children as much as we love ours. He created the Peace Corps because he felt that if we can't end our differences, at least maybe we can make the planet safe for diversity. Kennedy felt at home with his "New Frontier" because, unlike George W. Bush, when younger he actually got out to see the world.

Finally, there's C. S. Lewis, the Oxford professor and brilliant Christian thinker. Like Kennedy, he went by "Jack" and, in one of those strange historical crossings, also died on November 22, 1963. If you don't know Lewis, read his Chronicles of Narnia to your children or watch his life story in the movie *Shadowlands*.

Lewis is also known for his BBC radio commentaries, particularly his remark that "A man who was merely a man, and said the things Jesus said, wouldn't be a great moral teacher. He'd be either a lunatic – on the level with a man who says he's a poached egg – or he'd be the devil of hell. You must make your choice. Either this man was and is the Son of God or else he is a madman, or something worse. But don't let us come up with patronizing nonsense about his being a great human teacher. He hasn't left that open to us. He didn't intend to."

So, no, Christians need not hide their faith's basic tenets. A man may die, nations may rise and fall, but an idea lives on. That's what Kennedy told us.

Expressed views are the air we breathe, and, indeed, the strongest ones will transcend boundaries. But great ideas need to be dressed in great humility. And in today's war of ideas, we need a stronger vision with more imagination than anyone in Washington or anywhere else is offering.

Instead, in the crisis of our time, all we're left with are memories of wisdom from the past.

Like many boomers (born in 1965, I barely scrape in), I've had a fascination with the life of John. F. Kennedy: his silver-spooned pedigree and winsome smile, the uncertainty of the Cold War and civil rights movement, even his terribly self-destructive womanizing that now has become so much of the legacy. His assassination, with its eerie parallels to Abraham Lincoln's, only heightens the mystery.

Less advertised was Kennedy's dismal health, how he was read last rites several times in his ongoing battle with Addison's Disease and how his severe back condition at times reduced him to a cripple.

Combined with Kennedy's steadfast support of Berliners, this ripples into The Froese History Book. Look a few years before I came along and see my parents, an attractive and bright young couple, both therapeutic massage therapists in Canada at the time, being invited to (but gracefully declining) a Boston fundraising dinner for then Senator John Kennedy.

As Dad Froese tells it years later, he and Mom couldn't have known how far the senator's star would rise. Plus there were practical considerations like the cost of each fundraising potato for a couple of young German immigrants. (Dad's family was, by then, all in Canada; Mom's was back in Berlin.)

It was the meeting that never was, left as one of those "what-if" scenarios. In some other universe my sister, Heidi, and I could have run under the tables with the little Kennedys, Jon-Jon and Caroline.

The situation was that JFK needed a capable masseur in his inner sanctum. It's as far-fetched as it is plausible that Dad Froese, given a formal introduction, could have landed in the fold. In those years, masseurs in North America were sparse, which is why they were sought by the upper crust and, if good, kept very close.

Now nearing 77 and having a distinctive look that's somewhere between The Old Man and the Sea and Topol (from Fiddler on the Roof), Dad Froese is still practising full-time in Ye Olde Niagara Home. While masseurs half his age are leaving the work due to fatigue, 50 years after his initial training in Germany he's become a legendary massage guru, already awarded by Ontario's professional association for his longevity and contribution to the trade.

If JFK had only known.

33

Scattered, divided and weak

Sana'a, Yemen
March 22, 2003

"We're going to err on the side of caution and stay in the house for a few days" is what I told a friend during a phone chat yesterday morning.

Our self-imposed house arrest would mean Jean and I would miss a friend's birthday party and a weekly gathering of friends. Not much of a sacrifice, considering that a few hours later four Yemeni protesters, including an 11-year-old boy, lay dead on the streets of this capital city. They were killed by Yemeni police guarding the American embassy.

Yemenis killing Yemenis. That's part of the fallout of the strike on Iraq. It's the part you won't always see on the 24/7 war shots filling TV screens across the planet.

The deaths were perfectly preventable. But, as is often the case, a little stupidity got mixed with high emotion and, not surprisingly, guns.

To review, about 30,000 protesters, angry about the light show blazing over

Baghdad, decided to march to the American embassy, where they wanted to do what protesters do: chant and pump their fists, burn tires and garbage cans, call for death to America and Israel – all standard practices in this region, war or peacetime.

Compared to what we've seen globally, it wasn't a huge crowd. And I doubt it was terribly unmanageable. Remember, in Yemen guns are often slung over one's shoulder for honour more than anything. I've seen AK-47s casually brought into restaurants. If a few protesters had guns, that wasn't the biggest problem.

The concern over these protesters, I'm afraid, is that they decided to get together at all, let alone in front of the U.S. embassy. The terrible threat they supposedly gave is that, like protesters in Canada or any other free country, they marched on the steam of their own thinking. Imagine that.

In Yemen, you see, thinking for yourself – at least in terms of protesting where and when you want – is illegal. So if you hear that hundreds of thousands of Yemenis do demonstrate against war in Iraq, know that these are government-driven shams. Kids are let out of school. Folks get posters. Everyone has a good time.

Isn't it funny that, unlike those in the huge demonstrations in New York and London, many Arabs have simply been mute over Iraq? So when an autonomous crowd did get out for some fresh air yesterday, one of the few times this has happened in Yemen, folks didn't know how to handle the freedom. Next thing you know, somebody's boy is in a pool of blood. How sad. Sad because people are dead. Sad also because it shows this culture's terrible immaturity.

After the fall of the Ottoman Empire, the Arab world was exploited by foreign powers, namely the French and British. Now, after half a century of fake independence, it's again under the yoke of colonialism, that of its own leaders.

Today's Arabs are scattered, divided and weak. We know it. And so do they. In fact, they're embarrassed by it. As a *Yemen Times* letter writer put it, "If we remain like this, within a few years the whole Middle East will be called 'The United Emirates of America.'"

So despite the stereotype of the angry Arab terrorist, I honestly wouldn't worry about Arab masses truly rising against the West very soon. It's my observation that folks here, like kids who refuse adulthood, simply don't know how to take responsibility. Yesterday's slayings show it's easier to kill each other before organizing against any outside threat.

This frailty is also why both Arab governments and extremists encourage their masses to demonize Israel. Starving people need a scapegoat. And it's why real issues like Palestine's fate, or now this grand Yankee experiment in colonizing Iraq, is being decided by outsiders.

Yeah, like me, you may not like this war. But at least we have the freedom to say so without getting shot dead.

All in the family

34

Sana'a, Yemen
April 17, 2004

I hate politics. You can't trust anyone. I mean, if I was Maqtada Al-Sadr, the dangerously political Shiite cleric who's jostling for position in Iraq now, I wouldn't trust my grandmother.

The senior generation in that troubled country understands this because it knows how ugly things have been over the years. Lots of political blood has flown deep and wide.

You wonder if modern Iraq, created in 1921 after the Brits began serious meddling in this region, was doomed from the start. Western powers tried to merge archrivals Sunni and Shiite Muslims with ethnically different Kurds who were originally promised their own homeland. It's no surprise that Iraq's first monarchs and parliament couldn't hold things together. With newly discovered oil fuelling them, seven military coups unfolded from 1936 to 1941. To dissuade such things in the future, seditious generals were hung publicly.

But things worsened, and all political parties were eventually dissolved. In 1958, leader Nura al-Said was caught escaping the country while dressed as a woman. His body was chopped up and paraded in the streets. For good measure, Abdul Karim Qasim slaughtered Iraq's royal family.

Qasim, with a few thugs in the new Iraqi Baath Party, punished rivals brutally. When a coup against the pro-Soviet Qasim failed, he retaliated, including plenty of raping and pillaging of his anticommunist opponents. Qasim hung on until 1963, when his Baathist former friends killed him.

Then Abdul Salem Arif got on top, only to oust the Baathists who put him in power. President Arif somehow died in a helicopter crash.

Soon a young Baathist upstart named Saddam Hussein arrived. Known to shoot his enemies point-blank in the back of the head, he helped lead a 1968 coup. Later, Saddam would kill two of his own sons-in-law. The rest of his legacy you know.

Somewhere along the way – and this is what I really hate about politics – the guys in the white hats, in this case Uncle Sam, saddled up to Saddam. They feared his enemy, fundamentalist Shiite Iran, more than they feared Sunni-dominated Iraq. Remember the Iran-Iraq War? Nearly one million people died. Guess who armed Iraq?

Yes, in politics, the enemy of my enemy is my friend – all the more so if it involves blood relations. A well-known Arab adage puts it this way: "I and my brothers against my cousins; I and my cousins against my tribe; I and my tribe against the world."

Which brings us to the present. Now that the Americans are well inside the minefield of Iraq's unresolved family issues, they have both Sunni and former U.S.-allied Shiite camps hating them more than they hate each other. "Bring 'em on" doesn't sound so hot right now.

Yemen, by the way, has welcomed thousands of Iraqis in the last decade, some looking for opportunities while Iraqis suffered under Saddam and UN sanctions. Yemen, in fact, has among the highest Iraqi Shiite groups in the Middle East outside of Iraq.

Many had hoped to return home soon. Not any more. As one Iraqi here in Sana'a said this week, "I was hoping for security and democracy. Instead there's just killing and bloodshed. I've lost hope."

We know Iraq's unholy Islamic alliances can change easily. And now more than ever we know that civil war is likely still the biggest long-term threat to a rebuilding Iraq. It certainly will be when the Americans pull out completely, which they will sooner or later.

In the meantime, there's this rocky road to a so-called regime change. It obviously seemed like a good idea to enough important people at the time. But considering Iraq's long stream of political blood, do you not wonder if, from the beginning, nobody in Washington realistically asked, a regime change to what?

Humour needs such little explanation. Its first rule is, 'don't take yourself too seriously.' And I don't know what the second is.

I just know that one way to look at life as a big-time foreigner (there aren't many blond Arabs running around the Middle East) is to consider oneself a kind of galactic visitor trying to make sense of alien ways. Of course funny things are going to come to mind. I wouldn't expect visitors in my world to see anything else.

So if some of this material pokes some good-natured fun at the stranger side of life in a place like Yemen, that's okay. But if these columns are not really funny to begin with, well, don't blame me.

This section ends with a winding addendum on some experiences from South of the Snowy 49th Parallel.

Opposite page photo: *A Yemeni tradesman renovates the author's Sana'a apartment flat.*

The Lighter Side of Arabia Felix

Just kidnap me ... Please 35

Sana'a, Yemen
October 26, 2002

Jean is back in Hamilton to put final touches on McMaster University's November 8 symposium on international women's health. My wife has left me to fend for myself. But rather than take on our kitchen stove, I've decided it's better to get kidnapped.

Yemen is up there with Colombia and Russia among the best places on Earth to get snatched. The thing about kidnapping here, though, is that it's a kind of cultural education. No, really. How often can you see a semi-automatic Kalashnikov so close?

Kidnappers here are usually tribal folk. They visit checkpoints on rural roads to find tourists eager to see Yemen's ancient sites. Some roads in Mareb, where excavators are uncovering more ruins of the fabled Queen of Sheba, are kidnapping alleys.

In the past five years, 114 foreign tourists and 43 expatriate workers have been nabbed across Yemen. Italians go missing most often, followed by French and Germans. Kidnapped Americans are down the list at just nine. Canadians are barely on the map.

Of the 114, five died thanks to "rescue" operations of Yemen's military. That included one British-Canadian killed in an unusual 1998 incident, which led to the execution of one kidnapper.

But 109 hostages have walked free, most after just a few days. And in five years, some 350,000 tourists have visited Yemen.

So what's the risk?

About 30,000 kidnappings now occur around the world annually. But the Yemenis, God bless them, really do have a liberating approach. Parliamentary speaker Abdullah Ahmman put it this way: "Kidnapping is part of Yemen tourism. It's an adventure for tourists, because they'll end up learning about customs of the tribes as well as their good hospitality."

So while leaders of tribes – communities of hundreds or thousands – negotiate with Yemen's government for half-decent roads, water and health centres, or maybe the release of a brother from jail, they'll feed you well.

Italian tourist Giorgio Bonanomi couldn't be happier. "Too bad it's not possible to organize holidays like this. It was fantastic," he said, after his kidnappers fed him lamb and exotic fruits.

One tourist company owner went so far as to set aside $11,000 monthly for customer ransoms. Hey, bring the wife and kids. Tourism here needs it. It's lost about $1.5 billion since September 11.

Funny thing, some Yemenis feel embarrassed by it all. They think their country's image is being tarnished and blame conspirators from "foreign lands." That's code for Saudi Arabia.

Then again, this culture doesn't encourage one to accept blame for much. One doesn't admit to burning dinner if one can avoid it. For example, some Yemenis still maintain the wind is behind the terror attack on the French supertanker Limburg. More on that later.

Chinese accountants, French honeymooners and Polish diplomats have all been snagged by hospitable tribesmen. For my money, though, I want to go with a bunch of Germans. Having a German passport with Berlin as my birthplace will help. So will the blonde hair and blue eyes.

Indeed, Germans are big here. Yemen is Germany's developing-world pet project. Ambassador Werner Zimprich just announced $55 million in German aid this year.

In addition to expatriate workers, Germans visit for festivals, to share poetry, food and, naturally, beer, a rather uncommon commodity in the dry Muslim world.

I'm not a big drinker myself. But as Abdullah says, it's about cultural exchange. Peeking in at recent Oktoberfest celebrations at a swanky hotel here, I saw not only beer kegs and an oompahpah band from Bavaria, but also bony-kneed Yemenis running around in green felt hats and Alpine leather shorts. I couldn't wait for them to yodel.

The point is, gangs of kidnapped Germans could spread good cheer across Yemen's impoverished countryside.

I have only one fear – Iraq. U.S. president George W. Bush had already slapped around German chancellor Gerhard Schroeder for not supporting U.S. plans for Saddam. They'll get over it. But if the Germans spread beer through Yemen, some may eventually reach Baghdad. Oh, the consequences.

Anyway, wearing a ball cap and runners apparently boosts the odds of getting abducted. I'd better get ready.

Tell Jean not to worry. The stove is turned off.

Bound voyage.

Flowers for the wife?

36

SANA'A, YEMEN
June 8, 2002

So the poor Tories say they might clobber Ontario's smokers with higher taxes to bankroll new spending. Too bad there's not another easy target. Like qat.

Qat in Yemen is what hockey is in Canada. First brought here 700 years ago, it was a luxury for bored merchants and mystics. Now about 85 per cent of Yemeni men use the leaf. Some other places, particularly Ethiopia, also have it. But Yemen is King of Qat. Folks here stuff their cheeks like chipmunks every day.

After being packed in one's jowl for a few hours, qat leaves turn into a green slime that releases the amphetamine cathione. It's like having a deep massage, six double espressos and a couple of spliffs. And group chews are important social affairs.

I tried qat once but just got thirsty and a headache. Other effects are more problematic. Some Yemenis easily spend 30 per cent of their income on it. Also, qat plants need water, a precious commodity in Yemen. Consider also that qat costs the country about US$6 million every day in lost productivity.

Still, qat kills virtually nobody – just a few hundred souls poisoned from pesticides not washed off. Compare that to the four million deaths caused by tobacco every year, 435,000 of which happen to be in Canada. Qat leaves no smell. And there are other reasons it might eventually overtake tobacco as the world's top weed. Here's the Top Ten:

10. *With their cheeks bulging, chewers look like a bunch of happy Louis Armstrongs.*
9. *Defending users of qat, which is illegal in some countries, is a lawyer's dream.* There's no proof of crime since chemicals in the leaves break down to nothing in 10 days.
8. *Qat socials negate the need to learn golf for high-level business deals.* Yemen shuts down for several hours every afternoon to facilitate chews.
7. *Qat has no confusing brands.* No Lights or Slims. The product is straightforward. Its only suitable name is High-and-Dry. That has singularity of purpose that folks really crave.
6. *There's no anti-qat lobby.* And while the World Health Organization is trying to control tobacco worldwide, qat continues to fly under the radar.
5. *Unlike cigarettes in packs with grisly warnings, when qat is wrapped it looks like flowers for your wife.* For about 12 dollars, a Yemeni can walk down the street with prestige while carrying a large qat bundle wrapped in pink or blue cellophane.
4. *Qat sells without sex appeal.* No need for the Marlboro Girls, the gals in short skirts who, in some countries, go to public places and hand out free cigarettes. Qat is an equal opportunity plant, easily marketed by any hairy-legged Yemeni in a robe. I'd name him Qatman, fill his cheek to bulge like a tennis ball, get him to rock concerts and beauty pageants, and put his image on racing cars, T-shirts and lunch buckets.
3. *Qat sharpens the mind.* Yes, qat chewers can really ask the deep questions. Looking at a bottle, a chewer asked one day, "Just what

is behind America?" Was his question socio-political? No, he was wondering what was behind America's landmass. His qat-chewing friend waved his hands and would have nothing of it. He knew the Earth is flat.

2. *Qat can balance East-West trade.* Cigarette sales are down in places like Canada, but tobacco companies now make billions in profits by targeting the developing world, where 70 per cent of smoking deaths occur and where 10 million smoking-related deaths are expected annually by 2025. Sending qat in the other direction returns the favour.
1. *Qat can, in fact, unite the world.* Don't think so? Did tobacco beat communism? No. Qat did. Case in point: Marxists, who used to run the former South Yemen, restricted qat chewing to weekends. They felt it made people "lazy." But the masses threw off their shackles because they understand they were fed only half the truth.

Sure, hard work won't kill you. But why take the chance? Millions of Yemenis now chew in perfect harmony, just like singing the Coke song. The rest of the world can now join in. Every dog, after all, deserves its season.

I later wrote another version of this column, after being away and returning to find that a qat market near our Sana'a home was gone.

Of course, a qat market can be as simple as the back of a beater pickup with the gate down, parked on the same road at the same time (lunchtime) every day, an easily accessible place for regular buyers. And that is what this market was, like a trailer selling fries and dogs, just with more chewing going on.

So upon its disappearance, my Yemen Times column ran with the satirical headline "Hey, what happened to our neighbourhood qat market?" The column incorporated a similar Top Ten list on why qat is a rockin' great thing. And the e-mails poured in, including from bright and educated Yemenis, wondering why This Scribe was supporting this scourge that thinking Yemenis believe is destroying their country.

A Yemeni website then posted the column, prompting one reader from Vancouver, Canada (only on the west coast, people), to ask if I could help him get some of the product.

I suggested to him that Canadian immigration officials might frown on this. Later, large warnings, complete with photos of an open suitcase filled with illegal qat, began appearing at Toronto's Pearson Airport.

Now in Uganda, I've been approached just once by a drug dealer. Sorry, dude.

Einstein tops "Booosh" 37

SANA'A, YEMEN
November 13, 2004

So, after one of the most divisive of U.S. elections in memory, George W. Booosh, as he's called here, is back for four more years. Yawn. Plenty of folks needed a Valium after a campaign that shook them with anger and fear. Not here. Middle Easterners were placid. Seems nobody believed John Kerry would offer anything better for Iraq and Palestine.

A cab driver shrugged and asked me limply, "Booosh? Kerry?" Media agreed. One Syrian paper said they had "the same passion for Israel." A Lebanese paper noted "no difference" between the two. A Saudi paper based in London said Arab governments simply "waited for their next master."

And my Yemeni landlord? "Booosh is bad for the whole world because he's crazy." Regardless, he prefers him over Kerry.

Some *Yemen Times* editor wrote the headline "Who Wins? Who Cares?" Then, in a pre-election poll, the *Times* threw in surprise candidate Albert Einstein. Incredibly, hundreds of Arab and expatriate readers voted for him. Yes, Einstein got 34 per cent of the votes, slightly less than Kerry but more than Bush.

Not bad for this demographic. Einstein is not only dead, but also Jewish; he was once even courted to run for Israel's government. Sure, some *Times* respondents used him as a protest vote. But U.S. Democrats could still learn how to win in 2008 from all of this. Bush may be no Einstein, but he did get some things right. For the challengers, here are 10 tips for next time.

10. *Have great hair.* No joke. Bald is better than a pouffed or matted look. This rule will help Hillary Clinton, but the candidate looking like he or she stuck his or her finger in an electric socket, like Einstein looked, will be loved most.
9. *Don't conform.* Einstein, who liked to write poetry, knew that great ideas rarely come through the establishment.
8. *Like Einstein, say something different.* Kerry could have stuck to his early anti-Iraq-war guns. The war has already cost America $300 billion, three times its initial projection. No wonder Bin Laden and his hoods want to bankrupt the United States, $7 trillion in debt. Now think of innocent civilians killed. And U.S. troops? Imagine life in a wheelchair, never knowing who your enemy really was.
7. *Don't be afraid to share your spirituality.* Some 18 million conservative Christians (a huge voting block that never questions anything Israel may do) gave Bush the White House because of his

stance on domestic moral issues. Einstein also brought God into his work. Like Newton and Galileo, he looked for the universe's secrets as if they were precious gems hidden by a Creator of beauty and order. Among his lasting quotes? "God doesn't play dice."

6. *Tell the truth.* Bush lied about Iraq. Americans cut him slack because Kerry was less believable. But have imagination. Every day in my office, I see an Einstein poster with his quote "Imagination is more important than knowledge." Considering that America needs to be a perpetual problem-solver, the Oval Office should have it.
5. *Show humility.* This is tricky, because the commander-in-chief needs to exude unflinching confidence. But humility brings trust. Pacifist and humanitarian Einstein once said any peaceful co-operation among people is based on mutual trust first, societal institutions second. Kerry, who appeared to enjoy the sound of his own voice, didn't beat Bush on the humility-trust barometer.
4. *Be warm.* Bush beat Kerry here. The gentle, grandfatherly Einstein beats both.
3. *Be simple.* Bush (don't laugh) easily beat Kerry here. And Einstein made discoveries like nobody else because he was able to see complex phenomena through the eyes of a child.
2. *Have a sense of humour.* Hey, Einstein chose that wild hairstyle. It was the outgrowth, maybe, of being Father of the Bomb. He once said, "If only I would have known, I would have been a watchmaker."
1. *Understand the human heart.* Einstein said the discovery of atomic power changed everything but our way of thinking. People here see nothing but suffering in Palestine and Iraq. They see Washington ignoring the first and plundering the second. It's a time bomb. It's ticking. And unless it's diffused, it can lead to the type of big bang that could kill us all.

Why attack Big Mac? 38

"Just another sign that we're being Coca-Colonized."

SANA'A, YEMEN
November 15, 2003

It's Ramadan here, time to party all night, sleep all day, pray with gusto and shop, shop, shop. Yes, in Holy Month, after sunrise-to-sundown fasting, you get in all the eating and drinking and merriment you can muster, at least under the circumstances.

Shopping without enough money isn't easy, especially for food that's often overpriced and outdated. And it's hard to smile knowing that kin in Palestine remain without a home while the Yanks continue to trample with their muddy boots all over Iraq.

Westerners here don't have it entirely easy either. Unless you're highly connected, you can't get a simple brew. Mohammed banned alcoholic refreshments in this region 1,400 years ago. There are other drinks, however, and casual observation shows Coca-Cola and Canada Dry are in a dead heat for Yemen's most popular beverage.

Before you salute the Maple Leaf, though, understand that Canada Dry in Yemen is not ginger ale but cola. Bottled in Yemen's port city of Aden, this Canada Dry also falls under Coke's trademark.

Yes, Coke, the 19th century nerve tonic that now generates about $15 billion in annual revenue – 80 per cent from foreign markets – is using the type of corporate slickness we'd expect.

Indeed, the suits at Coke are so clever, I haven't seen a single Yemeni even taste one particular competitor called Mecca Cola. It's an alternative now in some 45 countries. Tawfik Mathlouthi, a businessman from, naturally, France, launched it last Ramadan with the motto "No more drinking stupid, drink with commitment!" He says it's time to fight "American imperialism and Zionism by providing a substitute for American goods."

Still, stupid drinking of the world-famous beverage from the smart Coke people continues everywhere.

Even Pakistan, a country created as the ideal Islamic state, gives Mecca Cola only five per cent of its market. It seems the stuff simply tastes bad. Which, to me, is instructive for folks wringing their hands over the evils of American cultural imperialism. You know, Planet Hollywood and MTV and Big Macs from Belgrade to Bangkok – all signs of the Yanks' desire to Coca-Colonize everyone. Really, don't people accept the cultural trappings they want, without coercion? As an American told European filmmakers: "If you made movies as good as your cheese, people would watch them, too."

In this region, it's particularly strange when some Muslims rant that the United States is going to hell but then turn on U.S. shows. Saddam Hussein's son Uday launched Youth TV, using pirated Hollywood movies. His radio station had DJs blast George Bush as a criminal before giving a snappy intro to Madonna. Even North Korea's despot Kim Jong-Il idolized Michael Jordan, while heir Kim Jong-Nam loves Mickey Mouse.

And why wouldn't he? I recently saw Mickey in a Yemeni supermarket. Apparently some sensible store manager realized the Disney icon is not just American but a universal figure that can bring a smile to even the most difficult of days.

Sure, this may be soft American power. But such dominance is hardly new. Before satellites could beam anyone's propaganda or immorality anywhere, countries were miffed over U.S. brand bullies like Kodak cameras, Heinz ketchup and Colgate tooth powder.

That doesn't make everything coming from the United States good. But let's keep perspective. The U.S. empire isn't entertaining the masses by rounding up folks to throw to the lions in coliseums.

Some even argue that soft imperial power, rather than adding to global tension, enhances peace. Unlike hard power – that is, military domination – it promotes stability through commerce. Numbers since the mid-20th century support this: Liberal democracies virtually never go to war with each other, because they'd rather line up for burgers – that is, become economic allies – than fight.

Small wonder there's no McDonald's in Iraq, Iran or North Korea, the trio branded by Washington as an axis of evil. Come to think of it, Yemen doesn't have a McDonald's either. So let the protesters rage. I say bring in the Golden Arches.

Mickey Mouse is a start. But I need a Big Mac. And all indications here suggest others would enjoy one, too. With an extra large Coke.

Wanna burn some water?

39

SANA'A, YEMEN
February 23, 2004

I was recently riding my bicycle in this town of traffic ferociousness when I experienced an epiphany, the type that's either from indigestion or lack of oxygen to the brain or something truly, wildly, from above.

I suspect all three, because it was a big one, coming sometime after a dense plume of black smoke from a nearby bus floated into my airspace. Yes, it was then, after emerging from the haze, that I realized how much I miss Port Stanley. Then the next thought: *Can't anyone, anywhere, get an alternative fuel on the market*?

Mandating bicycle use is an option in some places. Not here. Not with ladies wearing burqas. Most don't even drive four wheels. No, let's keep our cars. Let's just propel them some other way. Like by harnessing the wind, or the sun, or, heck, converting water into fuel? Unless it's from one of the Great Lakes, water's clean.

Before I share the brilliance of this, realize that in developing countries if you don't die from smoking you go in a traffic accident. Yemen's cars, usually old white Toyotas, are held together with binder twine; some drivers seem barely out of diapers; and even goats would have trouble navigating some rough mountain passes. Best not to open your eyes more than you have to.

Also, here in Sana'a, during gridlock everyone lies on their horns until the guy in front of them turns six shades of blue and sticks his hand out the window, thumb touching his fingers, like the Italian gesture for "this is delicious." Here it means %4&*!@# or simply "please wait."

And wait you do. In 30 years, Sana'a has grown from 50,000 people to about a million. Nobody knows the exact number because the census takers are all out of town avoiding the traffic. That leaves traffic police, who stand at most major intersections in daylight hours to count the vehicles that blatantly drive past their outstretched arms.

But back to Port Stanley. I worked for some time as a reporter in St. Thomas, living on Highway 4, a 15-minute bike ride, with the wind at my back, from the beach. It was a fine place to watch the sun rise.

Yes, it was 15 years ago this month when I started the newspaper game. And my first reporting assignment, empty notepad in hand, green as Kermit, was to trot off and see a local inventor named Gary Sutherland. A chemical engineer, Gary already owned many patents. But one incredible day he believed he discovered how to burn water as fuel.

Gary had patiently tried to find a safe chemical that would break water into its base elements of oxygen and hydrogen, both of which are combustible. After going through the periodic table for years, one day he finally found the magic compound combination. "I phoned [my wife] Mary and cried like a baby," he told me. "I found it. I found it."

The chemist, who lived in a stately home also on that road to the beach, then tried to convince folks he was of sound mind. And he looked for ways to market his product, Aquaburn. It all put him on the speaking circuit. And it convinced me that this journalism thing would be a blast. My first story: water burns. My next: global hunger is solved. Oh, the Pulitzer.

Think of the impact. That hungry furnace? Just add water. Poor fuel mileage on that SUV? Who cares? Add more water. And so long Saudi. Canada, owner of one-fifth of Earth's fresh water, becomes the planet's new fuel mecca. We'd have everyone over the barrel. And we could fill it with our deep surplus of you-know-what.

So, since all good dreams – the crazy ones too – never die, after fully ingesting that ample dose of Sana'a smoke, I thought of Gary Sutherland. I had kept in touch with him and Mary, but he passed on, taking his secret, whatever it was, with him.

Now, Gary, where are you? We need help to handle these cold February blues. And my epiphany. Sana'a may be half a world away from St. Thomas, but some days it doesn't seem that far, especially from that peaceful stretch of road that goes to the beach.

Port Stanley, Ontario, is one of those underrated fishing villages that deserve more in life, a place that finally got its recognition with the antics of the Lake Erie Monster.

It was the supermarket tabloid Weekly World News that broke the story about this monster, with a front page photo of a massive brontosaurus-like creature cresting through the surface of the lake some miles south of Erie's Canadian waters.

An American yacht was left capsized, its boaters barely surviving, according to the report, which had Port Stanley folk understandably concerned and wondering what they might learn from other sea-monster locales like Loch Ness.

At the time I was a young, apparently bored reporter at the Times-Journal in nearby St. Thomas. So I took on this investigative follow-up, first checking the facts with the Florida office of the Weekly World News (which stood solid by its report) and then speaking to other sources.

The most helpful was a chap in Niagara, in St. Catharines, where I grew up, who was into monsters and other paranormal things. He was concerned about the bounty that Port Stanley's chamber of commerce had put on this monster's hide.

He told me about the legitimate marine and biological life that LEM (the catchy acronym for Lake Erie Monster) represented, and boy, people had better smarten up.

Understand, nothing is more dangerous than a bored reporter. So I wrote an entire series of stories on LEM. Then my editors wanted photos. So I put on some sunglasses and big fishing gear, grabbed that Weekly World News and, with our photographer and Port Stanley correspondent, went to the beach for an official monster search.

The entire affair then got splashed all over the Times-Journal. Which is strange. But then I won some big journalism award for it all and was told to go to Toronto to eat some oversized steak and get a couple of thousand bucks.

At the podium I didn't know what to say. It was the year when a sea of ink was spilled on Canada's sex-killer Paul Bernardo, who, with his wife, Karla, did unspeakable things to some St. Catharines school girls. Other scribblers on this story were centre stage.

Karla actually attended the St. Catharines high school I did, the one with a bulldog and Churchill's name. And she and her killer husband dumped their cut-up victims, in concrete blocks, in Beaver Dam, where I would ride in my youth for morning quiet times, like years later to Port Stanley.

So feeling rather awkward about the whole thing, there in my tux in front of Canada's finest media, I told the crowd I was in Toronto "just to catch a Leafs' game, and I, uh, took a wrong turn. Can anyone help me out?"

Everyone seemed to like that, so they invited me back the next year to eat more oversized steak and say more from the front. That time my words of sincere gratitude prompted an astute observer, a fine Calgary Sun cartoonist, to tell me that he thought I had, pardon the expression, rather large balls. This is because while baseball players are known to "thank the Good Lord" after winning the big game, journalists are not.

Now looking forward to it all, the next time I was on that podium list the big party got cancelled. Company cutbacks.

Now there's tabloid journalism and there's tabloid journalism. When it rolled its big presses on LEM, St. Thomas' city daily was not a tab, but a proud broadsheet that had served with dignity for well over 100 years: the community's oldest business, like newspapers in many other North American centres.

Neither was it a tabloid when it rolled the presses for Angela, the resident ghost of Alma College, a slightly haunted but very stately building that's among Ontario's historic heritage sites. Opened in 1881 by the Anglican Church of Canada, the lively St. Thomas girls school with the beautiful gardens hosted thousands of young ladies from around the world for a liberal arts education and reasons to be healthy and happy. Angela, according to lore, was a teacher some of these fine girls locked up along the way.

By the time I arrived in town, some 108 years after Alma launched, the school was in hard times, a shadow of its former self, now just rented for a few male students from east Asia. Halloween wasn't known to them, so when some read a lighthearted news account about Angela's haunting, they started hearing ghostly noises and got a little crazy. So they phoned the police, who informed our newsroom.

Sensible City Editor then told me to sleep at Alma on Halloween night to prove all was well. So I did that, with my Bible and Great Canadian Ghosts book, in a suitable old ivory tower.

The rumbling presses rolled out the story, including a photo of This Scribe at work in a sleeping bag. Angie never did show. But I became known as the guy who got into Alma overnight, something local guys had been trying to do for eons. One press operator told me, "Thom, you're going to turn this paper into a tabloid."

In a changing news world, the Times-Journal later did downsize to a tab. And I fought more boredom, eventually with drink: a smiling, tipsy reporter who downed five beers in an hour for police needing media to test their new Breathalyzer equipment.

The Times-Journal has now also lost those big rumbling presses. That's like losing a leg and an arm. Still, it survives, now trucked from Toronto every morn-

ing, kept going by former colleagues like Sensible City Editor and Faithful Community Columnist, who have now laboured in St. Thomas with dedication for over 30 years.

And the venerable Alma College? After several Herculean attempts to relaunch it as a public facility, it's now in the winter of life, all but buried: decayed and perishing, facing the wrecking ball, nothing but memories roaming its fabled halls.

And now this is just in. On this spring day in 2008, Alma College burned to the ground. Fierce flames that ripped through the old 19th-century Victorian-Gothic college could be seen at least 30 km away. Longtime supporters and the surrounding community are in shock. Two teens are charged with arson. The saga is over. While the suits in Queen's Park and elsewhere dithered, Old Alma was raped. And lost forever.

I live in a hockey book 40

Sana'a, Yemen
May 15, 2004

Confession time. Don't tell my wife, but I live in a hockey book. Okay, I live in a few. They're not like my living room, where I lounge my feet on as many tables as possible. They're like an open space, where I romp around and discover things.

My first relationship, if I can call it that, with a hockey book involved *The Bobby Orr Story* – a gentle read by John Devaney. Fronted with a colourful photo of the stealthy Bruin in action, it was a Christmas gift from my grandmother in Berlin. I was eight.

I idolized it. Pored over it. Embraced it. I loved skating. I loved playing hockey more. But reading this book helped me appreciate the finer virtues of the game. Indeed, *The Bobby Orr Story* never imprinted my flailing Pee Wee body into the boards of the local rink, like the Tow Truckers did. Memories.

Eventually, I moved into *The Game*, Ken Dryden's deftly penned behind-the-scenes look at the Montreal Canadiens and a particular hockey era. You see, Number 4 Bobby Orr aside, I was a terribly enslaved Canadiens fan. And in the late '70s, the prime of my wonder years, they were soaking in Stanley Cups like drunken sailors.

Day and night with my buddy Paul on the street outside our school, Maple Crest, I excitedly announced the play-by-play – "Robinson to Savard to Lafleurrrr!" – while Paul flopped around as Leafs' rubber-goalie Mike

Palmateer. Later, I'd replay the goals in my mind, slow motion, like the first time I kissed a girl. It felt so ... Canadian.

Years later, I actually read *The Game.* It was like discovering new rooms in the sprawling country home where one had grown up. And Dryden had such keen insights, like "He trudged along, unknowing what he sought, whistling as he went, for want of thought."

Okay, that's poet John Dryden. But Ken is better. And these things have all helped me adjust, somewhat, as a hockey nomad in a place like Yemen. It's not easy getting up at 3 a.m. for two-days-old playoff games called by strange Yank sportscasters who can't follow the puck.

Thankfully, I'm now shacked up in another book. Dave Bidini's *Tropic of Hockey* is a manic look at Canada's game in weird places. If San Jose bothers you, you may not want to know of Ivory Coast, Beijing and Transylvania. Our game is even being born anew in the type of global outbacks where you need to bring your own toilet paper.

The United Arab Emirates, an oil rich piece of earth that could cover its ice pads with gold, has an annual Mighty Camels tourney. They were started by the so-called Father of Arabian Hockey, Chris Reynolds, from Calgary. Desert Yzermans named Yasser and Ahmed play for what the NHL has lost: the pure joy and magic of the game.

In Yemen, where some folks think that sitting on a rock is a good time, my ambitions are more modest. With a few other Canadians here, I need to simply teach the basics. I'm starting with my landlord's boy, Ibrahim. He's nine. Like most Yemenis, he's a bit small. Okay, he's dwarfed by Sleepy and Sneezy.

So we've started with rug hockey, played in the place of honour in Yemeni homes, a top-level, lavishly carpeted and cushioned room called a *mufraj.* Later, for respect, and maybe for ball hockey, Ibrahim should have a Team Canada jersey.

I wear mine regularly. Jean says that when greeting me at the airport on my first visit to Sana'a, with my fire-red shirt amidst the white robes, she asked, "Lord, what have I done by bringing this guy here?"

Another time, at Frankfurt's airport, a clerk who let me in the airport's private business lounge must have confused me for a Team Canada player.

Anyway, oddities like Jamaican bobsledders or Eddie the Eagle aside, the task is large. If the Calgary Flames win hockey's Holy Grail this year, maybe Reynolds can help bring it to Yemen for viewing.

Otherwise, little Ibrahim may be my only hope.

I guess, in the end, though, if all else fails, I can always resort to getting him you know what: a good hockey book to live in.

Playing ball hockey in a Sana'a gym every other Thursday is among my fonder memories from the Arab world.

A handful of us were Canadian: an anthropologist from Alberta, a couple of teachers from the Maritimes, a teacher and his wife from Vancouver. My Royal Babe even went (willingly, I may add) in net when seven months pregnant.

We were hockey pioneers in Yemen, gathering other friends who were Swiss, British, even a New Zealander and, yes, some Yemenis. None knew Wayne Gretzky from Peter Puck, but everyone enjoyed it all.

In Yemen, I also acquired two NHL-size goal nets made by a welder, who, over their heavy red piping, put netting normally used to catch everything from snappers to sardines in the Gulf of Aden. The scene of my anthropologist friend, Gabriel, and I carrying these homemade jobs through Old Sana'a, a centuries-old time-warped piece of earth, is a juxtaposed postcard experience that I'll never forget.

Now the nets are here in Uganda, this time to be used by African hockey players who, if nothing else, might need some running shoes.

And little Ibrahim? We eventually brought him and two of his siblings to visit Canada, including for a youth camp experience in Ontario's Muskokas. The blessing came first from their father, and eventually – after a last-gasp personal visit from Jean and I to the Canadian Embassy in Abu Dabi, thousands of kilometers from Yemen – from Canada's Foreign Affairs

The wacky Iraqi

41

"Remember, war does wonky things to people."

SANA'A, YEMEN
April 25, 2003

Telling Lies in Iraq is my choice for the name of the flick we can only hope will be made about former Iraqi minister of misinformation Mohammed Saeed Sahaf. If it's anything like a satirical website on this new cult figure, a site that once had an incredible 4,000 hits per minute, this movie will be stunning.

There's Sahaf at the beaches of Normandy. *"What Americans? There are no American louts here."* Now he's at the Battle of Waterloo. *"Napoleon is beating the British on their heads with their own shoes and will soon storm London."* And his briefing at Gettysburg: *"The retarded Union soldiers can't read their compasses. They're lost in the woods."*

It's all so dizzying. Sadly, the spinmeister won't star as himself since he's AWOL. But the website lists Batman's Joker, Jack Nicholson, as a possible star to deliver Sahaf gems like "God will roast their stomachs in hell."

Or will it be Mister Magoo? How can anyone parade in his underwear so unashamedly?

First, Middle East culture doesn't have an intimate relationship with truth in the best of times. Denial means saving face, and that, my friends, seems to be everything in the Arab world. Also, remember, war does wonky things to people.

Sahaf wasn't always the front man of Saddam's irrationality. In fact, my *Yemen Times* colleague Mohammed Abbas, an Iraqi who knew Sahaf as a personal friend, says Sahaf was once seen as "an intellectual."

An English teacher by profession, Sahaf apparently headed Iraq's media moderately and held ambassadorial and ministry postings, including foreign affairs, judiciously in the three decades of Saddam's reign.

"He was among those in the Baathist party who didn't advocate force," notes Abbas. He believes Sahaf's recent wild doctoring was due to lack of information from higher levels of Saddam's collapsed government.

"There's a disparity between the attackers and the attacked. People like Sahaf try to put bravery into their people, not disappoint them. Some things are factual, but some need exaggeration. Even the Americans do this," Abbas adds.

True. Psychological warfare has been around since Cyrus the Great battled ancient Babylon. And, cultural nuances aside, Washington has its own information spinner in White House spokesman Ari Fleischer.

Since meeting Fleischer in the summer of 2001, I've been increasingly enamoured with his polished articulations and growing presence in living rooms around the world. So much so, I'm convinced that Fleischer is actually running the White House.

This, after all, is the man who said the Iraq war could be avoided if someone would just put a bullet in Saddam's head. You think George W. Bush has swagger? My motto is "Ari for president."

Jean and I were married just two weeks when I dragged her to a journalists' conference in Washington. She was with me in the State Department when during question period I asked Fleischer why the Americans wouldn't lift sanctions hurting innocent Iraqis more than Saddam.

His "Blame Saddam" response wasn't a Sahaf loony-tune. But it was still spun from the finest of propaganda weave, not unlike his recent comments on Syria's need to reform or face a big economic stick. Is this, as they say, déjà vu all over again?

The reality is, 12 years of burdensome sanctions disabled Iraq's middle class. They fortified Saddam's regime and undermined Iraq's intellectual movement, people who could have been involved with politics and public opinion. Starving people think of food, not resistance.

So the battle for hearts and minds of Iraqis started long ago. Now that a pile of trust is needed to rebuild Iraq, from where will it come? Iraqis may be running around in their underwear, but when it comes to spin-doctoring many Arabs see Uncle Sam, who initially armed and entrenched Saddam into power, as the real emperor with no clothes.

Not that Washington is much different from anyone else. It's increasingly hard to trust anyone stuck for long periods in the bureaucracy of big-time politics. Which is why Ari deserves a shot at the White House. Give his old job to Sahaf. And call Mister Magoo.

W

About the Mighty Yanks. Before I moved overseas, I met one, a young woman as far as I could make out, walking in an suburb of Chicago – the only place on earth that has more snow than either Canada or the North Pole – on a typical blustery Chicago winter day.

We were bundled like Sir Hillary on one of his expeditions, and so I had to listen hard to this person's muffled voice. Yes she was female, she was from Florida, and she loved water sports.

When she found out I lived close to Lake Erie and Lake Ontario, she asked what anyone from Florida might: "Lake Ontario? That's great. Do you have surfing there?"

Another time, while I was stopped at a Michigan gas station, an enterprising gentleman noticed my Ontario plates and noted to me how much he loved Canadians.

"Oh yeah?" I said. "Why so?"

He proceeded to explain how cool and clean Canada was, especially Toronto, and how well Canadians get along with everyone. "You guys even love your animals so much, you put them on your money!"

I hadn't really thought of that until, on Interstate 75, I saw all the dead deer left on the roadsides, kilometre after kilometre – I mean, mile after mile.

Or take the writer from USA Today who saw my card from the Times-Journal, from that St. Thomas on frigid Lake Erie. He told me how much he and his wife, in fact, loved St. Thomas, and could they visit me in the islands sometime?

Nobody can blame him for the mistake, because the Virgin Islands are very beautiful, and when I'm not in a parka, I do have that laid-back island way about me. Besides, he and I exchanged cards at the above noted Washington conference where journalists came from far and wide.

St. Thomas, Ontario?

I enjoyed the company in Washington because being a certain kind of journalist in Canada can be a lonely drag.

I had been invited by David Aikman, a former TIME Magazine scribe who had spent his career in hip spots – New York, Moscow, Beijing, Jerusalem – and at the time had just written 'Great Souls,' biographies of the likes of Mother Teresa and Alexander Solzhenitsyn. Aikman took it upon himself to gather journalists of all stripes from around the world – a process he said was as easy as herding cats – to mull over things like truth and trust and faith in the profession. It was at a time of one fabricated Pulitzer here, a Stephen Glass affair there, and journalists were becoming less believable than lawyers.

And so I learned that there are mainstream journalists who do think like I do, with that Mennonite instinct. They're just not in Canada. In fact, at any given time you can count the number of faith and ethics reporters on one hand and still have a thumb left over. (At the Times-Journal, my long-time beat was education.)

Aikman's view was that reporters like me could make a difference, at least so he told me one evening in the latter '90s while, by chance, we met and I drove him over some snowy Canadian roads to his hotel near Toronto.

And so he brought me to places like the Savoy in London, then down the

English highway to Chichester, then later to Washington, apparently sensing things about my future that I didn't: he once proudly introduced me to a Russian friend as someone who had travelled around the world when, in fact, I had barely travelled past my living room.

At the time I was enjoying the Times-Journal, but still knocking at other Canadian news doors, always with enough credentials to meet the boss, but no more. "Have your bags packed" is the best assurance I once got from a paper in Calgary, a few provinces west.

Hard times had hit the newspaper industry with the Internet, plummeting circulations and escalating corporate takeovers. In Canada you needed a crib sheet to keep up with who was about to own who, and who even believed this business of writing on dead trees had much of a future.

And while the best papers integrate spirituality into their mix because they recognize the powerful force it can be for many readers, during this season I was reminded that certain Canadian editors would never acquire much faith in faith. Like years earlier when I couldn't get hired in Lindsay at the so-called worst daily in Canada, I was left muttering, "Remember, if you don't get hired, there's a reason."

It was around this time that I was in New York on an Easter weekend visiting the work of David Wilkerson, who gained notoriety decades earlier as a skinny street-preacher working with the city's deadly youth gangs.

When I was 12, I read about it in 'The Cross and the Switchblade,' a powerful account of New York street life. And before the book, the comic. There, as I remember it, is Wilkerson on the cover, with that punk Nicky Cruz holding a switchblade to the preacher's throat.

Cruz: "I'm going to cut you into a million tiny pieces."

Wilkerson: "And every one of them will tell you that I love you."

Decades later (Cruz in the meantime became a preacher himself) Wilkerson was still in New York, now leading a church in Times Square.

It was there, on this particular Easter Sunday, where a smiling usher approached me. Here he comes, a short man with an awful orange blazer and brass name tag. After opening chit-chat, he now says this to me, quite seriously: "You know, God has a special calling for you."

Now understand, while I may frequent certain Sunday locales, I'm still skeptical about home-cooked prophecies that some deluded folks – not just Great Yanks, mind you – can give. Plus, I wondered, why wouldn't the Almighty tell me Himself?

"Uhuh," I said. "Says who?"

"Well," he responded, pointing to a woman some distance away. "As a mat-

ter of fact, that lady, who's the wife of one of our deacons, told me to come and tell you."

"Oh," I said, appreciative of the information. "Okay."

"So what's your name, and where are you from?" he continued.

I had to confess I was, in fact, a Canadian from St. Thomas, Ontario.

"Well," he finished, "we'll be praying for you." Which, for an American talking to someone from Canada, seemed fine and kind of expected. And interesting. And all likely nothing to do with the strange overseas life that This Scribe fell into not long afterwards.

At 12, I also read a certain American bestseller, 'A Walk Across America,' a book by Peter Jenkins, who did take the time to walk coast to American coast, with his dog Cooper, discovering, among other things, the deep faith many Americans have.

I was already familiar with this faith, expressed in other stories like 'Through Gates of Splendor,' a book and cousin comic book of 'The Cross and the Switchblade.' This one told of five Americans in Ecuador – Jim Elliot, Nate Saint, Peter Fleming, Ed McCully, Roger Youderian – who, in 1956, made first contact with an isolated tribe of Indians, the Waodani, a people who easily killed anyone they feared, including members of their own tribe.

After friendly initial contact, the five were speared and hacked, left dead in an Amazonian river basin, their photos and journal entries later spread across the pages of Life and Newsweek and Reader's Digest.

Incredibly, two of the widows, Rachel Saint and Elisabeth Elliot (with her toddler Valerie), then responded by going to live among the Waodani, their husbands' killers, and bringing many of them to a new peace.

This past Easter, 10 years after my experience in New York, My Royal Babe and I invited an American friend and his Brit wife over to watch it all in the documentary 'Beyond the Gates of Splendor.' And so I was reminded of some treasured words of Jim Elliot, that "He is no fool who gives up what he cannot keep, to gain what he cannot lose."

That's what that usher in the orange blazer was telling me. And so it all simmers.

(For more on the author's spiritual journey, see Window 51 and its addendums.)

Some issues are lightning rods. Gender issues in the Islamic world – often a volatile mix of cultural and religious traditions – are infernos.

A Westerner seeing a Muslim female in a balto might think 'That poor woman.' Apparently if we could just free such victims from those body coverings, all would be well.

In truth, some Muslim women believe the same about Western women, that they're in bondage. And some of the staunchest supporters of conservative modes in the Arab world are women.

Still, others are not happy with their culture's ways. Some have the courage to say so. Others are more fearful.

Wearing a balto (or burqa or similar facsimile), which some Muslim women do enjoy for the privacy it gives, is, in fact, the least of their worries. Larger concerns relate to personal health and safety, rights to make decisions for themselves and their children, and society's interpretation of their role in keeping that all-important family honour.

Traditionally such honour revolves around women's modesty, bearing children and maintaining the home fires. But that's easily abused by husbands and brothers and uncles and cousins more concerned about their own image.

I may not be the best gender to comment. Nonetheless, here are a few personal observations on the pain often associated with being a woman in the Muslim world.

Opposite page photo: *Covered in a balto and gloves on a hot day, a Yemeni woman seeks a handout through the author's car window.*

Fairness and the Fairer Sex

Leaving the 15th century 42

Sana'a, Yemen
November 8, 2004

One of the more fascinating things here, in the cradle of Islam, is how things run on their own time. This comes to mind in the holy month of Ramadan, a time to ponder revelations that Muslims believe came to Mohammed here in the Arabian Peninsula 1,400 years ago.

Yes, things slow down this month. The moon seems to hover longer. And don't try to do much of anything important. Folks rest during daytime when fasting and then stay up long past dark to eat. Children play in midnight streets that are abuzz.

It's not a bad thing. The West, which drives through life so fast you see just a green blur for grass and a red blur for flowers, could learn from it.

But there are other time warps here, too. Take the work week, Saturday to Wednesday. Some Western-minded countries in the region, such as Lebanon and Turkey, work Monday to Friday. But for Arab countries opting for the other, imagine their challenges in global commerce.

Then there's the Islamic calendar. It says we're actually living in the 15th century. To be exact, it's 1425 A.H. This Hegira calendar, with lunar years 11 days shorter than solar years, began when Mohammed emigrated from Mecca to Medina in 622 A.D. It's not used outside traditional circles, but it is interesting how this figurative step back in time does reflect daily life here.

Especially for the women.

During Ramadan, women actually have it harder than usual. In the countryside, fasting women work in the heat of the fields, fully covered, before having to make nighttime and pre-dawn meals for large families. They eat, as usual, only after the men.

In the city, things aren't different. Upon our recent return here, a Yemeni medical colleague of my wife, Jean, harboured a young woman in his clinic. The girl feared her family would kill her because of her out-of-wedlock pregnancy.

Women here simply have no real voice. Yemen's 301-seat parliament has 300 men.

It really does seem like the West's medieval era, when a universal hierarchy gave men a God-ordained control of society. The husband is king, his household his kingdom. Islamic family wealth and property also still often goes through the father to his sons. Women have few rights, even over their own children.

Like in those times of lore, women here also live in so-called modesty – and isolation. Talk about family ties that bind.

It all reminds me of gender issues raised by Shakespeare in plays like *Hamlet*. And a recent scene from Afghanistan in which a teacher stood in front of her female students and said, "I'm sorry if you've never heard of this, but today we're going to talk about something called civil rights."

Of course, the West hasn't modelled perfect gender relations. Maybe this is why some folks here believe wonky things, such as that Western women are terribly immoral, or at least living in their own bondage. Yes, a recent Yemeni newspaper column claimed wife-beating is "master" in Britain and that 80 per cent of marriages of American women aged at least 15 (as if that's legal) now end in divorce.

In truth, the West has liberties, but it didn't develop them overnight.

So the good news in the Islamic world is that at least some change is slowly plodding along. For example, Pakistan, a nation created as the ideal Islamic state, recently began treating so-called "honour killings" as what they are: murder.

The bad news is that, by definition, Islam bases gender relations on a very different historic stream. Looking at Mohammed's example, to his credit he banned the killing of newborn girls, common at the time in this region. Yet historians also tell us he married as many as 12 women, including his best friend's little girl, Aisha, when she was six. He reportedly consummated that marriage when Aisha, considered his favourite, was nine.

So the challenge of Islam is to move its gender relations not only into 21st-century values but also into a place that satisfies the deeper longings of the human heart. Living unequally doesn't really satisfy anyone of either gender. It seems to me that those who think otherwise are only hurting the future of their own community.

Strange fixations

43

Sana'a, Yemen
December 2, 2002

Life in Yemen is different. Still, a colleague surprised me not long ago when I invited some men from the office for an afternoon getaway at a local recreation centre.

"How are you enjoying it?" I asked Ramzy while he splashed away in its swimming pool, one of just a handful of pools in this city of one million.

"Oh, this is great," he said, looking up with appreciation. "I've never seen naked women before."

Ramzy, a twentyish Yemeni who will be married in a few days, meant he had never seen women, in this case Westerners, in swimsuits. That's because in public, Yemeni women always wear baltos, black head-to-toe drapes.

Even when venturing into water, like some female friends did in the Red Sea with my wife and I once, they still keep their soggy head-wraps on. Why? Because maintaining honour is the highest virtue in Islamic culture. Family reputations have traditionally hinged on the purity of their women. What you can't see, you can't lust for.

Which is why Muslims in Nigeria recently couldn't accept hosting this year's Miss World pageant. For them, they might as well host the Happy Hooker Show. There were 215 killed in riots over the morality of it all.

Are we surprised? No. By now we know about Muslim extremists. We know of, for example, honour killings, when Muslim women are killed by their own families for things like having a child out of wedlock. Yemen has about 400 such killings a year. Pakistan has more.

We also shouldn't be surprised that, despite best-laid plans to suppress sexuality, more than an ankle will inevitably show. In fact, when fixated on excessive covering, it takes only that ankle or wrist or set of pretty eyes from behind a veil to inflame passions all the more.

Just ask the 40 Arab sexologists who met at Oxford University in 2000. They talked about out-of-wedlock births, abortion and homosexuality in the Middle East, taboo topics for sure. They noted the religious rules versus what folks are actually doing.

Liberal Lebanon now even has a version of Dr. Ruth. *Al Shater Yahki* is a chat show with lively debate on things I won't mention. Except for AIDS. A UN agency estimates 440,000 Arabs have it. Yemen, along with Djibouti, Somalia and Sudan, is the worst hit.

The conclusion at Oxford was that Arab eroticism is based on trying to get out from under an unrealistic ideal. Most of us would agree. Swimming with the drape on? Come on.

Too bad the West sets such a rotten example of anything better.

Living upstairs from my wife and I are our landlord and family, including 10-year-old Tasbeer, a bright, gregarious girl who might someday want to come to North America, where she'd be caught in a vicious culture war. She'd see Pamela and Xena prance around half naked on TV. She'd see other shows and ads and end-to-end talk about sex: premarital, extramarital and barely imaginable, all targeted to titillate youngsters like her.

She'd find her school stocked with condoms and wonder why, in Canada, girls 15 to 19 have such a high rate of sexually transmitted diseases. She'd learn of a recent global survey that shows three in four teens say such diseases are their biggest life fears. Finally, she'd see our tide of marital breakdown and the pain in the eyes of her friends and wonder how this could happen in a place that knows so much about love.

Yeah, swimming with the drape on is weird. But so is taking off your clothes for the world without blushing. Which is why I don't see the Muslim world as an enemy as much as a culture that's marred by, among other things, the gender wars: a deeply wounded place, like ours; a scared part of earth seeking eternity and Eden, like places in the West.

The truth is, any culture has the potential for either madness or life to be written on its soul. We all need divine mending in our broken places.

While trying to figure out people here, especially in our post-9/11 world, let's not forget to check the mirror.

44 Guys, take a pill

SANA A, YEMEN
January 29, 2005

I'm not sure how it happened, but sometime while growing up I discovered reading. And recently, while finishing a particularly enjoyable book, a tattered paperback I bought at some used-book store or garage sale in Canada, I've been reminded again that a book is never just a book.

Left alone, any book, sitting there, minding its own business, asks very little of anyone. But open it, and it lives. It breathes ideas.

Like currency passed around, books are ideas that are not really owned by any one person. They're travellers, like on a train, where the journey is as meaningful as the destination. Unselfishly give yourself to the written word and learn that others, with thoughts of their own, are alongside.

How tragic, then, to be unable to read even a single word. It must feel like, if not a prison sentence, going through life like a blind man.

I wonder if that's how 70 million Arabs feel. According to a recent report by the Arab League Education, Science and Culture Organization, which represents the league's 21 countries, that's how many Arabs over the age of 15 now can't read or write. That's 35 per cent of the Arab world's adults. To give perspective, one per cent of Canadian adults are illiterate, according to UN definitions.

The percentage of illiterate Arabs has actually fallen in recent decades. But surging population means number-wise there are 20 million more than in 1970.

The societal impact is predictable, especially since about half of all Arab women are illiterate. For example, studies show a clear link between reading and birthrate.

Here in Yemen, with families averaging seven kids, they can't build schools fast enough. In fact, Yemen's population is projected to explode from 21 million to 50 million by 2050.

One expert calls it "the bomb nobody wants to talk about." It will affect virtually every other development barometer. Forty-five per cent of Yemenis already live on under $2 a day, and two-thirds of rural residents have no clean water.

Few officials, even here, would argue against educating women about birth control as the key to improve it all. But only 60 per cent of Yemeni children – boys and girls – are now enrolled in school. Also, there are powerful religious and cultural values telling families to have more kids. So while it's fine to preach to the converted, the bigger need is to work on the men: the fathers and husbands and brothers who set the family tone and house rules.

Sometimes necessity breeds ignorance. If children are our only social safety net, let's have lots. And if there's nobody else to feed the goats and plow the land, why choose Mary over Johnny to go to school? They're tough arguments. Especially when decisions about how families run get pawned off as God's preferences.

More often than not, the real issue is fear. Teaching a woman to read will empower her at the expense of men. She might determine if, and when, she'll have children and how large (or small) her family will be, even if she's happy with just one girl. Many men in Yemen, and elsewhere in the developing world, just can't accept this. In fact, many young men here are quite open about not wanting to marry a woman who's been to university. After all, if these uppity girls aren't lippy and argumentative, they're at least interested in careers of their own. How threatening.

Slow as it is, cultural change is always possible. Some richer Arab oil states have made literacy strides for both genders. And certainly outside help is always needed. But as crucial as foreign aid is, I'm afraid the West can talk about global visions like the UN's millennium goals and renew its commitments to the poor until the Third World cows come home. The deeper need is for basic heart change. Men over here simply need to appreciate that both genders are equally and inherently valuable. And donor groups that want to help bring lasting improvements need to understand these cultural and human issues and then face them head on.

Otherwise it's just like the blind leading the blind. And those jail doors won't budge.

W

Heart change, of course, is needed by not just Arab men but men everywhere, and I've been a man long enough to know this. So I've prayed.

The first prayer goes like this: "I am a man. But I can change. If I have to. I guess." Canadians will recognize this from the Possum Lodge scene that closes every episode of The Red Green Show, a fine comedy that may not depict Canadian men entirely as they are but, maybe, just enough.

Before I married, I had the chance to say this golden supplication along with some buddies from my social network (the Over-30 Unclaimed Precious Jewels Club) with Red Green at a studio taping of the show in Toronto. With the help of this duct-tape guru, our prayer was beamed across the nation.

While single, I was also influenced while reporting on Promise Keepers, which in the 1990s blew across North America and prodded men to gather in big numbers and pray something like Red Green: "I am a man. But with God's help, I can change, where I need to, I believe."

While untold thousands of wives celebrated and pushed their husbands out for more, TIME Magazine put the strange affair on its cover. Nobody could fig-

ure out why men would go to football stadiums to talk at all, let alone about loving their families.

Meanwhile, the picketers and naysayers lashed these dudes for not allowing women to come in and say the same prayer. So as part of my reporting, This Scribe noted this all: Promise Keepers oppressed women. Promise Keepers were homophobic. Promise Keepers caused the Oklahoma City bombing. Promise Keepers were going to steal the White House. Promise Keepers were green-eyed hairy monsters. (Okay, I just made this one up.)

But really, I guess being single is what made it harder for me to understand the stone-throwing logic. I personally watched 40,000 guys pray in Atlanta, 70,000 in Detroit, and around a million kneel on the grassy mall in Washington. Each time they seemed rather decent and cleaned up after themselves. Susan B. Anthony, a Quaker who was among the first mothers of feminism, would have been proud.

Even when PK came north over the snowy border, the stones followed. They finally stopped a few years later when anyone who was going to say the prayer apparently had and all the guys went back home, I'm guessing, to carry things out.

Today everything is calm again. David Sweet, a former president of Promise Keepers Canada, is now a successful member of Parliament for the Hamilton riding of my family's Canadian home. When he came to my door to ask for my vote one summer day, I saw no pickets.

Those America stadiums are being used for football again.

And reruns of Canada's Red Green Show are now shown in several countries. We can only hope they'll someday reach the needy Yemens of the world.

Who is God? How should we relate to Him? These questions dominate the Muslim mind.

I had barely arrived at the Yemen Times when I was peppered with questions about "the Christian view" on various contemporary moral issues.

My new colleagues first assumed that, as a Westerner, I must be a Christian. They further assumed that all Christians have monolithic views. So my responses likely didn't fully satisfy.

Still, they appreciated that, upon their request, I walked with them through the words of "Coloured People," a song by the Christian rock band DC Talk that these young Arabs had just pulled off the Internet.

On the Arab Street, where Muslims have 99 names for God, and in Yemen, officially 99 per cent Muslim, such is God Talk. Unlike in the post-Christian West, it flows freely and publicly. Naturally it's in a fully Muslim context. Still, some Yemenis have a growing curiosity about the outside world.

It's also noteworthy that many Arabs live with an overpowering fatalism. Thus the phrase inshallah (if God wills) is often sprinkled into everyday conversation. See you for dinner? "Inshallah."

Yemenis know that God especially wills the timing of one's death. So pedestrians rarely look when crossing the street. Who's then responsible for the ensuing fatality? And who's responsible for other preventable deaths or social ills, like, say, women dying in childbirth?

You get the idea. It's why cultural change takes so long.

Here's more on the complex undercurrents of God and the world's two largest faiths: Christianity and Islam.

Opposite page photo: Students of Islam study the Koran.

And Now, A Word from God?

WINDOWS

Islam's wake-up call

LONDON, CANADA
October 6, 2003

45

Irshad Manji doesn't come across as your typical religious reformer. With stylish glasses and punkish hair, this pint-sized woman is better known as a TVO journalist and gay rights activist than as a Martin Luther nailing his *95 Theses* on Wittenburg's church door.

But Manji's new book, *The Trouble with Islam: A Wakeup Call for Honesty and Change,* is a cannonball about to splash into the Muslim world's pool. Released in Canada and Germany and awaiting publication in the United States, Britain and France, this book tries to revive *ijtihad*, Islam's long-lost tradition of independent thinking.

Manji suggests – at her peril – that Muslims should question their faith if they're going to bridge the gap between Islam's idealistic theories and its often-questionable practices. She suggests Muslims stop blaming others, especially Jews, for their troubles and get on with making their faith relevant to modern sensibilities.

Some thoughts:

First, Manji, who spoke here in London at the University of Western Ontario in 1999 about things such as God and homosexuality, does not represent mainstream Islam. Nonetheless, she articulates the feelings of at least some strait-laced Muslims who wonder, if Islam is the greatest of the monotheistic religions – Christianity and Judaism being the others – why do so many Muslims around the world struggle with things such as basic human freedoms?

It seems this type of critical thinking has not been mastered by some religious so-called scholars. As a result, many of the world's one billion Muslims are left unable to speak their minds for fear of reprisal from state-sponsored mullahs who have closed the door to reinterpreting the Koran in a modern context.

So Manji and her allies likely won't find many friends in places such as fundamentalist Saudi Arabia. But they may find interest in places such as Iran, where six million university students and recent grads are full of questions.

"They are not anti-religious, but they are anti-fundamentalist," says Iranian sociology professor Hamidreaz Jalaeipour. "They refuse to be blind followers."

That's not a bad thing, really, for anyone, in any discipline. Give differing views a forum, and let people make choices based on their honest investigations. Truth has a way of rising to the surface.

Second thought: Reform is not easy. When Luther and company led the Christian reformation 500 years ago, they put the faith's entire theology on the operating table.

Let me illustrate. If a young criminal broke into a home and killed the owner's wife and children, the owner, naturally, would want revenge. To kill the criminal, or at least lock him away forever, would be justice. To forgive him would be an act of unusual grace.

But if the homeowner had the criminal released, adopted him, cared for him as kin and gave him a future, that would be a supernatural, even outrageous, grace. Luther brought the Church back to that foundational truth, and thousands were martyred defending it: that salvation is based on this type of divine grace, and nothing more.

No surprise, then, that Western culture, with its Christian heritage, tends to show more mercy and tolerance than virtually any other society in history.

Conversely, it's no surprise that Islamic society, which has historically focused on divine justice rather than grace, is being hijacked by the likes of Osama bin Laden.

That's not to say that God can't meet humans, in their place of need, through the cultural and historic contexts of their religions. God is big enough to get around to a mosque on Friday, a synagogue on Saturday and a church on Sunday. But if Muslims are really going to experience reform, they're going to have to accept the trauma of some major surgery.

Some cherished beliefs may have to go. But it could also be life-saving. And we should encourage open dialogue, as threatening as it may seem, to continue.

Can't God decide? 46

Sana'a, Yemen
April 17, 2003

Jean and I are packing to return to Hamilton to deliver our first child. And at the top of my to-do-in-Hamilton list, besides "get diapers for the bambino," is watch a big fat movie. There's a single theatre here in Sana'a, a town of one million, but considering it's infested with rats or something similarly revolting, I've avoided it.

For my re-entry to Canada's cinematic world, I'm eyeing *Gods and Generals*. At almost four hours long, this American Civil War epic seems enough to meet even my impregnated need. Curiously, this show, which explores themes of war and Christianity, is produced by media mogul Ted Turner.

You'll remember Turner once said Christianity was "for losers," blaming his divorce from Jane Fonda, his third wife, on her new-found Christian faith.

By some miracle, Turner has now reportedly soaked $80 million into *Gods and Generals*, a movie that sees the Civil War largely through the eyes of pious Confederate General "Stonewall" Jackson.

Most reviewers seem rather unimpressed, which can be a good sign. More so, this movie is particularly timely because it asks a question that has deeply permeated the Iraq disaster. If He cares, where does God sit in times of war? All sides in the Iraq war, like in America's Civil War and the Super Bowl and the odd Leafs-Canadiens game, claim the Almighty is squarely in their corner.

But can God be with Pope John Paul II and antiwar protesters and with U.S. President George W. Bush and with Saddam all at once? He may be divine, but even God can't be for and against the same thing simultaneously. Can He?

Which brings us to Easter, this season of reflection and renewal, and a recent conversation I had with a journalist friend I've grown to admire here in Yemen. We were talking about Islam and Christianity and their commonalities. Eventually we arrived at the cross, the rugged, bloody one that Christians believe Jesus died on.

"Well, there may be slight differences," my friend said, noting Muslims believe Christ was a prophet who was never crucified.

"It's no slight difference," I responded. "For Christians, the cross is everything. It's the foundation of the house. Take it away and everything falls."

The New Testament, of course, is filled with what Christ's cross and resurrection mean for humanity, both in this world and beyond. "It's important," I said to my friend, "because if Jesus is alive, just like you or I am sitting here, then His spirit is actually living in me."

So, no, all worldviews are not the same. Easter tells us this. So does our common sense. We simply cannot hold differing ideas that are mutually exclusive. Christianity is not Islam is not Scientology is not some wacky Shirley MacLaine New Age psychosis.

So then, whose side is God taking in the Iraq war?

He's on the side of the soldier, regardless of uniform, who lays down his life sacrificially.

He's on the side of the child, regardless of nationality, searching for his family in the rubble that was once home. He's with the grief-stricken, the lonely, the desperate and the broken-hearted.

This God, who knows suffering so well, is also with those like the disgraced criminal dying on a cross beside Christ, who asked Jesus to simply remember him when entering His kingdom. Yes, Easter's God, it seems, is rather passionately on the side of these so-called "losers."

And what might this mean for Iraq?

Turn to Abraham Lincoln, who found his own faith when asking whose side providence took when 600,000 Americans lost their lives in that brutal Civil War. "It is quite possible," Lincoln said, "that God's purpose is something different from the purpose of either party."

Imagine that. God has his own ideas. Like when you think you need to look for Him, and He finds you.

One of the more common misunderstandings about the Muslim view of God relates to the question, do Muslims and Christians worship the same God? Or, who is "Allah"? Without getting into a theological sinkhole, the short answer is that Mohammed chose the word Aliah, the higher form, male term for God that was common in pre-Islamic Arabia. He stripped the term of its polytheistic past, infused it with new meaning, and used it for the one, high god, Allah. This term "Allah" is linked to the Hebrew El-Bethel, El-Elohim and Eli / Eloi in Aramic. So etymologically, Muslims and Christians worship the same God. In fact, Arab Christians also call God "Allah" because they have no other name.

With this said, Muslims and Christians also have some stark conceptual differences in God's character. For example, the one name that is missing in the 99 names Muslims have for Allah is "Father" or "Abba," an integral concept in the Christian view of being adopted into God's family as a rightful heir of His many promises.

Jesus with the Muslims 47

Sana'a, Yemen
April 8, 2004

Okay, let's not be totally surprised that Jesus wields power outside the West. He did, after all, live in the Middle East. But after its big splash in North America, did anyone – I mean anyone – expect *The Passion of the Christ* to be allowed in the Islamic Middle East, let alone break movie records here?

In Lebanon, a record 58,000 people recently watched its first weekend, 80 per cent of all theatre admissions for the week. Then it opened in Jordan to best-ever crowds. And in Syria, a police state with a Christian population of just five per cent, *The Passion* has been seen by more people than any other movie – ever.

In Qatar, the first Middle East country to open the show, a Christian viewer noted, "The Muslims sitting around us were being moved – gasping, crying and reacting with disgust to the brutality that Jesus faced."

You have to live on this side of the world to understand how incredibly bizarre this is. Consider the orthodox Islamic view that Jesus was just another prophet. Yes, a unique prophet. So unique He will someday return to judge the world. So special, He's the *nur,* or "light," of the world. But according to Islam, Mohammed, not Jesus, is God's final and most noteworthy prophet.

Muslims also deny that Jesus was crucified. Why? Because God would not allow His own to be so brutally dishonoured. Muslims maintain Christians simply have both their theology and history wrong. No cross, no resurrection, no atoning sacrifice for the forgiveness of your sins and mine.

Further, for many Muslims, it's a transgression to leave the faith, severely punishable, even by death, if not by the state then by family wanting to preserve that all-important honour. No surprise, in places such as Yemen it's illegal for nationals to have Bibles. The Gideons just don't leave them in hotel rooms here.

Okay, that's what we know. So why are so many Muslims scrambling to see a movie that contradicts their core and cherished religious tenets? Why, on the streets of Jeddah, Saudi Arabia, for example, were bootlegged copies of *The Passion* selling like hotcakes weeks before its North American release?

One theory is that, if the movie is anti-Semitic, Muslims want to spread some good Jew-bashing. I don't buy it. Closer to the truth may be that now, when it's more politically unpopular to repress your people, Islamic governments are allowing the movie to show how tolerant they are.

Another explanation is that everyday folks across the Islamic world are simply curious about a show of one of their prophets.

Whatever their motives, though, one can't help but think that, while sitting in front of such a poignant movie, viewers are also being prodded by some basic life questions, namely, "If the story of Easter is true, what does it all mean for me?"

Interestingly, technology also has a role in this affair. Yemen, the poor cousin of the region, is a 99 per cent Muslim state. But few people will see *The Passion* here, simply because there are no Cineplexes. A Muslim friend of mine notes, "They can't keep it out. I can download it off the Internet. It might take three days, but I can do it."

Pirated movies from outside the country are also easily had here. Street shops everywhere rent poor-quality movies dubbed onto CVDs. But Yemen's censors generally do a good job keeping out what they want to.

I know of one government official who sits in a small dark room all day, opening folks' personal mail. He has confiscated cartoon videos showing Jesus (Islam prohibits any artistic depiction of prophets), home videos of children's christenings, bottles of wine, "anti-Islamic" movies such as *True Lies,* and Nintendo games.

Still, in the end, efforts to suppress truly revolutionary ideas always do seem hopelessly useless. History proves that. Change, like a rushing stream, is inevitable – sometimes in ways we least expect.

If nothing else, this is what *The Passion* phenomena shows. Interesting, we're in the midst of its swirling vortex.

Can't stomach The Passion?

48

SANA'A, YEMEN
April 3, 2004

So, *The Passion of the Christ* is making movie history, and critics who predicted nobody would watch its so-called anti-Semitic gore are eating crow. Another sign of how some of our darling media elitists are terribly out of touch.

Of course they don't flinch over explicit sex or violence that has far less to do with reality. Remember the last R-rated Jesus film, *The Last Temptation of Christ*? Martin Scorsese, lauded as a film genius, directed Jesus as a confused, if not neurotic, Messiah who could barely do up His sandals.

I recall it well because, disappointed in its lack of authenticity, I walked out just prior to Jesus' crucifixion. From my front-row seat. Up the long aisle. Past everyone.

Little did I know it was the instant when Christ's boldest disciple, Peter, denied he ever knew Him. With hundreds of eyes watching me, all I heard was the rabid charge against Peter, in thundering surround sound, "He's one of them! He's one of them!"

I hear some viewers have also left *The Passion*. Strange thing though. Apparently, unlike my escape from Scorsese's 1988 farce, many have returned, sometimes in tears, drawn back by the movie's powerful theme.

Unfortunately, since Yemen, 99 per cent Muslim, has no Cineplexes, *The Passion* will get here only sporadically via pirated dubs. In the meantime, I'll have to trust critic Roger Ebert, who calls it "the most powerful and important interpretation of Christ's final hours on film, because it deals directly with what happened, not sentimental, cleaned up, postcard versions."

Yes, the gore is exactly the point. Jesus crushed is a profound metaphor for the sin that disfigures and destroys our lives. More than a polished piece of silver jewellery, the cross was a gruesome instrument of death. In fact, Jesus' pain was so terrible, a new word – *excruciating*, or "out-of-the-cross" – was created to describe it.

Experts believe Jesus was flogged to show His veins, muscles and sinews. With great blood loss, a racing heart and stalled kidneys, He was in critical shock already while carrying His cross. Nerves in His hands and feet were then shattered by Roman spikes. And after His cross was hoisted, Jesus' shoulders would have dislocated. Then, slow asphyxiation.

To exhale, Jesus had to push on His feet, tearing them, to ease His stretched diaphragm. Over time, fluid collected around His lungs and erratically beating heart. Eventually, after hours of fighting for each breath, heart failure.

Finally, rejected and alone, marred beyond recognition, Jesus died. Willingly. For you. For me.

Is that brutal? Absolutely.

No wonder Muslims, who revere Christ as a prophet, even calling Him the *nur*, or "light," of the world, deny the crucifixion. They can't swallow God allowing one of His own to be so cruelly dishonoured. (As if God ever asks for our opinion.)

Ironically, though, Muslims in several Middle East countries are now watching *The Passion* in record-breaking numbers. And it's also interesting that, culturally, Muslims do value atoning sacrifices. Bloody ones. That's why millions of lambs in the Muslim world, including one that was running around our house, were slaughtered recently during Eid al-Adha, a Muslim holiday that, paradoxically, has an echo of Easter.

Yes, thanks to our landlord's invitation, I've now seen a lamb butchered up close. It really wasn't very pleasant. So why would anyone expect a movie about the death of Jesus, who's called the Lamb of God, to be any different?

It seems to me, then, that *The Passion* is resonating with people worldwide because it poignantly reveals the mysterious, if not outrageous, love of God. The heart of that love is Christ's sacrifice: to give us, like Peter, a second chance. And much more. Surely that's worth the ticket price and a couple of hours of our time.

Nonetheless, if you find yourself curious about why this movie is causing such a stir but fear you can't stomach it, here's some advice. Don't go. Instead, this Easter, read the original, including Jesus' spectacularly brilliant resurrection, in the New Testament.

Then, in the quietness of your heart, think about what it may all mean for your own life. No doubt, Someone will smile.

The late, great planet lives 49

Sana'a, Yemen
February 26, 2005

I treat most things said here in Yemen about Jews with skepticism.

The latest gem came from a Yemeni colleague ranting, in an unpublished column, about the so-called Jewish conspiracy. He cited the *Protocols of the Elders of Zion,* purportedly Jewish texts from the late 1800s describing Jewish plans to enslave the world.

The *Protocols* were debunked as early as 1921 as anti-Semite fabrications plagiarized in Paris with help from Russia's secret police. Of course, the truth didn't stop fascists like Hitler from using them. And today they're still dredged up. Egyptian TV promoted the *Protocols* as fact as late as 2003.

Nonetheless, living in this region does help one see the age-old Arab-Jewish conflict through a different – dare I say more accurate? – lens. I was first awakened to this after meeting a Palestinian, Ahmed, here in Sana'a. A gentle spirit, he's a pharmacist, exiled in Jordan since 1973. When modern Israel was birthed in 1948, his family was forced from its home by the newcomers, in this case Jews from Iraq.

What if that happened to you? At gunpoint. No questions. Just pack your memories and don't come back.

Modern Jews wanting a homeland recognized this dilemma as early as 1898, when two rabbis from Vienna went to Palestine on a fact-finding mission. Their message back? "The bride is beautiful, but she's married to another man." Still, an estimated 700,000 Palestinians, like Ahmed's parents, eventually left their homes to make room for incoming Jews. How did this happen?

Before the Holocaust and subsequent world sympathies for Jews, two forces were working against the Palestinians. One was political. Through statements like the 1917 Balfour declaration, the British supported the dream of a Zionist homeland in Palestine because they wanted an ally protecting their empire's trade routes through the Suez Canal, particularly to their jewel, India.

Meanwhile, one view of Judeo-Christian eschatology, called premillennial dispensationalism, was roaring to life via British theologians like John Darby. This interpretation of ancient biblical prophecies linked the birth of modern Israel to the end times and the imminent second coming of Christ.

Interestingly, experts like Colin Chapman, author of *Whose Promised Land?* say that at the time there were actually more Christian Zionists than Jewish Zionists wanting a Jewish state. Dispensationalism has since become hugely popular. I recall reading Hal Lindsey's blockbuster *The Late Great Planet Earth* in the 1970s. He predicted Christ would return by 1988, what he considered one generation after modern Israel's birth. More recently, dispensationalists Tim LaHaye and Jerry Jenkins have sold 50 million of their end-time *Left Behind* novels.

The problem, besides pernicious date setting, is that dispensationalist theory is just that: a theory. It's one interpretation of mysterious prophecies, and it may or may not be proven the best. But by taking theory as fact, proponents (tens of millions of evangelicals, including powerful policy-makers in Washington) see Arab-Jewish issues through certain blinders. And one wonders who else, besides Palestinians, would so many Christians deny basic human rights to, while ignoring things like international law, to fit their particular interpretation of our times?

Chapman, a Christian and former lecturer in Islamic studies at Near East School of Theology in Beirut, uses *Whose Promised Land?* to support another view, called covenant theology.

When recently visiting Sana'a, he told me, "When I read what was being written by the evangelical community and how far off the mark it was of what was happening on the ground, I was appalled. I felt I had to offer an alternative." I, for one, appreciate his blending of history and theology, using justice as a starting point for understanding.

Another noteworthy expert is Palestinian-Christian scholar Elias Chacour. Like Chapman, he chafes at the long silence of Christians, especially in North America, about lingering injustices in Palestine. In his home of Galilee, he's responded by building peace centres inaugurated with the drama *The Diary of Anne Frank,* showing that Anne could easily be a modern Palestinian girl. It's helped bring Jews and Palestinians together and restore dignity.

It's a shame, however, if such voices are left like calls in the wilderness. Certainly now, with new hope for the peace process, it's time to carefully consider them.

Need surgery?

50

Sana'a, Yemen
January 15, 2005

Ever hear of the poor guy who kept pulling his own hair out because he was so worried that he was going bald? Ever feel like him? I do. After all, life can be uncertain, and when one feels very fortunate, there is always opportunity to worry that one's treasures might somehow, someday, all be lost.

Maybe I'm a bit like Job. You know Job. This ancient Middle East figure had everything, but in a strange twist of fate, lost it all overnight. His children, his vast riches, and finally his health: gone. All Job had left were his wife and his so-called friends, who told him to curse God and die, or at least 'fess up that he was being punished for some secret wrongdoing.

Interestingly, this timeless story begins by noting that, like the man pulling his hair out, what Job greatly feared is what eventually fell upon him.

In my case, I fear surgery. Of course, anyone else's surgery can be interesting. In the outback of Congo, I was once rather intrigued while photographing Hamilton doctor Philip Wood. A tireless worker in Congo's hardness for much of 30 years, he performed a surgery with only the early-morning sun for light.

The surgery I fear, however, is another type. In my better moments, I know there really is no need to worry (for tomorrow has enough worries of its own). But lately, maybe like you, I've been reminded of how dreadful this surgery can be by the terribly unexplainable tsunami disasters in southeast Asia.

It's the surgery of suffering.

In our more honest moments, we not only fear suffering, we also have this terrible knowledge that we can't really avoid it. True, we can cause our own suffering. Smoke, and get cancer. Don't exercise, and get heart disease. But cancer and heart disease can also strike anyone. Yes, suffering has this ugly lurking randomness. We innately know if it didn't come like a killer wave in 2004, it will hit in '05 (Happy New Year), or in '06, or some other inopportune time. How disturbing.

Lost jobs, lost relationships, lost health – it can be one type of shattered dream or another. That's not 150,000 dead, but it still registers on our personal Richter scale as an incredibly brutal upheaval. In fact, if your experiences are anything like mine, you feel like you're being stretched, arms spread open, for some unseen force to rip into your insides and do things that you don't think are really all that necessary.

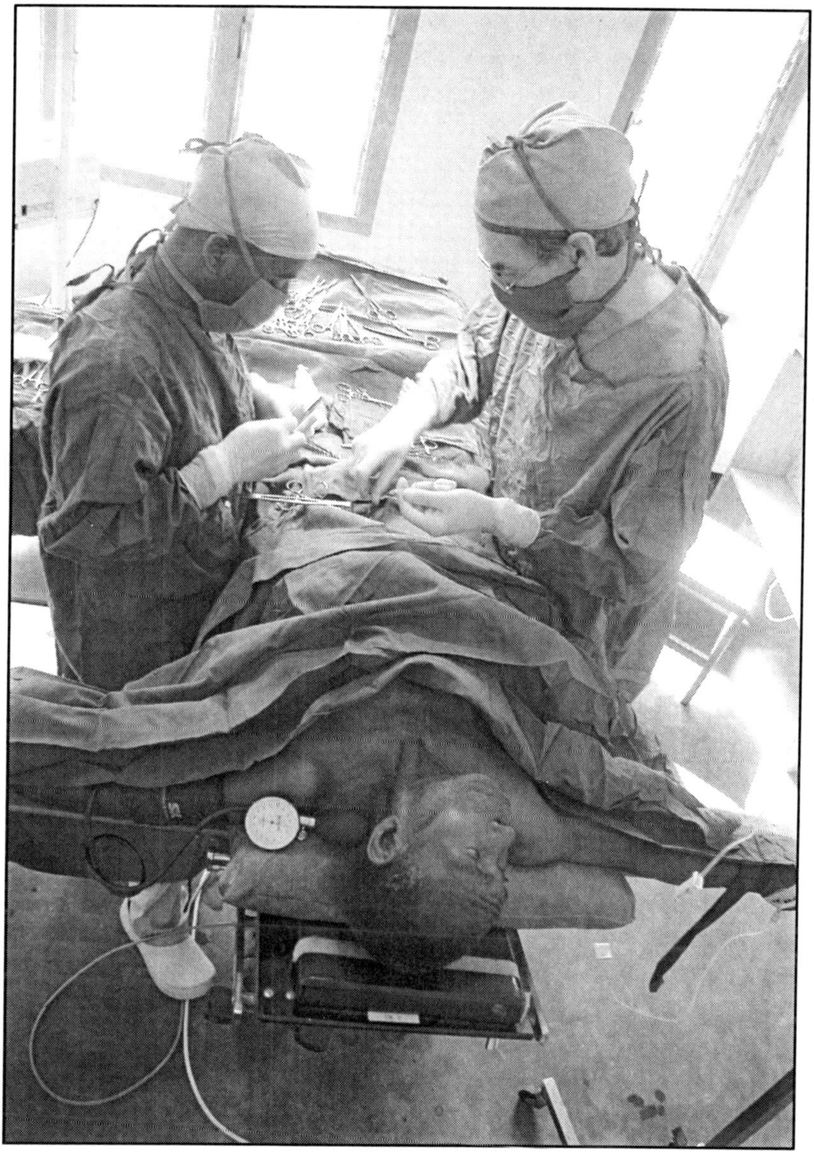

Thankfully, Job's misguided friends were wrong. When he finally got his personal meeting with the Almighty, Job was vindicated by a powerful yet loving God who blasted the others for their rotten advice. During our own hard times, that's comforting. And this should also help us deal with wonky people who claim that victims of disasters, especially natural disasters, are being divinely punished for their moral waywardness.

Regarding the tsunami disaster, that is what some Muslim preachers here are telling the masses (not unlike some Christian leaders elsewhere talking about, say, AIDS). Incredibly, these Muslim clerics then vilify the United States, as usual, for its foreign policies, while America is among the largest deliverers of aid to tsunami victims, who happen to be largely Muslim. As a Yemeni colleague of mine says, "How bizarre."

There's a mystery that says this life is like a hazy mirror. We can't see everything clearly, yet. Job was never told exactly why he had to suffer. Similarly, people in the developing world, already impoverished, may never know why they're the members of the human family who get more than their share of natural disasters. Sadly, this may even increase, as population and migration patterns move more of the world's poor closer to Earth's dangerous fault zones.

Yet, another mystery says, "*Blessed are those who mourn, for they shall be comforted*". Maybe this is why, in my observation, people in the Third World tend to have more humility – and even joy – than those in the "I-have-it-all-together" West. It seems that's what heart surgery does.

Maybe it can do the same for us spectators. No matter how much we may fear it all.

Dirty feet

51

SANA'A, YEMEN
March 26, 2005

I wonder if the Prodigal Son had blistered feet. And I wonder if Vincent Van Gogh, if he were alive, would come to Yemen to paint them.

You likely know Christ's parable of the prodigal. A young man abandons home, taking his inheritance early. He lives wildly, then winds up alone and broke and eating in the company of pigs. When he finally returns home, hoping to be just a hired hand, his lovesick father runs, ridiculously, likely almost tripping on his robe, to meet him in the distance. He throws his arms around his son. And he throws a party.

It's a universal story. Ernest Hemingway tells it well in *The Capitol of the World* while writing about a runaway teenage son. After a lengthy search, the longing father takes out a Madrid newspaper ad. "Dear Paco, meet me in front of the newspaper office tomorrow at noon. All is forgiven. I love you." The next day 800 men named Paco are at the office wanting to restore a broken relationship.

It's Rembrandt who painted a scene of the prodigal being held in his father's arms. The painting has such impact that Catholic priest and scholar Henri Nouwen once travelled to Russia just to see the original. He stood in front of it for four hours and then noted that it shows humanity's "yearning for a lasting home."

Van Gogh painted similar themes. And I'm reminded of this whenever I drive the dusty and busy streets of Yemen and slip Don McLean's song "Vincent" into my tape deck. The lyrics explain how Vincent painted "weathered faces lined in pain." He put "frames around ragged men in ragged clothes." He "tried to set them free."

You have to be here to appreciate the imagery. You have to see Yemeni feet. They are not Paris feet. Or London or New York feet. Yemeni feet are not Toronto feet. They are not even Hamilton feet. For one, they're all in sandals. Riding a motorcycle? Working in construction? Going to the mosque? Sandals. And not surprisingly, like poorer feet of the ancient world, Yemeni feet walk, long distances sometimes, in sandals that are battered and torn. Yemeni feet are scarred. They're bruised. And dirty.

So, in Yemen, Van Gogh could find inspiration to paint the Prodigal Son's feet. And there's something very Easterish about this. Because after Jesus finished eating and laughing with His friends, after He hung out with the hookers and tax collectors and other prodigals of His time, to make His lasting point unmistakably clear Jesus washed their filthy feet and went off to die for them.

How interesting, then, that in this Muslim country where there is not one Christian church for 20 million Yemenis, there are everyday pictures that are so biblical and so much more vibrant than in the planet's more sophisticated places. It's something I'll keep in mind tomorrow morning when my family joins a couple of hundred other expatriates in an Easter service on a nearby rocky plateau as the sun rises.

The other thing one can't help but ponder is Van Gogh's disillusionment. As a young man, before becoming a painter, he wanted to, in his words, "sow the words of the Bible" to the poor in London's slums, in the grimy coal mines, in nearby farm fields. Later, painting the realness of such men and women, he said, "Christ is more of an artist than the artists; He works in the living spirit and the living flesh; He makes men instead of statues." Yet this gifted and spiritually rich man, who was born this week in 1853, died, young and hopeless, by committing suicide. Why?

Putting aside the 19th century's lack of treatment for mental illness, one can't help but conclude that the deeply depressed Van Gogh couldn't absorb the rejection of having his work (worth a fortune today) go unrecognized. Apparently nobody understood, or could be bothered to understand, the different language of his colours, the strange composition of his brushstrokes, no matter how true and loving they were.

Rather than stopping, even briefly, to look at what was a unique window into eternity, people simply walked by. Blindly. Like some do with Christ. It's something to think about. Tomorrow. Or any day.

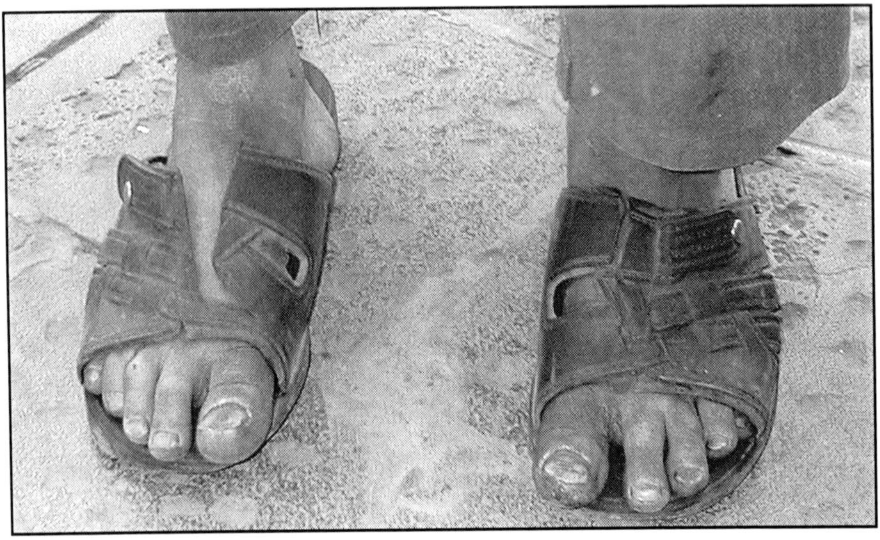

My own spiritual journey started at Gemeinde Gottes, a church in Kitchener, Ontario, made of German families who came to Canada looking for a better life after the Second World War, a hellish time when Germany was a land of terror. (Dad Froese tells how, towards the war's end, his father was taken to a POW camp in Siberia while he, as just a boy, was left back home to, at times, make coffins for loved ones who starved to death.)

In the subsequent post-war years, Gemeinde Gottes, or Church of God, helped sponsor German refugees. A good number from the Froese family settled across Canada from Ontario to British Columbia, others south to Indiana.

It was after arriving on the scene some years after all this that I was then taken to the Kitchener church by Dad while visiting relatives. At one point, some members met in a gym, which is where I was first awakened to something that even then, when I could barely tie my shoes, I sensed was big. There He was, this Jesus, on the huge screen at front, on a cross between two others, soldiers nearby with their helmets and ladders, their hammers and laughter, a terrible and dark feel to it all.

Perhaps shown for Easter, this movie scene is my earliest recollection of a spiritual experience, something divine touching a deep part of my being.

Those German families later built Pioneer Park Church on Old Carriage Drive in Kitchener. It was there where I would witness the prayers; usually in German, spoken out loud, long and earnest, often by babushkas wearing head scarves, while everyone stood. I saw the men, with big creviced hands, often folded, *sturdy men with dark suits and deep baritone voices when they opened their German hymnals.*

I was not in this Gemeinde Gottes very often, and, beside Sunday morning TV, my family had no church. But my home life in Niagara fostered a reverence for the Judeo-Christian God and for seeking truth. At the dinner table Dad Froese especially enjoyed reading the more philosophical devotions of E. Stanley Jones, a long-time missionary to India who had a wide exposure to world faiths and a vibrant way of revealing Life. "To l-i-v-e backwards, like the spelling, is e-v-i-l."

Through such influences, while young I grasped my need to be saved from, if nothing else, myself.

Kitchener's Pioneer Park Church of God now has services in English, some traditions gone in order to stay relevant to current members from the new neighbourhood.

And I'm now 42. I've have had time to look at things more thoroughly, time for higher studies that confirm the veracity of Christ's claims and the historic impact of His resurrection. I've had time to ask honest questions, time to learn from others who have travelled this road. I've had time to understand how my journey might fit into a bigger world, one that's not just pluralistic but also hurting. I've had time to learn that all truth is God's truth.

I appreciate the mystery of it all, the mystery of this so-called Hound of Heaven. I think of the time I crossed paths with a young man in Berlin, in the busy square Breitscheidplatz, near the ruins of the Kaiser Wilhem Memorial Church, an old building the drug addicts urinate against nightly. There he is, his hair spiked like the Statue of Liberty, playing a flute, wearing a black muscle-shirt with a picture of Christ, crucified, upside down, with the words "Jesus didn't die for my sins. He died for his own."

And so he plays. Gospel.

Gospel?

"It's easiest," he tells me.

The poor fellow was running from Dutch authorities. And from songs in his own heart.

Other everyday mysteries speak to me.

Not that long ago I received notice from an editor with, in his words, the "lousy news" that after some years his newspaper, a key market for my work, was dropping my regular dispatches. I felt devastated – until I realized this came 20 years to the day after I left home. (A memorable time, because while my departure led to my vocation, it was also seen as the act of a prodigal son and therefore a time of suffering.)

And now this, 20 years to the day? What are the odds?
Yes, life does have divine patterns and cycles and seasons.

W

This is the type of thing that makes me feel like when I was younger, with expectancy, not in a manner of religion but life, and life so deep and vast and immensely worth discovering.

We tend to fool ourselves in these matters, like the little girl who got lost. After looking all day, the townspeople stopped their search at dark. But her father carried on. All night. Until he found her curled up, asleep, hopelessly lost in the woods. Awakened when he bent down to kiss her, the girl reached up, put her arms around him and exclaimed, "Daddy! I found you!"

No, all of this isn't about anyone finding God. It's about God finding us: all the travellers, the wanderers and the vagabonds, even the prodigals with dirty feet, looking for our way Home.

(For more on the author's spiritual journey, see pages 154-155.)

W

There's no time like Christmas.

True, in a Muslim nation that has been largely closed to outside influences for centuries, Christmas comes and goes in Yemen with the masses largely not even aware of it. Still, even in this isolated pocket there are enough foreigners to give a general feeling of the season.

Some shops in Sana'a cater to expatriates, and in these it's easy to find a decent Christmas tree. In fact, toy shops in Sana'a abound, and they're remarkably well-stocked 12 months a year, a visible testament to the priority that children are in many Yemeni families.

So while we missed the snow of our Canadian home (sort of), My Royal Babe and I never had a problem creating a fine holiday spirit in our little ground-level apartment flat.

Christmas also has enough magic to venture into some different places with one's writing. It's a time when Story and Reality meld, when a child might say, "Daddy, is it true, is it really true?" and the only response is "Yes, it's truer than you'll ever know."

(To put it more succinctly, consider J.R.R. Tolkien's thoughts on what he called "eucastrophe" – the event that turns catastrophe on its head; the moment in the Story when the tide turns, when the wind moves in a new direction, when dawn finally breaks; the moment of divine surprise.

As Tolkien elaborated, "The birth of Christ is the eucastrophe of Man's history. The Resurrection is the eucastrophe of the Story of the Incarnation. This Story begins and ends in joy. It has pre-eminently the 'inner-consistency of Reality.' There is no tale ever told that men would rather find is true, and none which so many skeptical men have accepted as true on its own merits.")

So the following pages have some things a little different, such as Christmas letters home from Yemen, plus some introductory pieces from Africa, to stir the heart and imagination.

A couple of selections that explore the historic Jesus are pulled from the vault, written during that previous life while This Scribe was a reporter at the Times-Journal, that city daily in St. Thomas, Canada.

Opposite page photo: *Expatriate youth in Sana'a perform a Christmas pageant for other Westerners.*

I'll Be Home for Christmas (Sort of)

Truth, lies and Christmas 52

HAMILTON, CANADA
December 27, 2003

Jean and I are in Canada for the holidays, but still in the thoughts of our landlord's family back in Yemen. These Muslim believers have nicknamed our little girl, Elizabeth, "Mariam" or Mary, in honour of Jesus' mother.

That's interesting, but not a total surprise, since Jesus and Mary are revered by most Muslims, who also agree with the orthodox Christian view of Jesus' virgin birth.

That's more than can be said for the Jesus Seminar, a group of so-called scholars who surface every Christmas and Easter to tell us who Jesus really was. With names like Robert Funk and Walter Wink, these clowns in recent years have written off virtually everything the biblical gospels tell us about Christ.

For example, they argue that Jesus could not have fed 5,000 with a few loaves and fishes, because, well, that's not "natural." I guess Jesus just cued everyone to pull out a bagged lunch from under their cloaks. Funny? Well, Funk actually claims that Jesus was more like the first Jewish stand-up comic.

Don't get me wrong. It's good to debunk myths. Like the one that more people commit suicide at Christmas because they're more disillusioned over life. Studies show suicides actually decrease over the holidays, which I find quite remarkable because the season's cultural garb does drive some of us mad.

Firstly, of course, December 25 is not Jesus' literal birthday. It was picked for cultural reasons, similar to the Muslims' annual Hajj to Mecca, which replaced a seasonal celebration held before Islam was born in the 7th century.

And those three kings from the "Orient" who gave Jesus gold, incense and myrrh? In fact, they likely came from Babylon, modern Iraq, which at that time had a large Jewish community, or from Persia, modern Iran, another home of the priestly caste of Magi. They were not kings, but experts in medicine, religion and astronomy.

Further, the gospels say that Magi, and not necessarily three of them, gave their gifts when Jesus was a young child at His house, not at His manger. I could go on, but the point is, we need to let the story tell itself.

And like urban legends, any faith needs healthy skepticism.

Novelist John Updike puts it well, noting that "looking at some of our present-day ayatollahs and Fuhrers, the devil is, in fact, the absence of doubt. He's what pushes people into suicide bombings, into building extermination camps. Doubt may give your dinner a funny taste, but it's faith that goes out and kills."

With that said, nobody does well in a culture of unbelief. True, it's not easy to accept someone's claims to forgive sin. And men normally don't rise from the dead. But what's the difference between that and creating the world from nothing, or parting the Red Sea, or turning water into wine? Is one supernatural event harder than another?

That's what the Funks and Winks of this world don't get. Jesus' actions were never meant to be natural. The question is, are they true? Because, despite the slogan that "we can always find our own private meaning in just the story," in our hearts, truth matters very much.

And for that, my money goes to bone-diggers like journalist Lee Strobel. An ex-skeptic, this former Chicago crime reporter and author of *The Case for Christ* tried to debunk his wife's newfound faith by doing his own exhaustive investigation into Jesus with various global experts. Problem was, he kept coming across unexpected information.

For example, based on events – some out of the control of Jesus, such as where he was born – mathematician Peter Stoner calculates the odds of anyone but Jesus of Nazareth being the fulfillment of Old Testament prophecies as one in a trillion to the power of 13. All Strobel found is that based on empirical evidence of history, literature and science, it's more reasonable to believe in the orthodox biblical Jesus than not to.

That's why this season has always been less about evidence per se and more about the choice to celebrate or not. Christmas doesn't ask, "Who is Jesus?" It asks, "Who are we?"

Santa, can you spare a dime? 53

SANA'A, YEMEN
December 20, 2002

Dear Santa:

Thanks for last year's gift, the *Gulliver's Travels* book. I enjoyed the Houyhnhnms, those horse-like characters. So bright. So noble. And those savage Yahoos. So dim. So lost. Poor Gulliver couldn't see himself in them.

But Gulliver really was a traveller. Like you, Santa. That's why I'm writing. Distribution problems down here are getting worse.

Start with my street. Soccer, or "futbal" as they call it, is all that Middle East kids love. The boys in the hood play in front of our place all the time.

Their ball, though, beaten and deflated as folks here feel, looks like it's been through the war.

These kids aren't David Beckham. They won't make *TIME* magazine. But is anyone who kicks a ball around worth $9 million a season? How much is that a goal? Average NHL plunkers now get $1 million to lace up their skates. And, incredibly, Michael Schumacher pulled in $80 million last year for driving his race car.

There are bigger problems, though. Like toilets. I don't even like to think about it. But a concern I had when arriving in Yemen this year was that we wouldn't have decent facilities. Thankfully, in our home we do. But many Yemenis are among three billion folks on earth who don't have a pot to call their own. That's half of the world's people.

What's with that?

Granted, things could be worse. It's easy to complain that we don't have shoes until we see someone without feet. Yemen's neighbours in Ethiopia are running out of food. Fast. They say 15 million might die in the next few months. Usually, the children go first.

Guess they won't need any toilets.

Ethiopians are actually beautiful people. Some come to impoverished Yemen for a better life. Jean and I know several. Guess poor Yemen will have to do more. Westerners apparently have something called donor fatigue. Is that like free will?

It's not like there isn't any money. On your trip to Ethiopia, look down on nearby Djibouti. That's where the Yanks are playing war games. Keep an eye out for those Predator drone planes though, the kind that just killed some al-Qaeda suspects in Yemen's countryside. A new Predator goes for $4.5 million.

That comes from the $400 billion or so the United States now gives its military every year. That's six times what Russia spends. Guess we all need protection.

About clean water. A billion people now don't have it. But there is wine. Canadians apparently are drinking more these days. Can you turn some into water? And then back again? For the Ethiopians I'd recommend a white Valle Berta Gavi from Italy. It's rich on the palate but still crisp. Clean as a vicar's conscience.

Yeah, for some people, this Christmas kind of stinks. But you can cover the smell easy. Hugo Boss is nice for the guys. Give the ladies a more luxurious aroma, something romantic but sophisticated for the times.

Nobody will think about Louis IX and Marie Antoinette. While their parties at Versailles were swinging, revolution outside was brewing. Eventually things exploded with quite a bang. That left everyone with the smell of blood. That's less pleasant than frankincense, for sure.

Frankincense was a valued trading commodity in ancient Yemen, when this region was known as "the ends of the earth." You know, for the right person frankincense is still a great gift idea.

Yes, that person is you, Santa. Frankincense and myrrh from the ends of the earth. Merry Christmas. Do enjoy it. After all, Christmas really is all about you. It's about your honour and your glory.

It's about Someone Else's glory? No, Santa. You know you're the one who loves us so much.

Anyway, I think this year Jean and I have all we need. We have each other, and more.

But please. Teach us to be thankful every day. Teach us to be generous throughout the year. And wherever our travels may lead, please do help us all find some horse sense so that we don't live our lives, short as they are, like a bunch of Yahoos.

Thom

Will the real Mister Christmas please stand up?

54

ST. THOMAS, CANADA
December 22, 1997

> *"Dear Editor: I am eight years old. Some of my little friends say there is no Santa Claus. Papa says, "If you see it in the* Sun, *it's so." Please tell me the truth. Is there a Santa Claus?"*
>
> Virginia O'Hanlon, 115 West 95th Street, in a letter to the *New York Sun,* September 21, 1897

Among my favourite Christmas movies is the original *Miracle on 34th Street*, the tale of one Kris Kringle, Santa Claus at New York City's huge Macy's department store, a Santa so real he even sends shoppers to competing stores to ensure children receive the best gifts. That the jolly guy is fingered by a mental therapist as a public threat doesn't bode well for him when he's before a court determining if he should be committed.

Still, Kringle has a few things going for him, like an amazing Santa look, solid Claus know-how and a true giving heart. Children testify he's the real thing. If he's not, is there evidence? What about the 1897 *New York Sun?*

One hundred years ago, the *Sun* published a now world-famous editorial responding to Virginia O'Hanlon, a very real eight-year-old girl who wrote simply: "Papa says, 'If you see it in the *Sun*, it's so.' Please tell me the truth. Is there a Santa Claus?"

These stories are enjoyable because they're credible. As *Sun* writer Francis Church replied, "The most real things in the world are those that neither children nor men can see."

The original Saint Nicholas, a fourth-century bishop from present-day Turkey who was canonized after an exemplary life of giving, would agree. Sadly, he would frown on many of our modern modes of observing the season.

That's because there is much that is neither holy nor real. Near the time of Nicholas, Emperor Constantine jammed Christ's birthday celebrations into *natalis solis invicti*, an agricultural solar festival of the Romans. It was a top-down approach that has left the modern world sifting Christmas's deeper significance from its pagan roots and ever-evolving folklore. Accordingly, in North America, gift-giving has become a holiday sickness, and, like Nicholas, Jesus has become a mere shadow of His historic self. If He's not poking His head through extra tinsel, little Jesus is left in His manger, sleeping in heavenly peace, implications of His birth all-too-sanitized by our culture's obsessive compulsion with Mister Clean.

I was reminded of this on the opening night of this year's St. Thomas Holiday Fantasy of Lights while in front of a rather unconventional nativity scene with Mary, Joseph, animals, straw, the manger, and...no baby Jesus.

"People don't get it," said a nearby woman who helped make the work. "He's risen."

"Oh," I said, lights going on. "Yes, of course."

Allowing Jesus out of His manger runs against the season's homey sentiments. Even when we let Him grow up, we still prefer a Jesus who's palatable, with conventional, if not effeminate, features and a message that's prudently balanced, like that of an Aristotle.

Yet Christ's birth, brief ministry and death were all unconventional. As magnetic as He was, Jesus was puzzling and even infuriating. Deserted by His friends, called a devil, and nailed to a stake of wood, He was hardly the picture of an integrated, happily adjusted man. Journalist-author Philip Yancey asks in *The Jesus I Never Knew* what government would execute a Mister Rogers or Captain Kangaroo who told people to be nice to each other?

So, yes, this is Christmas, and what have we done? Why do I, like others, feel such a strange ambivalence to much of it? Is it because glib cheeriness simply isn't in the original? If God truly did enter the world's stage in the flesh, He clearly played by its harsh rules. Born in a barn? A mule could have stepped on Him, for heaven's sake.

Christ even chose a family tree filled with public skeletons. His bloodline runs from Old Testament scandals, including incest, prostitution and not-so-royal adultery covered by murder, showing a God less interested in avoiding disgraces than in transforming them.

This is what the gospels tell us God offers us. Himself. Not a gift peddled by store management to make a buck, but an appropriate gift perfectly suited for humanity's children.

Did the maker of all things really descend to our fifth-rate dirty little ball of a planet? Asking the question seriously changes Christmas from a shallow time of coziness to a meaningful event in the proverbial courtroom. There we can listen to the untainted story of a mysterious Jesus, the Christ of an empty manger, and reach a verdict.

We can be hallowed and lifted and, like the *Sun's* bright editorial of 1897, say, yes, with faith we can push aside the curtain and be filled with the reality of Christmas's joy.

Or we can be left in a thinly glossed celebration of dissatisfaction, hounded by the season's contradictory forces and the world's unredemptiveness.

Do we need to ask the real Mister Christmas to stand up?

Walk on water with me?

55

Somewhere Between Africa and Canada
December 19, 2005

It's madness to wear ladies' straw hats to church.
We should all be wearing crash helmets.
Ushers should issue life preservers and signal flares.
They should lash us to our pews.

Annie Dillard, American author

Ever wonder why Jesus asked Peter to walk on water?

Of course, like with the miraculous account of the first Christmas, not everyone believes, or even knows, the story. But the same gospels that tell one, tell the other: a man, Simon Peter, jumped from a boat to walk on water one night some 2,000 years ago, apparently with some success, in a kind of reckless joy in seeing Christ Himself on the waves.

I've never found it hard to let such stories speak for themselves. The God of Christmas pursued me early in life. He's encouraged me in ways that I can't express, surprised me too many times to remember, and gave me enough evidence about His reality that the jury of my heart reached its verdict long ago.

My problem, if you can call it that, is indifference. You know how hard it is to leave bed some days, never mind a boat. Maybe lunch beckons. Or the bus is coming. I have things to do. So it's been good to live in Africa, because for all their daily challenges, many Africans freely worship God in that dangerous Peter-like manner.

Now it's hard to know what anyone might mean by the word *worship* these days. I can say I worship the ground my wife walks on, but that's not literally true. In more honest moments, some of us might admit we tend to worship ourselves. But I was reminded about meaningful worship on a recent night after dropping into a small chapel at the Ugandan university where I live.

Unaware that I was listening from the back, a student sat alone in the brick and wood sanctuary, at a simple piano, pouring out her heart in song in such an intimate way that she reminded me of the woman who once poured expensive perfume on Jesus' feet before she washed them with her tears and dried them with her hair. Appropriately, beside my rear-pew seat stood a sign: "Caution, worship in progress."

I felt a similar spirit when once watching an Ethiopian youth being baptized in Yemen. His joy was so deep and so overwhelming that one could easily forget this was in a Muslim country without a single Christian church for millions

of indigenous Yemenis, where outsiders, especially underclassed African refugees, take their chances with any public expression of Christianity.

"Caution, worship" – that vulnerable giving of our deepest selves – "in progress." What's one to do with a warning like that?

Think of Aslan in *The Lion, the Witch and the Wardrobe,* the C. S. Lewis story now in theatres around the planet. "Then he isn't safe?" asks Lucy when first hearing about the majestic lion.

"Safe?...Who said anything about safe? 'Course he isn't safe," responds Mr. Beaver. "But he's good."

So good that Christmas came to our world. And if Christmas is for children, which it surely is, then all this has something to do with walking on water. The message from Peter's boyish jaunt is just what the mystics say: we are more than we know. Over time we've simply forgotten our real identity, forgotten our real home, forgotten that, as Lewis once said, "You don't have a soul. You are a soul. You have a body."

And isn't this the story of the postmodern West? It's grown so mature, so sophisticated and comfortable, so safe, entertained and distracted that it hasn't really killed God, as Nietzsche said. It's just domesticated Him. The spirit of the age isn't skepticism. It's ambivalence. A hero-less, broken and aimless ambivalence.

Into that, Christmas still comes around to give direction, if not a good shake. With that thought, I'm anticipating my own holiday home in Canada. In fact, it's very possible that as you read this, Jean and I and our two little squirts, Elizabeth and Jonathan, are flying over the sea. But one day, in another place, I'm going walk on it. No, I'm going to run. It will be a blast. And I hope you'll be there beside me.

Pantywaist affairs 56

Kampala, Uganda
December 1, 2006

I received an e-mail the other day from a Christian in Ontario upset over, in his words, "the pantywaist liberalism" of his employer. He had offered to say the dinner blessing at his company's upcoming "seasonal party," but his employer didn't want reference to any "supreme being," lest anyone of any faith, or of no faith, be offended. Thus the writer encouraged his e-mail friends to, like him, boycott such neutered holiday gatherings where participants are insulted when forced to acknowledge the simple fact that it's Christmas.

Fair enough. Nobody likes senseless political correctness run amok. There are few things worse than even church leaders who deny Christmas orthodoxy like the virgin birth. But why is it so easy to get worked up over this type of thing, the so-called removal of Christ from Christmas, and so hard to get angry over other liberal attitudes that creep from culture into everyday Christian living?

Like, say, the lax response to God's demand for justice for the world's poor and oppressed.

This Christmas, at least half of Earth's 6.5 billion people will be malnourished. This low class lives on $3 a day or less. Many are in sub-Saharan Africa. No gifts for these kids. Just brain damage from a lack of protein.

Next up the ladder is the lower-middle class, more than a billion people earning about $1,000 to $5,000 annually, in places like Bolivia or former Soviet countries – places with a brighter future but still lacking frills like decent health care or education.

Then there are more than 500 million in the upper-middle income lot, earning about $5,000 to $12,000 a year in places like the richest Latin American countries.

Finally, at the top are those who can help: more than a billion people in the high income class, earning $12,000 a year or more, mainly in North America, Europe and Japan.

It's a sobering picture. Year-by-year the affluent minority lives more like monarchs and the destitute majority like serfs. Jesus may have said the poor will always be among us, but never in world history has human disparity been so stark.

In fact, researchers say that if today's world had 100 people, 50 would be malnourished, 70 wouldn't be able to read and 80 would have rotten housing. Incredibly, six would have half the wealth. Just one would have a college degree.

Canadians tend to think of themselves as generous, but we're not really. The journal *Foreign Policy* recently ranked Canada 10th out of 21 rich nations in its commitment to global development. Americans scored 13th.

One might think Christians in North America are more generous, but no. Traditionally they've tithed an average of less than three per cent of their income. Most of that doesn't get from the church to the world's most needy.

Granted, poverty has a complex web of causes, including poor choices on personal or national levels. Government corruption, for example, hurts many African countries.

Problems are also globally systemic. The average Westerner may not like that an agricultural subsidy ensures that more money goes to a cow in Europe than to a human in Uganda, but feel there's little that they can do.

Still, Christmas is a good time – perhaps the best – for Christians to ask how they can do better. One way is to simply keep their theology straight.

Economist John Maynard Keynes said what every diabolical Christmas advertiser knows: "Consumption is the sole end and object of all economic activity." Jesus said, "*Do not store up for yourselves treasures on earth, where moth and rust destroy*".

Who has more insight into the good life? And what are the results, individually and collectively, sooner or later, of following one road versus the other?

Liberalism, by definition, is what causes our thinking to be shaped by culture rather than by biblical revelation. Unfortunately, we tend to pick our favourite revelations and walk past others.

So while it's fine to fight to keep Christ in Christmas, maybe it's even better not to get too distracted by what might be simply pantywaist affairs. In the end, they'll only blind us to God's broken heart about other things and how we might live in response.

Something happened. Something big. 57

St. Thomas, Canada
December 18, 1999

"Jesus Christ. Superstar. Do you believe what they say you are?" The jingle from the popular rock opera *Jesus Christ Superstar*, catchy as it is, is an incredibly sad reminder that there are people who don't have an inkling of this season's joy.

Thirty per cent of Canadians say Jesus isn't for them – a figure relatively unchanged from the mid '70s. Pollster Angus Reid says the rest of us believe, at least intellectually and somewhat privately, the basic tenets of historic Christianity: that Jesus is divine and rose from the dead.

One should not be too hard on doubters who must suffer the season to varying degrees. Many are very nice people. Their arguments, however, are nonsense. They usually revolve around cursory studies that suggest that if Jesus lived at all, He was a legend built over time. He may have been a revolutionary, a sage and an iconoclastic Jew, but no more.

Some luminous beacons suggest Jesus tapped into our own potential in a new way. Yes, Jesus is a powerful symbol to lead people to do great things. But born of a virgin? No. Jesus Himself never said He was divine. He didn't die on any rugged Roman cross and He certainly did not rise from the dead. He moved to India and got married.

Accepting any worldview, religious or otherwise, requires faith. Yet there is compelling evidence that makes crossing the bridge to the traditional Christ reasonable.

Consider that Jesus is the only leader of any world religion who claimed power to forgive sin, who claimed His miracles were signs of His own kingdom and who foretold His own death and resurrection. Many eyewitness accounts have Jesus claiming that those who saw Him saw God – a claim that enraged both Jewish and Roman authorities.

Consider that the Bible, regardless of particular modern translation, is amazingly reliable. Why? In ancient literature, the more copies found, the better comparison to reproduce the original text.

For example, historians have uncovered seven copies of Plato's *Tetralogies* and 643 copies of Homer's *The Iliad.* The New Testament? More than 5,000 copies in the original Greek alone. Princeton professor Bruce Metzger calculates copy distortion within 0.2 per cent.

Also, Jesus' definitive biographies, the four gospels, were written 30 to 60 years after His crucifixion, a newsflash for the time. Compare them to the earliest biography of Alexander the Great (400 years after his death) or Virgil (300 years) or Caesar's *War Commentaries* (900 years), works considered generally reliable by history's yardstick. In addition, of the 24 ancient sources that concern Jesus' divine nature, seven are secular.

What about Jewish prophecies that created a fingerprint of the coming Messiah? Based on events – some out of the control of Jesus, such as where He was born – mathematician Peter Stoner has calculated the odds of anyone but Jesus of Nazareth being the fulfillment of Old Testament prophecies as one in a trillion to the power of 13.

Then there is circumstantial evidence. If early disciples did not see a raised

Jesus, why would they die for a lie? More so, 30,000 Jewish men were executed during Jesus' time. Yet five weeks after His crucifixion, 10,000 Jews were following Him, claiming He initiated a new religion. What, if not Christ's empty tomb, is the epicentre of the quake sending cultural and sociological shock waves over the centuries? Something happened. Something big.

In our time there are plenty of clues showing that the Jesus of faith is the Jesus of history. Lawyer and former Chicago Tribune legal editor Lee Strobel shows a good number in *The Case for Christ*, a fair investigative work drawing on renowned experts in science, history and literature. Similar to brilliant thinkers such as C. S. Lewis and Alexander Solzhenitsyn, Strobel himself was an ardent skeptic prior to his personal search.

Still, after the proverbial bones of antiquity are dusted, the issue remains.

We see what we want. So the question is not only, who is Jesus? It is, after 2,000 years, if the rough and earthy drama of the first Christmas is true, who is allowing it to have authority over their own hopes and dreams, their fears and losses – indeed, their very existence?

This holiday season, millions are doing so while singing "Emmanuel, God is with us." It's a reasonable song to sing, not because it sounds nice but because, in the end, superstars don't change lives.

Neither do dead men.

On the lighter side of journalism is what's known as the published screw-up, and the preceeding column had among the better ones that I've personally seen.

Originally in the London Free Press, a fine regional newspaper, a slight error was made in the tagline that identifies This Scribe.

It was meant to read "Thomas Froese is a journalist living in St. Thomas." This was accidentally amputated to "Thomas Froese is a journalist living"

Of course, I accepted the editor's apologies without concern. It happens. But coming right after the column's last two words on "dead men" ... Come on, what are the odds?

In their most innocuous form, published mistakes really can be fabulous entertainment. I've never been involved in anything too drastic (but for the grace of God go I), but one does hear stories from papers of all sizes and stripes.

A journalist might leave a note in an electronic story file, and it may be accidentally published. No problem if the note is just "Spelling of Waltter is correct." But if it's "Spelling of Waltter (who by the way is in bed with the mayor) is correct," then that might need some explanation. Journalists' heads have at times rolled.

One personal favourite is from a sports page at my former home at the

Times-Journal in St. Thomas, where two briefs – one of an Olympic track star under suspicion of taking drugs, another about a local prepubescent hockey star – were accidentally sliced and married. So the public learned about the big track star tearing up local hockey rinks and the poor local hockey tyke getting his urine tested for stimulants.

His parents, I'm sure, were not impressed.

A donkey walks beside a Land Cruiser. Buildings reach like giant gingerbread houses into the blue sky. Dust swirls and gets in the mouth. Men with ceremonial jambias tucked into their belts walk past women draped in black baltos looking like giant walking bowling pins. This was my opening taste of Yemen.

Some 40 months later, the strange had become a familiar friend.

The Times evolved. It became the first independent newspaper in Yemen to own its own press. While I prepared to move my family to Africa, my good friend, editor-in-chief Walid al-Saqqaf, made his own move for work and studies in the United States. (His sister, Nadia, took the newspaper's helm, a female ripple in a sea of men.)

War in Iraq and continuing trouble in Palestine had worsened East-West tensions. And the event of our dear friends being shot dead by an Islamic extremist lodged itself as a poignant memory.

Yet, through such experiences I grew to feel comfortable with this unusual land that's still waking up to the world, and the world to it. This historic and unique patch of hard earth and soft people had become another home, a place to return to anytime, and a meaningful first chapter in my young family's own story.

In early 2008, Darling Doctor Wife and I did return, Two Royal Younglings in tow this time, and with a refreshed vision to eventually expand Jean's Save the Mothers program into the region.

And so my goodbye to Arabia Felix is becoming more like "until we meet again ... and, I hope, again and again."

Opposite page photo: *The author plays with a camera and mirror in his Sana'a apartment-flat.*

WINDOWS REFLECTING

Walid, meet Danny

58

SANA'A, YEMEN
March 12, 2005

> *May you grow up to be righteous, may you grow up to be true,*
> *May you always know the truth and see the lights surrounding you.*
> *May you always be courageous, stand upright and be strong,*
> *Forever young, forever young, may you stay forever young.*
>
> Bob Dylan

If I had things my way, which I usually don't, someday I'd like to see two of my friends meet each other.

One is Daniel Pearl. You'll recall that Danny, an American journalist, was abducted and beheaded by Islamic extremists in Pakistan in 2002 for no real reason besides that he loved the truth.

The other is Yemeni-born Walid (pronounced Waleed) al-Saqqaf. He's now packing to catch a plane to Washington, D.C., to start work at the *Wall Street Journal*'s Washington bureau. It's where Danny worked for several years.

Until recently, as editor-in-chief of the *Yemen Times*, Walid was my boss. Now, like Danny, he's simply my friend.

I've never actually met Danny. I know him as a friend only through a posthumous collection of his writings, aptly called *At Home in the World.* From there, I feel Danny, who loved talking to strangers, really has given a personal hello: from the many exotic locales in his Middle East and southeast Asia beat to a tiny office cubicle, complete with beach chair.

By all accounts, Danny, who was Jewish, was a remarkable man: skillful, unconventional, and one of those rare people who, although young, had both the nature and opportunity to help change the world. Which is why I think he and Walid, who's just 31, would enjoy furthering Muslim-Jewish dialogue in, say, some juice bar in Tehran with Bob Dylan playing.

As it is, Walid is off to Washington on a Daniel Pearl Fellowship. It's a new part of the Alfred Friendly Press Fellowship Program, which, for more than 20 years, has given journalists from dozens of developing countries the opportunity to work in American newsrooms. None have ever come from Yemen. Which says something about Yemen. But something more about Walid.

"It was my destiny to be a journalist, and it was my fate to lead this newspaper in particular," Walid wrote in his *Yemen Times* farewell editorial. After the *Wall Street Journal,* he'll stay abroad for higher studies. Interestingly, the last *Times* issue under his helm was number 820, which corresponds to his birth month and day.

Walid began leading the *Times* several years ago, after the death of his father, Abdulazia, who founded the independent paper. That was not long before I arrived in Yemen. As fate also has it, he's now leaving Yemen just before my own departure to Africa. I feel fortunate for our time together. And I will miss him.

I'll miss watching him do business with a phone in each hand. I'll miss that sheepish feeling I always had after complaining about his country's befuddling laxness. I'll miss our laughs together over what Danny would call the *absurdités de l'existence*, like Walid needing permission from Yemen's minister of information to now leave his editor's post.

Walid's take on it? "The minister said yes. What else could he say? But I taped him." Yes, Walid has a courageous intellect. He's been able to both scold and befriend high officials. He's been a cultural bridge and ambassador while already routinely representing Yemen abroad. And many Yemenis will miss him because they see a likeness of his father. Shortly after becoming the only Arab to receive the U.S. Press Club's International Freedom of the Press Award, Abdulazia died in a traffic accident. He's heralded as a Yemeni martyr for human rights.

It all seems fitting. Because if you look inside Walid's copy of Danny's *At Home in the World*, after a personal note to Walid from the Pearl family, you'll see the book's dedication: "For Danny's son, who will know his father in words and spirit."

No, Walid won't ever meet Danny in this world. But he too will now know him in spirit. And you know, Danny's son, who was born shortly after his father's death, is now big enough to reach up and say hello.

At this time Walid is in Sweden, with his family, studying for a master's degree in global journalism. But since we both left Yemen, we've kept in touch.

When I was recently visiting Yemen for the first time in several years, I e-mailed him. "Walid – I know you're over there in Sweden, not in Sana'a, but believe it or not, I'm in Yemen."

In a few hours I had a reply. "Thom," he wrote, "you won't believe this, but I just arrived in Sana'a on a flight at 2 a.m."

It was another sign that our friendship is meant to be. And so it continues.

Reflections

59

Hamilton, Canada
June 18, 2005

A humorous story: I wasn't much past kindergarten when my chum Paul and I were adventuring like boys do. Looking through a hole in a board in the back of a neighbourhood corner store, we saw the "big eye." The really *big* eye.

"Thommy, Thommy!" Paul screamed. "There's a big eye in there and it's looking right at me!"

"Yeah!" I said, taking his place and looking through the hole. "Now it's looking at *me*!"

It was a monster eye. Ugly and hairy. Probably a killer, I thought.

"Yeah," said Paul, looking again. "It's a big brown eye!"

I looked. Brown? Afraid to blink lest the murderous eye change colour, I said, "It's blue!"

"No!" Paul said. "It's brown."

"Blue!" I argued.

"Brown!"

Back and forth we went until we courageously walked into the store to tell about the monster and ask if we could go and see it. So we were led into a storage room where there was ... a mirror facing that hole in the store's outside wall.

A mirror reflecting our own eyeballs.

Most things in life are never as scary as we think, even in a boogeyman place like Yemen.

Some years ago, talking about my upcoming new life in this mysterious Arab country, I would joke to former colleagues that I was "going to the desert to live in a tent." In fact, the tent turned out to be a nice apartment in Yemen's capital, Sana'a. Middle East weather, I learned, could actually be cool, and Yemenis, despite global politics, very warm.

With such things in mind, while my young family now moves its overseas base to Africa, here are some quotes that reflect my time as a Canadian in Yemen – and an editor at the *Yemen Times* – for most of the past 40 months.

"Are you American?" – A customs official, after I first landed in Yemen in 2002. After I said I was Canadian, he smiled and nodded, "Canadian okay. Better than American."

"Hold it this way." – Me, to an Aussie asking how to hold a hockey stick. I regularly gathered expatriates from various countries, plus willing Yemenis, for floor hockey in a Sana'a school gym. I'll miss it more than anything.

"If women don't cover, we're always gazing at their loveliness. When

they're covered, we don't even notice them." – Ramzy, an office colleague, telling me why women should be covered head to toe.

"It's like a bad dream." – A friend, commenting on the death of Christian aid workers Dr. Martha Myers, Kathy Gariety and Bill Koehn. The Americans were killed by an Islamic extremist at a hospital in the Yemeni town of Jibla in 2002. Incredibly, my wife Jean – one of just two Western obstetricians in Yemen, the other being Martha – was originally scheduled to be there when the killings occurred.

"We like your new name." – *Yemen Times* colleagues, after I took Jamil Abdul Karim as my pen name for my column "East and West." It means "Beautiful Servant of the Most Gracious One." I adopted it in tribute to Bill, Martha and Kathy and the legacy of their decades of service to Yemenis.

"Can't I buy one that's pre-tied?" – Me, about the Arab head-wrap that I attempted, too many times, to tie, to wear in public for security when the Iraq War broke out.

"Like at the end of any good story, the hero should die." – My always quotable landlord, after Saddam Hussein was captured in Iraq.

"Thomas, you're not eating enough." – My landlord, before stacking my plate, again, whenever Jean and I joined his family for meals.

"What we're giving them are tools so they can help others." – Jean, commenting on a 2003 donation of hospital equipment worth tens of thousands of dollars to Yemen from Outreach International, a program of Hamilton's Sisters of St. Joseph.

"The U.S. news media won't tell the truth. The only way to get the truth to the American people is through the mail." – Someone, in one of the many wild items that crossed my desk while I was editing the *Yemen Times.*

"Assalaam alaykum achree." A common Arabic greeting, meaning "Peace be upon you, brother." I didn't learn much Arabic, but I liked to use this often.

"Sweetie, do you have any TP?" – An all too common question I'd ask Jean before visiting any public washroom, which usually didn't have such essentials.

"You want to travel?" – *Yemen Times* editor-in-chief Walid al-Saqqaf, before referring me to the Salzburg Seminar, a forum for dialogue on global issues. I was later awarded a US$5,000 scholarship to attend a 2004 Salzburg session in Austria.

"Dear Thom: I read your article on-line and it was truly touching. Be assured that the Yemen Times and its staff will always remember you, regardless of where you are and what you do." – Walid, in an e-mail from Washington, where he is working through the prestigious Daniel Pearl Journalism Fellowship, responding to a column I wrote about him (headlined "Saying Hello, Saying Goodbye").

Saying hello. Saying goodbye.

It's what life is all about, and the phrase reflects my memories from a place that also won't ever be forgotten.

My hope is that my correspondence has shed at least some light on some of its mysteries.

I tell people that my job is simple: follow Darling Doctor Wife around and write from wherever I wake up.

Occasionally, though, here and there – in Europe, in South America in recent years – I've woken up in an airport or hotel alone. This type of thing has happened so rarely, there's not much more to say. Except that here are some scribbles and shots from a few of these travels.

These jaunts include a visit to Salzburg and, after hopping a late-night train, to Venice. The photos at the end of this section, on page 221, are a few from these picturesque European cities. If you want to see more, plus a fuller collection from Africa and Arabia, please visit www.thomasfroese.com and go to the link "99 photos."

Opposite page photo: *An early-morning view from the author's hotel room near the Piazza San Marco (St. Mark's Square) in Venice, Italy.*

An Interlude from Elsewhere

Hello

60

Salzburg, Austria
September 18, 2004

I love my daughter, all 15 months of her, for many reasons. One is that she's more like her mother than me – especially while flying. My wife, Jean, and I are aid workers in the Middle East and Africa, so this is often. In fact, diaper-clad Elizabeth-Katherine has already been on more than a dozen flights and four continents.

The Squirt knows just one word. Just one. It's *hello.*

But words can be powerful things. I personally don't like to use more than I have to. This is because, by nature, I am – or at least I once was – painfully shy. Playing hide-and-seek with me as a child meant calling search and rescue to find me.

Elizabeth, on the other hand, will say "hello" to anyone (of any colour), anywhere (of any political or religious stripe), anytime (even if you're trying to sleep). She'll give a snappy "hello-hello-hello" or a more deliberate "hel-looooohh!" with a wave and toothy grin and playful swat to your head. Realize, though, that her "hello" can mean anything from "good night" to "I'm hungry" to "I have a stinky."

Now, flying around the planet, glamorous as it seems, has its challenges. Even before sky terror, staying alive was one. The airlines don't want you to dwell on this, so they offer various in-flight distractions. For example, Air Emirates, based in oil-rich Dubai, wins awards for things like video consoles for everyone. Entertaining, yes. But they just numb and dumb us down.

I mean, in case of that panic-driven descent, does anyone believe that, as safety rules say, putting your head between your legs will help? Think about this. Upon impact, where will your head go? Does anyone really want to be found like this? And life jackets? Have you ever heard of even a single rescue from the Atlantic?

So I use my flight safety-drill time to build my nest. Shoes off, books out, pillows and blankets everywhere, along with a noticeable yawn, so anyone sitting nearby (besides my wife, of course) understands I don't want to say "hello." Elizabeth, standing on the seat, if possible waving to her fans, does enough of that. Jean, an obstetrician, also seems to genuinely enjoy interacting with virtually anyone.

It all works quite well, except on the rare times when I fly alone, such as here to Salzburg, where I'm attending a conference on how globalization affects poor countries. It's a reminder how humanity truly is a global family, how we're accountable to each other, how we need to, in essence, say "hello" to one another more often.

No, private personalities or not, we all have a profound effect on each other. My strengths and joys, like my weaknesses and disappointments, reach beyond me. They touch those around me, sometimes in very distant places. Economically, globalization shows what's true relationally: "No man is an island entire of itself; every man is a piece of the continent, a part of the main."

It's been said that this great truth, first penned this way by poet John Donne, is both comforting and disturbing. For me, this is especially clear when flying, vulnerably, at 40,000 feet. I get perspective on the petty worries that seem so large on the ground. I see how vast the ocean is and how small my boat is. I see how my little girl, like all children, lives more like the rest of us are meant to live: closer to heaven.

So now, you and I have met. This isn't a total surprise, considering my ties to the Waterloo region. Born in Berlin, I lived with extended family in this area after arriving in Canada as a preschooler. Later I returned to study journalism at Conestoga College. Now continuing more studies, I'm likely the only Canadian to ever have University of Waterloo exams sent to Sana'a, Yemen's capital, our overseas home.

Soon we'll return to this impoverished Muslim country, an ancient and complex corner of the world. From there, I'll write more, while Jean continues her work improving women's health, with a focus on death during childbirth, a terribly under-reported global blight. More on that later.

And Elizabeth-Katherine? I suspect she'll keep learning things about this world that we might not imagine.

Until next time then, from each of us to all of you ... hello. And hello again.

Bang! You've been shot 61

Vicosa, Brazil
January 23, 2006

Here's a thought for today: *BANG!* You've been shot. Shot through the heart. Can you imagine it?

Your body is warm as blood pours from it, but you feel so cold. There are screams. Someone tries to lift you, but all you feel is your last breath leaving, like air from a punctured tire. Your eyes roll back. All goes black. And that's it. You're dead.

Such a waste. The bullet wasn't even meant for you. Or maybe it was. It doesn't really matter.

Such are the streets of Brazil, a place that gives perspective to gun problems in the Toronto and Hamilton regions. This country of 185 million has an incredible 40,000 gun murders annually, one every 12 minutes. That rate is falling, but it's still higher than the United States and among the highest globally.

Teeming cities like Rio or Sao Paulo, with populations over 16 million each, are brutal. Guns and drugs mix. Life is cheap and death is senseless. "You hurt my feelings" or "You're on my turf" and – *BANG*! Even here in Vicosa, a university town of 70,000, just before Toronto's Boxing Day gun shocker a professor was shot dead as he was getting his daughter from a grad party.

I'm talking about it all with Carluci Dossantos at the Universidade Federal de Vicosa. He's among 900 Christian university students, from Brazil and beyond, attending a congress here to talk about their future careers and how to engage and heal their society. To take part, some have travelled for days.

Nearby, one student wears a T-shirt, one of the few in English, reading "I would die tonight for my beliefs." In a culture of violence, the irony fits all too well.

Dossantos, a Brazilian PhD student of theology at the University of Toronto, tells me about Brazil's slums, its poor infrastructure and its need for public programs. He's amazed at the free activities that his kids can access in their Toronto public schools. In Brazil, that's only for the rich. Just 16 per cent of Brazilians now graduate from high school and seven per cent from university. Experts say that youth here fear, besides death itself, being disconnected in a techno age and being left behind in a competitive market.

What strikes me about Dossantos is his observation that many youth in the Millennial Generation, whether Brazilian or Canadian, simply crave love, something no amount of legislation or public campaigns can give. "The government and community can expose the horror of guns, like it does with drunk driving. An agency can take a kid from a bad home. But it can't love them. It can't make a family love a kid," Dossantos says. "But we can love them."

Guns and broken homes are core issues that are too often minimized, he says. Fatherless boys, orphaned in spirit, are ripe for the street.

Listening, one also realizes there are people in faith communities willing to live for their beliefs, not only, as the nearby T-shirt says, to die for them. And while it may irritate secular sensibilities, their expertise and involvement should be in the mix.

The so-called Boston Miracle, which saw Boston's murders plunge by 75 per cent in the 1990s when pastors initiated street programs with police and politicians, is a success some Torontonians are now arguing against. Why?

Of course gun owners – in Brazil, they're officially 3.5 per cent of households – have beliefs of their own. In fact, thanks to the gun lobby and its clever lawyers, a recent national referendum supported continued sales of guns countrywide.

Brazilians wanted protection against the hoods, and they didn't want to relinquish their rights. They also took the opportunity to thumb their noses at the government, a lesson, maybe, regarding similar gun ban ideas in Canada.

So, back to *BANG!* You've been shot. Shot through your heart. Can you really imagine it? No, most Canadians, even now, can't. It's too far removed from our collective experience. For this we can be thankful. But if we want to keep it that way, we absolutely will need to pull together. Because with easy guns in hand, the Grim Reaper doesn't really care where he is. Or who's next.

von Trapped in mythology

62

ST. GILGEN, AUSTRIA
October 2, 2004

Okay, for the record, nobody rocks like Mozart. But Julie Andrews made plenty of Austrian stores come alive with the sound of ka-ching, after her famous opening to *The Sound of Music*, filmed 40 years ago on a mountain near this lake-district resort town.

The movie initially raked in a cool $165 million, about $800 million in today's dollars. Now tourism cash still flows from it like a river, especially an hour from here in Salzburg, Mozart's hometown, where the visitors never really leave.

The popularity of all things *Sound of Music* is matched only by Salzburg's

famous music festival and the grandeur of its historic churches and castles or *schlosses.*

One is Leopoldskron Schloss. After the Second World War, some Harvard grads made this 18th century rococo palace into the home of an American institute that hosts debates on pressing global issues. Since 1947, some 20,000, including yours truly, have graduated from these "Salzburg Seminars," better informed about world economics and things that suggest we know more about the planet's mess than we do.

The link is that in 1964 some *of The Sound of Music* was filmed at Leopoldskron, at least outside, since a Salzburg Seminar was in progress inside. Interior shots of the schloss were recreated elsewhere. Which is where things get interesting, because Hollywood, of course, loves to create its own geography, literally and otherwise.

Yes, the real von Trapp "children" (none were named Liesl, Friedrich, Brigitta, Louisa, Kurt, Marta or Gretl) were actually age 17 to 27 when the musical family escaped Nazi-occupied Austria in 1938. They travelled by train to, first, Italy, not on foot to Switzerland. They certainly didn't go over the Untersberg, Salzburg's closest mountain, which would have led them into Hitler's lair in the Bavarian Alps.

These filmmakers, though, did better than most. I find it more curious that *The Sound of Music,* Hollywood creation that it is, is treated by most Austrians with cool indifference to active dislike. Many haven't even watched it. You'd think they would at least look at the goose that laid their golden egg.

Then there's the pristine image of this family classic. Are you surprised to learn that the young actors didn't have to act like they feared Christopher Plummer as their harsh father? They did fear him. For example, Plummer, who for years called the show The Sound of Mucus, said of little Gretl at the final mountain-escape scene, "I'm not carrying that bloody fat kid." A thinner double was found.

And "Edelweiss"? No, this song is not Austria's national anthem. It was written for the movie by Rodgers and Hammerstein. "Edelweiss"? "Edelweiss"! Say it's not so!

To me, this is all like sullying rather holy ground. I've identified with the movie in a very personal way. I lived near the Austrian-Bavarian Alps as a child. Later, my sister (aptly named Heidi) and I sometimes saw our austere German father, a widower, through the lens of Plummer's more sensitive moments. And we felt the softness of a Julie Andrews through a loving nanny who did sing "Edelweiss" to us.

None of this is to say that mythology is bad. The following generation of von Trapps now runs a resort lodge in Vermont, and I wouldn't mind visiting, exactly because it carries that *Sound of Music* mystique.

But even when our culture's stories are proper and meaningful, let's recognize them for what they are. Because if we don't, what does that say about our inability, or lack of desire, to recognize myths that we may have about other cultures, like, say, the Muslim world in a post-9/11 era?

Somewhere here is a lesson about what every advertiser knows: perception plays an incredibly powerful role in our lives. I think of this especially after my recent Salzburg Seminar relating to Third World aid and now on the eve of my young family's return to a somewhat labelled country like Yemen.

We tend to see life not as it is but as we think it is, through personal and cultural prisms. To see things as they truly are, we need divine help. The rest, I think I will have to mull over later, even in the Middle East, with the help of some Mozart.

Thirty-five years later I still keep contact with the former Canadian nanny I refer to in this column, the woman who sang "Edelweiss" often and freely when she helped care for me in my primary years. In one of those tricks of the universe, Evelyn entered the picture at that time after showing up at Ye Olde Niagara Home for a nursing job, not realizing the owner, Dad Froese, was the widower of Hannelore, a friend of Evelyn's from years earlier when both were in nursing training in Montreal, when young Hannelore was a new immigrant to Canada.

Evelyn has since given me a music box that plays "Edelweiss." And I now play it for my Two Royal Younglings. Someday we'll make it to the von Trapp lodge.

I have no memories of my earlier childhood near the Austria-Bavarian Alps. This is just another serendipitous footnote, this one about my caregiver in Germany, Frau Hildegard Mueller, a fine woman and close friend of my mother – who was sick in Berlin at the time.

Years after my time with her, I tried to look up Frau Mueller when visiting Germany. All I knew was her name, as common as Smith, and her location of 25 years earlier, near Munich, in Aufhausen, of which there are several. No surprise my search failed. (But I did receive, from my mother's sister – my family's last surviving relative in Berlin – a pile of old photos, letters and writings of my mom's.)

A handful of years later, this phone call from Dad Froese.

"Do you remember the name Hildegard Mueller?"

"Yes."

"Well, she's here in Canada. And she wants to see you."

Hildegard, then about 80 and a rather independent and seasoned traveller, wanted to meet me in Niagara Falls.

Working as a young scribe three hours away in St. Thomas, I listened.

"Friday?" I finally said. "In Niagara Falls?" It was the day I had planned to travel to the falls with a friend, for a rare visit myself.

Travelling with family, Hildegard barely spoke a word of English but managed to get the number of Dad Froese and Ye Olde Niagara Home from the local directory, where it's been for some decades. So amidst translation and laughter, we all met and closed a chapter for good.

The last I heard about Hildegard was from a newspaper clipping sent to me that featured her as a then 86-year-old traveller to Africa, moving some 6,000 km across the south, staying in homes and lodges along the way and having the time of her life.

She commented to the reporter, "Man musste nur manchmal aufpassen was man sagt, den die sind sehr konservativ..." (You have to be careful what you say, because they're so conservative.)

Her next trip? "Siberia," she told the reporter. "I'm saving my money."

(For more on the author's personal background, see Windows 27, 51, 78 and 95 and their addendums.)

A trapped princess 63

Dubai, United Arab Emirates
April 9, 2005

En route to Africa, I'm in filthy-rich Dubai, where the favourite pastimes are making tall buildings and shopping. Yes, Dubai is the tourism prom queen of the Middle East, the sparkling fashion girl everyone wants to date.

In just 40 years, since oil's discovery here, this city has gone from rags to riches. It's as opposite as imaginable to Yemen, from where I'm coming. The fact that Yemen has named 2005 its "Year of the Tourist" only makes it look more longingly to its glittering cousin and wonder if its day will ever arrive.

Of course, Dubai gets no travel warnings. And now, after a $5 billion facelift, Dubai's international airport, which is like a giant mall, has room for more gold watches and pearl necklaces. Or get a raffle ticket for a Ferrari or Porsche or Rolls-Royce. They're on display. Or take the draw's winnings in $400,000 cash.

If you ignore the warnings from foreign affairs in Ottawa and somehow do get to Yemen's gate in Sana'a, expect less. Less than in Saskatoon. If Dubai's airport is Beatlemania, then Sana'a International is the Swinging Udders. Its latest excitement is getting green paint over orange. That hasn't helped it get close to the 21 million people that poured through Dubai's airport last year.

It seems Yemen, which has just issued its first credit card, needs a shopping blowout. Recently, the 10th annual Dubai Shopping Festival had a whopping three million folks come from around the world to shop, shop, shop as a global village. Sorry, "Ladies Only" day on Mondays is discontinued. But visit the daily Treasure Hunt and everyone wins. Get some Jet Skis.

Or win a stay at Dubai's City Centre. It has a view, because, you know, nobody does buildings like Dubai. Pisa, Italy, may be planning a second leaning tower, but for $900 million Dubai is erecting the world's tallest building. By 2008 you will be able to stand in the Burj Dubai and swoon from 123 floors. That's 700 metres. All to give tower envy to Toronto and that sky-needle on the lakeshore.

Which brings us to what Yemen does have. Great buildings. Tourist estimates for Yemen in 2004 range wildly, from 10,000 to government claims of over 150,000. Whatever the number, many visit just to see the mud-stone architecture. In the highlands of Sana'a, think giant gingerbread houses. No surprise that Sana'a's historic quarter is a UN World Heritage Site. These buildings, found only in Yemen, are now even in a promo-trailer for the new Tom Cruise movie *War of the Worlds.*

It's one of several recent screen highlights for ancient Arabia Felix. French actress Emmanuelle Beart, the heroine in *Mission Impossible I,* was just on Yemen's island of Socotra for the popular French TV series *The Unknown Land.* It films how personalities adjust after they're dropped in some offbeat place for a week.

Yemen also now claims to be the first country in the Arabian Peninsula to make a full feature film. *New Day in Old Sana'a* is a 90-minute movie about a young man marrying for love rather than arrangement. The $2.5-million cost of the film, produced almost completely in Old Sana'a, was raised locally. Also, almost all of the cast and crew are Yemenis.

When it's shown in film festivals, this movie will help bring Yemen – often an embarrassment to other Arabs – to the outside world. This is good. Especially for Dubai. Folks can see it here in their own Dubai Film Festival and be reminded of Arabian culture's soul.

Yes, Dubai has oil. Five times what Yemen pumps. And while Yemen has strained under the weight of civil war, Islamic extremism and government corruption, Dubai has managed itself smartly, diversified its economy and attracted outsiders. In fact, only one in five of the 3.5 million residents across the United Arab Emirates are now native citizens.

Which is likely why when I travel through Dubai, it feels so hollow. It's like being surrounded by heaps of gold that's been spun by Rumplestiltskin. It makes you wonder if folks aren't trapped, like the princess in that fairy tale. And if their spirits wouldn't do better if some of this stuff turned back into straw again.

Welcome to Africa. You'll have the time of your life. Welcome to Africa. Now run for your life. Somewhere between these truths I've learned to love and fear life on the so-called Dark Continent.

Winston Churchill once called Uganda, a lush Garden of Eden, the "Pearl of Africa." He was right. "Throw a seed on the ground and find a tree in the morning" is how My Royal Babe puts it. Lush landscape teems with all kinds of life. Our favourite neighbours are the monkeys. And the people? As warm as the days.

But they have gone through much, these people. Disease and poverty still visit regularly. And this has bred a certain fatalism. Simple changes, often life-saving, tend to run on African time. Regardless of the pain involved.

Come look at the sorrow of AIDS, or the risk of other deadly bugs, or the all-too-bloodied face of the broader continent, an image that, pretty or not, someone has to hold a mirror to.

It's not hard for one's heart to break over it all.

I also think of what Mark Twain once said, that "Travel is fatal to prejudice, bigotry and narrow-mindedness. Many of our people need it sorely on these accounts." Yes, that's true. But it's also true that even travellers (like This Scribe), somehow expecting a quicker pace of change, can get jaded.

So it's my hope that, as this mirror is held up, these selections are not only true and fair, but still somehow hopeful and observant to the potential of tomorrow.

Opposite page photo: *A mural of Africa's faces at a global mission conference in Urbana, Illinois.*

WINDOWS

Welcome to Africa

Serendipity in an untamed land

64

Kampala, Uganda
October 18, 2003

This country is one of contrasts. Red-dirt roads cross lush-green landscapes. People familiar with war smile easily and greet you genuinely. Beauty meets ugliness, plenty meets want, and life meets death here. Uganda may be, as Winston Churchill said, the Pearl of Africa. But, if so, it's a tarnished jewel.

It's said that Idi Amin's reign of terror piled Ugandan bodies so high that they were dumped in the Nile, where even the hungry crocodiles couldn't keep up. Hundreds of thousands more died in a civil war that followed. Decades later, the impact lingers, especially in the north where children are forced into guerrilla warfare and atrocities I won't mention. Then AIDS.

A strong public campaign emphasizing abstinence until marriage just as much as condom use has cut Uganda's HIV rate from almost one in three to about one in 15. That's a model for the rest of AIDS-ravaged Africa. Still, orphans, perhaps as many as 1.5 million in this country of 25 million, are everywhere.

Such is this untamed country. And, after barely unpacking our bags in Yemen, I'm here with the two women in my life – Jean and our four-month-old daughter, Elizabeth – to help shoot a promo video for Save the Mothers, a program being birthed to deal with another problem: women dying during child delivery. Uganda's maternal death rate is more than 100 times that of Canada's. More orphans.

Set to launch at Uganda Christian University in two years, Save the Mothers is a master's program in public health leadership. Jean's brainchild is based on the premise that if Ugandan professionals, including non-medical people – politicians, lawyers, journalists – were trained in maternal mortality issues, they could build the social infrastructure needed to solve the crisis. It's a more enduring solution than just offering more medics or clinics.

Thanks to producers from Crossroads Communications in Burlington, who filmed at Hamilton's St. Joseph's Hospital before bringing the cameras here, the video will help promote this vision. Jean realistically calls the long-term work "a spit in the ocean." But there's reason for optimism.

For one, unlike those in some other struggling countries, Ugandans are open about their problems and willing to work for change. You see an improved capital, Kampala, for example, partly because industrious Ugandans were willing to take economic medicine prescribed by international aid groups such as the World Bank.

On a more esoteric level, I also think of certain footprints we walk in. If you're not familiar with Dr. Lucille Teasdale, a charismatic Order of Canada recipient, watch *Dr. Lucille: The Lucille Teasdale Story,* a noteworthy Canadian movie that chronicles her career. Originally from Montreal, Dr. Lucille worked more than 30 years in Uganda with her Italian husband, Dr. Piero Corti.

The movie shows how they survived the Amin era and turned a bush clinic into a successful 500-bed hospital, one that still operates. Dr. Lucille died in 1996 of complications from AIDS – contracted years earlier in surgery from sharp bone fragments – but not before giving countless Ugandans dignity when they needed it most.

I feel a particular bond to the story because, when it first aired, I used it as a first move to date Jean. At the time, all I knew of my charming New Doctor Friend was that she had already worked short-term in Uganda and that she had a resemblance to the attractive Marina Orsini, the actress who played Dr. Lucille.

Three short years later, here we are, a young family (Lucille and Piero also had one daughter), making plans for Uganda to be our future overseas base. Some might call such a trick of the universe *serendipity* or *synchronicity* – either that or the hand of a personal God, One who does more than just watch our lives quietly from a distance.

That's not to say that Jean's future will ever be compared with that of a Canadian hero like Dr. Lucille. But who wouldn't feel fortunate to stand on the shoulders of such giants who have gone before us? Now let's see how the rest of this story unfolds.

A handful of years after writing this, I still see parallels between Dr. Lucille and Darling Doctor Wife. And once in Vancouver, at a medical conference where she spoke, I couldn't help but wonder about Jean's future legacy.

There were docs from across Canada, and a pharmaceutical company was promoting Jean's book 'Where Have All the Mothers Gone?' The drug company had bought a couple of thousand to promote the cause.

There in the conference lobby, the gal behind the book's display booth, however, needed some motivation, barely putting out a book, (they were available for free), apparently more interested in the scenery and the smell of her own perfume.

So I casually walked by, looked at a lone book and opened a conversation with this woman that went like this:

"Oh, is this Dr. Jean Chamberlain Froese's book?"

"Yes."

"You know, I've heard a lot about her."

"Have you?"

"Oh yeah. I see her name everywhere."

"Really?"

"Sure. I'm not a doctor myself. I'm in the media, you know. And Dr. Jean is famous."

"Is she really?"

"Sure. She's been in the press quite a bit: in Maclean's, in the papers, on TV. Last Mother's Day she was on the front page of the Globe and Mail for her overseas work."

"She was?"

"Picture and everything. You know, someday they'll make a movie about her."

"You think?" said the woman, now getting a few more books and straightening up.

"I think she's going to be like Dr. Lucille Teasdale. Do you know who she was?"

"No. I don't."

"She was a Canadian doctor who worked in Uganda. That's where Dr. Jean is launching her program Save the Mothers. Then she wants to take it to other countries."

"I never knew that."

"Is Dr. Jean actually here at this conference?" I continued.

"Yes, she is. I believe she's in the hall speaking right now," said the lady, quite alertly now.

"She is? Right now? I'd love to go hear what she has to say."

"Yes, you should do that."

And so I did, while some more books were given to folks.

Dr. Lucille's honours were many: Order of Canada, Canadian Medical Hall of Fame, a commemorative stamp. People like her, like Jean, truly aren't about this. But recently Jean was nominated for the 2008 Teasdale Humanitarian Award from the Royal College of Physicians and Surgeons of Canada, just one of her honours.

Like with Dr. Lucille, the real honour, though, is leaving something behind: a work that others down the road can pick up and run with in a greater way.

Dr. Lucille, who was a surgeon, pointed out that her best achievement was creating a "patient first" attitude in her hospital in Lacor, which still runs in northern Uganda.

Working in less-glamorous infrastructure development, Jean has the same desire, to create a "mothers first" attitude in Uganda and beyond.

Will someone someday make a movie about this type of thing? Maybe. Maybe not. In either case, apparently I'm in charge of the entertainment.

(For more on Dr. Jean's work, see Windows 96 to 99 and their addendums. For more on Dr. Jean and the author, see Windows 1 to 3 and their addendums.)

The heartbreak of AIDS - 1

65

KAMPALA, UGANDA
November 2, 2005

We're in what's called the Pearl of Africa, where red-dirt roads cross rolling green countryside, where elephants get the right-of-way when on safari, and where, even in the capital, wild monkeys might run across your tin roof and wake you in the morning. It's an enchanting place that can capture and break your heart at once.

Jean and I are here shooting a video about a certain crisis, that of mothers dying. It's estimated 6,000 Ugandan women die every year, among the half million who die in the developing world annually because they have no access to basic health care during child delivery.

The video is for a new educational program known as Save the Mothers. Jean is the executive director. More on that sometime later.

Better known is AIDS. It has killed some 1.5 million Ugandans in 20 years. Coffin makers build their wooden caskets right on the roadsides here. It's one of the more startling things I've seen.

Another was meeting an old woman who, by herself, was caring for her nine grandchildren orphaned by AIDS. Such are today's Ugandan families.

Then there's our driver, Paul, who took us on a potholed trip in the lush countryside to see "the tombs." We thought we were going to a cemetery to film. Instead we ended up in his home's backyard, where virtually his entire family is buried. AIDS again.

One day, after the disease took her fifth child, Paul's mother sat down and cried, he explains. At that moment she too died. Heart attack.

She's buried beside Paul's father, who was shot dead in his own home during Uganda's civil war. That war killed 300,000. That was after the Idi Amin era, which killed even more.

But I think the saddest thing I've seen here has been in a hospital, a relatively well-run university facility, where, in the corner of a hallway, lay a little bundle, neatly wrapped, with a tag indicating a dead baby was inside. It was there five minutes, 10 minutes, 20, 30 – I really don't know. It was still there when I left.

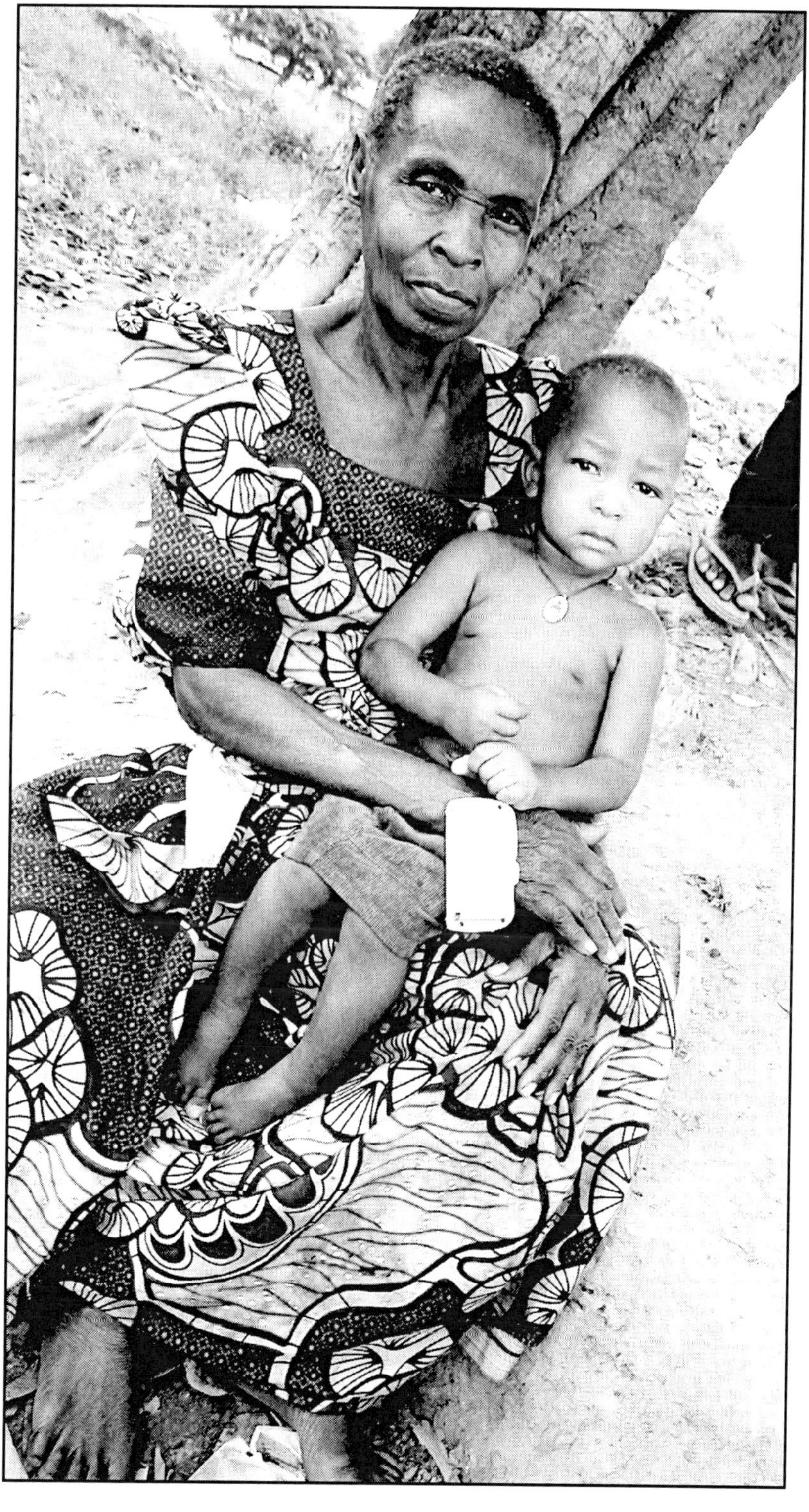

Yes, Ugandans, among the most pleasant people you'll ever meet, know suffering. Still, there are islands of hope in this sea of despair.

For one thing, their AIDS rate has dropped from about 30 per cent to five per cent, thanks to a public campaign promoting sexual abstinence outside of marriage in addition to condom use. It's considered a model for Africa, where 30 million AIDS victims make up 70 per cent of the world's cases. And, thanks to unyielding lobbying from aid groups such as Doctors Without Borders, rich countries, led in part by Canada, are now changing drug patent rules to finally allow the developing world access to cheap generic AIDS anti-viral drugs.

They can't come soon enough. Just one in 30 AIDS sufferers in the developing world receive treatment. The rest can't afford it.

That's no surprise when you survive on about a dollar a day, as tens of millions of humans do. Three years ago, antivirals cost as much as US$1,000 a month. Now that the generics are about US$30 a month, Uganda's government is among those planning to foot the costs for its people.

This, obviously, is very good news. But it's taken rich countries far too long to help. And while the antivirals may give AIDS victims another 10 years or more, side effects aren't known. They won't prevent new cases. And without a huge focus on now getting trained health workers to where they're needed to administer these drugs, millions of people will still be left to die, needlessly.

So the West shouldn't make another mistake and think that by simply sending these drugs, everything is fine. It's not. What's really needed here is an influx of hands-on care that will give a new desire for life. Because it seems to me that, like that bundled baby in the hallway shows, folks around here are already all-too comfortable with the everyday feel of death.

The heartbreak of AIDS - 2 66

Kampala, Uganda
March 20, 2004

We're reading the papers in the heart of Africa, and this is what we see: How a woman's derriere needs the right jeans. Photo included. A cartoon of a married fellow who'd rather give up drinking than sex on the side. And a story about *boda-bodas* – the motorcycle-taxis everyone here uses – and how ladies of the night like to proposition drivers while on board. One driver says he gets headaches if he refuses.

Such are Uganda's two national papers, tabloids, like Beavis and Butthead. Television is worse. Africa's highest-rated show ever is *Housemates*, a voyeuristic so-called reality show with, besides the usual banality, something called "shower hour."

Meanwhile, 38 million Africans, the largest group worldwide, have AIDS. The disease now kills about 20,000 North Americans annually but more than 100 times that in sub-Sahara Africa. One country, Botswana, has a 44 per cent infection rate.

New antiviral medicines will give some victims a few more years – if trained health workers go where they're needed. But the UN believes AIDS will still kill 50 million people worldwide in the next decade.

Those are just numbers until, like Jean and I, you visit a man who's buried most of his family in his backyard or meet a grandmother raising nine grandchildren, until you hear the laboured breaths of an innocent two-year-old girl infested with the disease or until you see the many coffin makers that dot Kampala's roadsides.

Yes, it's the innocent who suffer, often the faithful wife of a playboy husband and the children. Uganda has 1.5 million orphans.

Fortunately, to counter the sexual recklessness spread by pop culture, other Ugandans have been trumpeting a clarion call to a better way. Even Ugandan president Yoweri Museveni and his wife have repeatedly declared the obvious: no sex outside of marriage means no AIDS.

In fact, by promoting not only condom use but also abstinence outside of marriage, Uganda has cut its AIDS rate from 30 per cent to less than 10 per cent. Open talk on the radio, on the street, in the markets, in sex education helped Uganda become a symbol of what's possible for the rest of Africa to become: a place of hope.

One official told me, "We can't die now. We're not finished yet. We have work to do."

Of course, some people will always insist on running like suicidal lemmings off tall cliffs. They're in Uganda just as they're in Canada, where AIDS is not such a mainstream problem but where responsible sexual conduct still needs to be the foundation of a healthy society. They run. But why follow them?

How strange, for example, that while it's now almost impossible to find a child to adopt in Canada, 100,000 abortions are performed there every year. And why, when teen girls have the highest rates for STDs (sexually transmitted diseases) of any group, do most health officials maintain the notion, which I find silly, that condoms are the best answer for hormone-raged teens because they're incapable of controlling themselves?

How often do you hear the public message that plenty of people – Jean and I for example – were virgins until they marry? In truth, restraint is neither impossible nor weird. Not only will no body parts fall off, people who wait for sex wind up with more trust and better relationships. Being disease-free is simply a bonus.

Really, we all need to take responsibility for our sexual choices, especially when cultural licentiousness leads to love in all the wrong places. Because, contrary to what the Beavis and Buttheads of the world say, all decisions are not equal. And casual sex is not a victimless pleasure.

If you don't believe me, look again at the many tears that are shed by innocent people because others simply won't rein it in. Honestly, isn't it time to stop running blindly off that cliff?

Killer bugs

67

Kampala, Uganda
October 11, 2005

Two weeks into my new life in Uganda, I'm quickly learning how precarious life can be when living with the threat of infectious diseases. Take malaria.

"I guess I've been inducted as an African now," a Canadian colleague told me after recently suffering for the first time from the mosquito-spread disease. In a best-case scenario, it's like going 15 rounds with extreme flu.

Africans, meanwhile, might get malaria dozens of times. "You mean this year?" said one when I asked how many times he's had it. But their built-up resistance means they suffer less during recurrent bouts than "Muzungos," as whites are called here.

Globally, about 200 million people survive malaria annually. But make no mistake, this old scourge still kills. The engineer building my family's Ugandan home lost his mother to it when he was 13. In fact, malaria is on the rise in Uganda, killing about 70,000 a year, mostly children younger than five.

Across sub-Saharan Africa, malaria kills at least one million every year. It drains about US$2 billion from the economy. In some African countries, up to 60 per cent of hospitalizations are malaria-related. AIDS may be higher profile, but it's clear that malaria also threatens to destroy Africa's economic and political institutions from the inside.

Now add a pile of other infectious diseases. They take on a very personal dimension when one needs to protect one's own, like now, while I've been setting up my family's home here at Uganda Christian University.

Mosquito bed-netting is part of that preparation for my wife and our two young children. They are all scheduled to be here by the time you read this. Three of the four of us – our 10-week-old Jonathan Thomas is still too young – take antimalarials daily. And we're all immunized against a list of other diseases as long as your arm.

Meanwhile, unlike most of Uganda's 26 million people, we'll have potable water. That's thanks to a new water-treatment system at this growing university of 4,000 students that sits in gently rolling green countryside near Uganda's capital, Kampala. So we won't have to boil our drinking water to avoid other killers like typhoid and cholera.

The clean water is a sign of good things possible in this unique corner of the world, a continent that can so easily capture your heart and break it at the same time. The challenge is getting such projects to spread faster than any infection.

When rock concerts for aid become a memory and the television is click-clicked off, is there really much hope for such sustained progress? Maybe, if donor nations spend a dime wisely now to save a dollar, and an uglier mess, down the road. UNICEF notes, for example, that for a country of five million people, it would cost just $400,000, or eight cents a person, to implement an antimalarial program.

Corruption is an ongoing problem. Uganda's health ministry is currently being investigated for how it's managed, or mismanaged, some of its Global Fund to Fight AIDs, Tuberculosis and Malaria. Its US$201 million share of this UN initiative is now frozen, at least until the probe's end.

But the corruption card is always easy to play for rich donor nations, like Canada, when they haven't met their own obligations, like reaching the long-standing international benchmark of giving 0.08 per cent of GDP for foreign aid.

Living in the sanitized West, it's also easy to think one is immune from killer infectious diseases. Yet history shows pandemics have never respected borders. Consider that after the First World War, which killed nine million, the Spanish Flu took 40 million lives worldwide in one year. With easy global travel, such nightmares are just as possible today. Some health officials, in fact, argue that it's not a question of if but when a global pandemic of something like avian flu, which currently has no vaccine, will occur. They say it's no exaggeration to think of tens of millions of deaths again.

The reality is that nobody is entirely safe. Some of us just live closer to certain immediate threats. Now we're trying not to lose too much sleep over it all. Especially when considering the children.

In the past 30 months nobody in my family has contracted malaria. Except for me. Twice. Both times I was taking prophylaxes. So now I'm on nothing. And I haven't had a problem for a year.

Keeping up appearances

68

Kampala, Uganda
October 28, 2006

Beautiful women and mobile phones might not be the first pictures that come to mind when you think of Africa. But even here, image sells. So much so that Venatia Otto, a statuesque 18-year-old Namibian, is the latest African beauty to be made wealthy after being chosen the 2006 Nokia Face of Africa. Picked from thousands of hopefuls, Otto and nine other semifinalists from across sub-Saharan Africa were jetted off to Nokia Fashion Week in Sun City, South Africa, where 30,000 watched their final runoff.

Otto, who has Grade 10 schooling, has now catwalked to a three-year US$150,000 modelling deal in New York City. She has a new mobile phone, plus enough jewels to shame the Queen of Sheba.

Africa has an uglier side, more like the unsightly chicken-chested Congolese man who once stared humorously into my camera, apparently befuddled by the technology. Look closer at Congo, where this year more than 1,000 people have died every day, mostly from preventable diseases, from what's been called the planet's worst conflict since the Second World War.

Or look east to Somalia, where Islamicists are returning that country to civil war; or south to Zimbabwe, where inflation is 1,200 per cent; or north to Sudan, where you can't even get a bar of soap in some regions; or here to Uganda, where more than one million northerners live in refugee camps.

The other side of Africa's face is rather dirty. And bloody. And worn. Still, between such beauty and despair, the daily beat of life goes on, and, surprisingly, plenty of folks love presenting a good image of themselves.

At the Ugandan university where I work, many students may come from homes without enough food, but their clothes are always neatly pressed and "smart." If I have a wrinkle or two, I'll hear from my house help. "Mr. Thom, you can't go out like that!" And Ugandan women easily spend a week's pay on their hair.

Yes, one is to look and act properly, despite the price, because unlike in the individualistic West, this culture is based on community. It's not unlike the Arab world, where maintaining honour and avoiding shame is the goal of any interaction.

So, many everyday Africans are keeping appearances admirably, with a spirit of gentleness and courage that would humble some of the world's wealthy. They're making the best of the limited options they have. Many sacrifice dearly to chase, even idolize, education – such as it is, automated and rote.

At the same time, this social paradigm can easily become a pseudo-community. Good manners and nice people may dominate, but if nobody knows how to resolve everyday frictions and conflicts, they simmer and boil over all the bigger.

And with a weak sense of self, few people can lead. Thus, African dictatorships have come easy. In fact, it can be argued that the key, and challenge, to build a new infrastructure and future for Africa is to develop societal leaders in what is, in essence, a culture of followers.

There's a certain criticism, especially from some Africans, that the West has defined, and still defines, Africa's identity. Maybe. Global trade barriers have hurt developing nations. And it's certainly true that we all hold mirrors up to each other in some fashion. No man, or continent, is an island.

But Africans have also had the freedom to create their own reality and present it to others in ways of their choosing. Colonialists left African states independent 50 years ago. Since then, this continent has seen 26 major wars and gone from being a huge food exporter to being one that can't even feed itself.

Twenty years ago, a couple of African nations could feed the whole continent. This year, 22 sub-Saharan countries, the same ones those Nokia judges recently toured, have suffered severe food shortages, not mainly from regional drought but political turmoil.

By now it seems painfully clear that, alone, sub-Saharan Africa in particular can find neither the sustained development nor the deeper healing it so desperately needs. The challenges are only growing.

If it cares, the rich side of the world needs to risk and partner and work for a new future that goes beyond keeping its own appearances.

I have no problem with keeping up appearances and being culturally sensitive. While in a pork-free zone like Yemen, I never ordered bacon with my eggs or kissed my wife in public or showed off my legs, such as they are, in public. But at the sunny Ugandan university where I now work, I do run in shorts and a Team Canada cap often, which I suppose is one reason why the university has introduced a new dress code. Get out the socks.

Understand that Uganda Christian University prides itself as a place set apart from other regional schools. And dressing up really is an African thing. But can this code thing be a bit confusing? Do you think some of those raving Old Testament prophets looked a little dishevelled some days?

Of course, in the beginning it didn't matter. In the Garden, even Gucci wasn't on the scene yet. Head to toe, we were buck naked.

After our pride got exposed, in shame we tried to cover up with those teeny fig leaves, but, as the story goes, it was the Creator who came to our rescue with more lasting animal skins, a precursor to His final covering of forgiveness in Jesus Christ.

So it seems to This Scribe that even looking hip and smart can be distracting, which is why Jesus later told us to stop fretting over things like clothes and look at how our Father dresses even the flowers of the fields.

Being at a theological centre, I felt it was okay to say all this, and a little more, in a guest column in the Standard, the Young Campus Paper that I do, after all, coordinate. That prompted several responses to me, all to the effect of "Thom, I really liked that. Have you been fired yet?"

On shame:

See Young Important Reporter, one of the interns on Young Campus Paper, a bright young man who likes to dress for success. One day, not realizing how sensitive this might be, I asked him to carry a small mat from my house to the nearby news office.

Young Important Reporter agreed. Until he got to my home, where, seeing a gardener nearby, he refused to come closer and instead stayed around a corner out of sight, not wanting someone on a lower social strata see him doing such a menial task.

My best lesson on avoiding shame in Uganda, though, came recently when I was waiting with some Canadian colleagues for Henry, a Ugandan driver, to take two visiting colleagues to the airport in Entebbe for their flight back to Canada.

Getting a little nervous after Henry didn't show up at the university on time – twenty minutes, thirty minutes, forty minutes late – we began phoning him on his mobile. We made several calls, each time getting more exasperated, each time asking, "Henry, where are you? You're supposed to pick up the Canadians to go to the airport."

Each time Henry told us where he was, each time getting closer to the university. When finally arrived on campus, he calmly told us on the phone that he had arrived in "the classroom."

"Henry!" I finally said. "We need you here at the guest house. Now! We're going to be late and miss the flight!"

Pause.

This Henry, it finally came out, was not the right Henry. No. This Henry was a university professor who, as it happened, like the driver Henry, was also late.

Oops.

Now, one would think the good professor might have mentioned this a little sooner. But in Uganda, this is not the way.

And the driver Henry? He finally showed up, late due to having the taxi van in for repair.

The Canadians did make their flight.

And my lesson was learned.

Even as a veteran of overseas life, I'm still learning these kind of cultural nuances. I'm also finding that the young scribes on Young Campus Paper also appreciate certain themes of Western culture.

Their training from This Scribe, in fact, has included watching movies like 'Dead Poets Society,' which prompted conversation particularly about that thematic line from Henry David Thoreau: "I went to the woods because I wanted to live deliberately, I wanted to live deep and suck out all the marrow of life, To put to rout all that was not life and not when I had come to die, discover that I had not lived."

Any two-year-old can tell you that power isn't easy to handle. But in Africa, power madness is a certain disease.

A few months ago Queen Elizabeth and the heads of 50-some Commonwealth countries met down the highway from me for smiles and wine and their biannual Commonwealth Summit. Everyone was cheery, and the good queen noted how life has improved since her last visit to Uganda. That was some 50 years ago.

She didn't ask why, since the British colonialists left around then, there has not been even one peaceful transfer of power in this East African country. To observers like This Scribe, that is a bit bewildering.

And many Ugandans, especially those knowing yesteryear's political horrors, are left in nervousness, or fear, or anger, or all these. (Note the photo of the generous beating given to a supporter of Col. Kizza Besigye, leader of Uganda's opposition. Besigye, a former personal physician and friend of President Yoweri Museveni, in fact, saved the president's life when the two fought side-by-side in Uganda's bloody civil war of the early 1980s.)

Old tribal issues are part of today's underlying uncertainty. Kenya, which blew up for the world to see in early 2008, is a next-door example of how this can fester under the surface of otherwise calm days.

And so, like with other development issues, on the evolution of government we wait. And wait. Or we just accept that certain countries in Africa will never be cut out for Western-style democracy.

Following are more thoughts on such things, which actually touch on the deeper struggles of the human spirit: not on just power per se, but on identity and forgiveness and all that's needed to understand and give and receive such life-sustaining breath.

Opposite page photo: *Ugandan police beat a supporter of Col. Kizza Besigye, leader of the Federation of Democratic Change in Uganda, while Besigye rides in an election campaign vehicle.*

WINDOWS

Power Struggles

The everyday feel of death

69

Mukono, Uganda
April 23, 2005

On a recent evening, as we drive though the darkness, two things are out of place. One is the furry moose head, complete with maple leaf, dangling from the rear-view mirror. The other is Roger's talk about forgiveness.

From Entebbe International Airport we motor at Highway 401 speed towards Uganda's capital, Kampala. Roger, my driver, explains that the moose head is from a Canadian friend. I smile.

People are everywhere. On motor scooters. Bicycles. Foot. The odd truck tries to make three lanes of two. Lights come at us. Everything whizzes past. The moose head swings.

Roger talks about wanting a better life. About his car. His family. The West. The "circus" of government. How entire towns, including much of Kampala, are dark due to power outages.

I ask him about a certain Ugandan ghost, Milton Obote.

"Obote," he says, "is irrelevant." He then adds, "We need to forgive and move on."

Forgiveness.

Obote, exiled in Zambia for the past 20 years, is a two-time Ugandan president. His first rotten government gave rise to Idi Amin, a devil who liked to kill people by, among other means, bludgeoning them with sledgehammers. Some 300,000 Ugandans died during Amin's reign of terror.

After Amin, Obote returned in 1980 as elected head of state, only to keep Uganda on its knees. A military coup in 1985, led by today's president, Yoweri Museveni, forced him out for good. But not before hundreds of thousands more Ugandans died.

Now Obote, at a ripe 81, plans to return. Within weeks.

It's an African thing. Amin also tried, unsuccessfully, to leave his exile in Saudi Arabia to die on Ugandan soil. In this case, Ugandan's government initially said Obote, by law, could indeed return to a furnished home, chauffeur, security guards, secretary and domestic staff. Museveni has since said Obote must first explain his crimes. Obote says he's coming anyway.

Forgiveness.

The papers here are full of the story. Obote, in fact, is writing the entire history in his own words for one national daily. The other competing story is

Museveni's push for a constitutional change allowing him to run for the presidency. Again. Twenty years of power isn't enough. He wants it, apparently, until death.

Not that Museveni has been bad for Uganda. He's been good. Brought stability. But in 53 years, since the British gave independence to what Churchill called the Pearl of Africa, Uganda has not seen one peaceful transfer of power. Power madness is the disease of African leaders.

So there is unrest here. British rock star Bob Geldof, echoing Western donors, has even weighed in on the need for more democracy. Political parties are still banned in Uganda. That's because, when drawn along tribal lines, they have their own demons. Ugandans know. They've memorialized Rwandans whose body parts have washed onto Ugandan shores, via Lake Victoria, long after Rwanda's 1994 tribal genocide.

Forgiveness.

Recently some Ugandan religious leaders travelled all the way to The Hague, asking the International Criminal Court (ICC) not to indict Lord's Resistance Army (LRA) leaders. In the north, the LRA has kidnapped some 17,000 kids to make into child soldiers. It has terrorized countless Ugandans. Now these thugs might be simply reintegrated. My future neighbours, maybe.

Nigeria, meanwhile, wants the ICC to let Africans, not outsiders, deal with Darfur, Sudan, where 180,000 have been killed since 2003. And, of course, South Africa handled apartheid's crimes against humanity though its Truth and Reconciliation Commission. All examples of how – unlike the West, which focuses on the crime and punishment – African justice focuses on restoring community balance.

It sounds very fine. And restorative justice has its place. But I've seen Uganda before. And as Roger talks about forgiveness, I know the morning will reveal the many coffin makers on the roadsides. Their coffins, largely for AIDs victims, come in all sizes. For kids too.

In this land of uncommon beauty, and life, this is the everyday feel of death that Ugandans have. So while, like other Africans, they're telling the world they can handle their own justice, I wonder what that might really mean. And that scares me.

Because already, even prior to my family's move here later this year, this place has captured my heart. And I fear it will be broken. Forgiveness or not.

The African Way 70

Kampala, Uganda
February 6, 2006

If man is by nature a political animal, as Aristotle said, then the best place for the best politicians is in the wild.

This is what I've advised the president of Uganda (in my mind): "Yo, go back to the bush. Get some perspective, man. Really. Return to your roots."

You'll recall from previous dispatches that President Yoweri Museveni has so much going for him that, to ensure Ugandans can keep him, he's changed the law to allow unlimited presidential terms. Winning Uganda's national vote February 23 would extend his reign to 2013. That totals 27 years. In dog years, that's a couple of German shepherds. And even by African standards, a very long time.

It really defies, up to now, the African Way.

The African Way is this: A government is elected. A rebel group opposes it. It ousts the leader in a coup. There's civil war. Atrocities occur. Millions starve. Rock stars sing about it. The UN intervenes. Peace is restored. The cycle restarts.

Yes, no continent on earth is wracked with more mindless bloodshed than Africa. It needs a sign at every port of entry: "Welcome to Africa: Now run for your life."

Think of 3,000 killed in the United States on 9/11 and multiply it a thousandfold to get an idea of lives lost in the brutality and mayhem of recent decades. Sudan, Ethiopia, Somalia, Sierra Leone, Ivory Coast, Liberia, Angola, Rwanda – take your pick.

Museveni knows it. As a guerrilla rebel leader in Uganda's bush country from 1980 to 1986, he fought like a lion against former president Milton

Obote. Hundreds of thousands died before Museveni's National Resistance Movement (NRM) won the day.

The resisters then settled down to govern. With some stability. The NRM brought Uganda's army under control, built a macro-economy, helped reduce AIDS, initiated free primary education and even helped restore the decimated elephant population.

It's all very fine. And last week the NRM celebrated its 20 years in power with plenty of tanks and jets and whatnot to show how secure and hip Uganda is.

Still, the opposition complains. Corruption is wild. Poverty is up. The north, where the cultlike Lord's Resistance Army operates, is a neglected disaster. Three million Ugandans need food aid.

Now, with the recent imprisonment of the opposition leader for several weeks, democracy itself is threatened. The critics want change. And if it's not through the vote, there's always, you know, the African Way.

Which is why I advised the president (still in my mind) to forget the state house for now and return to the bush. "Take some mobiles and laptops and resist the establishment again," I said. "Run an opposition campaign. You'll look and feel 20 years younger."

"You think?" he said.

"Yes sir. In Africa, resistance is always the future. Besides, when you're so darn good, a Museveni versus Museveni match is the race everyone wants. Think about it. You can't lose."

"You're right."

"It's tricky," I added. "It's one thing for Moses to set up in the wilderness to battle Pharaoh. It's quite something else for Pharaoh to battle Pharaoh. But you can do it."

"I can. I will," he said.

"Remember," I added, "as long as you're resisting leaving office, or resisting the government, both of your personas can keep 'resistance' in your party names."

"Great."

"But one of you needs to ditch your 'peace, unity and prosperity' slogan. Instead, use this: 'The only thing worse than a present African leader is the next one.' It will seriously hurt the opposition. Just be careful which one of you uses it."

"Yes, of course," said the president.

"The two of you should also mimic each other. Have the same walk, the same facial expressions, the same voice, you know. Then your current self will always be seen as youthful, and your past self will be seen as experienced."

"It's brilliant. I like it all," he told me. "But how can I be in two places at once?"

"That's where the computers come in," I said. "Do the *Wag the Dog* thing. Remember? The Dustin Hoffman movie? Today's technology can easily show you in a virtual world that doesn't really exist."

"Yes, yes, I remember. But didn't they have to start a fake war in that movie?"

"Exactly," I said. "And isn't that better than the real thing?"

Power struggles 71

KAMPALA, UGANDA
February 20, 2006

Okay, who turned Uganda's lights out? More important, when do they come back on?

On the first question, blame the dry weather and short-sighted politicians. For the second, folks here need to check their savings. In any case, thanks to a power crisis that dwarfs Ontario's 2003 blackout, millions of Ugandans are now aboard a rather uncertain ride through the dark. And one can't help but wonder if their country is not about to come to a grinding halt.

Not that this piece of Africa is a fully serviced kind of place. Mobile phones, interestingly, abound. But lanterns and candles are still commonly used by rural residents, over three-quarters of Uganda's 22 million inhabitants.

Kampala, though, is different. It isn't Space Shuttle Central, but this capital region of about two million people has industries, businesses and homes as reliant on hydro as anywhere you are. Sugar plants are one. And there are schools and offices and supermarkets, not to mention my house, now facing a new load-shedding schedule that cuts power up to 12 hours a day.

Due to a couple of truck batteries, my home has backup to run low-voltage lights and small essentials like computers. In fact, I'm on backup as I write. But don't open the fridge. Please. Not until we get a generator.

Most Ugandans, and small and medium-size businesses, can't afford that $500 minimum cost or gasoline, pricier here than in Canada. One hard-up contractor lamented to me about his inability to weld trusses: "What would take me one month will now take me six."

It will have a devastating ripple effect. Manufacturing stops, businesses close and the jobless will likely return in an exodus to their home villages. The fortunate, like my family, will undoubtedly pay more for what goods and services remain available. (We already pay more for groceries than in a typical Hamilton supermarket, where, of course, the refrigerated milk isn't sour.)

One might imagine this is the big issue of the current election campaign.

Wrong. Front pages are using more ink on the soap opera of alleged rape and other "secrets" of President Yoweri Museveni and his main competitor.

In a recent two-page newspaper commentary, Museveni, who's particularly popular among uneducated rural voters, gave a single paragraph to the power crisis, to blame – naturally – the opposition. Otherwise, the government assures it won't be long – about 2010 – before hydro from new thermal sources is available.

One culprit is regional drought. Power-generating Lake Victoria – the world's second-largest freshwater lake – supports the livelihoods of 30 million Ugandans, Kenyans and Tanzanians and has dropped to its lowest level in 80 years. Unchecked deforestation, which slows the rain cycle, has contributed to that.

Typical bureaucratic mismanagement and carelessness have worsened it all. Uganda's politicians have known for years that they need new options, especially since decaying power lines rule out importing hydro. They simply blame everyone else, including international planners.

I doubt that average Ugandans in my neck of the woods really care whose fault it is. They just want to be able to find their socks again. And have a job to wear them to.

And by the way ... African election campaigns are never ladylike affairs. But campaigning for Uganda's February 23 vote went beyond routine ugliness when the home of government MP Jessica Eriyo was burned down for her alleged hand in the death of her rival Clara Vuni.

Eriyo had earlier defeated Vuni in a party primary. Vuni, 27, who died in a car crash, was reportedly speeding to police to file a complaint about Eriyo, who was in hot pursuit during the deadly crash. Later, angry relatives and friends nabbed Vuni's body from hospital, placed it in front of Eriyo's house and torched the place.

On the same day, President Museveni's motorcade was hit with gunfire from an unknown source. The president, safe, continued campaigning. "We still have our old devil of a gun," he said at a rally afterwards. "There's no need for you to scare away development from your area. I'm a cattle-keeper like you. You can't scare away a cow when you want to milk it."

And you thought Ottawa was a tough place.

Making your bed

72

Kampala, Uganda
March 6, 2006

Join me along a main drag, congested and potholed as it is, into Uganda's capital. See the rather ragged election banner of President Yoweri Museveni? It's hung like that for weeks, as big as the beer ads here, crooked and torn, saying in not so many words "nobody cares."

Thousands of presidential supporters have seen its damage. The president's campaign team undoubtedly has. When nearby, Museveni likely has also.

Still, there it blows, a testament to the fact that nobody here seems overly concerned about much, least of all that Museveni's recent election win makes him, in effect, Uganda's emperor king.

While he once said no African leader should rule more than ten years, Museveni now reigns for 25, to 2011. *Big Man* is apparently still in the lexicon of African politics. This is because unlike Canadians, who will turf governments over, say, corruption, Ugandans, remembering yesteryear's despots, are happy with leaders who allow them to go to bed without getting shot or raped before morning.

"He brought us peace. We love him," is how our housekeeper, Alice, put it. So let the torn presidential banners blow over potholed roads. And if democracy has to stay in its nappy stage, so be it. Freedom, after all, is relative.

The downside is that one still has to sleep in the bed one makes. Corruption already puts an estimated $175 million annually into the wrong pockets. Ugandans just entrenched such sleaze as a regime maintenance tool.

By holding their tongues on government neglect of the war-torn north and Uganda's hydro crisis and rotten health care, voters just tacitly accepted them too. By re-electing a government that perpetually weakens the opposition, not to mention civic institutions like media and courts, they've made it even harder for new leaders to emerge.

And by recrowning Museveni after he changed the law to allow unlimited presidential terms, Ugandans have isolated themselves. International donors, who provide about half of Uganda's revenue, are already trimming support. Uganda is also out-of-step regionally, now the only East African country allowing more than two terms.

Ironically, things aren't all great for Museveni himself, because this election was about more than leading Uganda for another five years. It's about 2013, when the East Africa (EA) Federation – 90 million people in Uganda, Kenya and Tanzania – is scheduled to become a political and economic union under one president. Museveni is eyeing that, but will EA want his Big Man image? Kenya, for one, is becoming more democratic than ever.

Ugandans, ultimately, could keep their man until 2019. At 75, he'd have to leave by law. Unless he changes it.

Museveni won his third term largely on the female vote. In fact, not one woman, my wife included, told me they'd vote for main contender Dr. Kizza Besigye. My theory is that Museveni's facial features are softer.

Twenty years since assuming power, this is just his third term, because after Uganda's 1980-86 civil war, Museveni ruled de facto for nine years. Two five-year terms followed. To clarify from a previous column his desire for "seven more years," Museveni still has Uganda's 2011 elections before that potential 2013 EA presidency.

Meanwhile, other African presidents are catching third-term fever. Chad's Idriss Deby has changed that country's constitution to run for a third. Courting disaster, Nigeria's president, Olusegun Obasanjo, is considering the same.

Besigye, a former ally who saved Museveni's life during the civil war, campaigned between jail time plus 27 court appearances on trumped up treason and rape charges.

And Besigye's supporters? At a recent rally, some of them crowded and threw rocks at a military lieutenant's car. So the officer shot three of them dead.

With voter turnout topping 60 per cent, Museveni garnered 59 per cent of over six million votes. Besigye got 38 per cent. International observers acknowledge voting irregularities but say official results are solid. Besigye's camp disputes them.

Is that poor losing? Consider more on how the winners play. When early polls streamed in and Uganda's independent newspaper, the *Monitor,* released its own running tally, the government blocked its website and jammed its sister radio station's frequency.

As our yard help, Paul, said, "I voted Museveni, not because I wanted to but, if he lost, we'd have a war."

This morning, not far from where that torn sign of Museveni's hung, I ran into the back of a pickup. And, never losing a chance to get a fresh word on the street, I asked the driver (while we went to the garage to get his light fixed), "So are Ugandans happy with their government?"

"Half and half," he told me, which I figured was diplomatic enough for a taxman with the Ugandan Revenue Authority.

But to be fair to Mr. Museveni and his political legacy, potholes or not, he does remain a popular leader. Here are a few more notes, this time from today's papers.

Here's Elivania Kanyonga, 120-something years young. She doesn't know her exact birthday (many adult Ugandans don't), but does recall, she says, something about the Berlin Conference of 1884 when the major Western powers negotiated control of Africa, the beginning of today's, for better or worse, political partitioning.

Elivania apparently just crawls now, but is still up at 6 a.m. for prayer. And she's a diehard supporter of President Museveni. There's her photo, with card held high.

Flip a page to see Colonel Muammar Gadaffi, an African bad-boy-turned-sometimes-good, who has run Libya for some three decades. Looking like an aging rock star, he just showed up in Uganda to thundering applause (with four planes and a kilometre-long motorcade) and told President Museveni to never retire.

This is because, as the good colonel explains, presidential term limits are simply an invention of Western democracy, which, for a revolutionary place like Africa, just won't work.

"We need zeal and vision," he says, and "what we are asking from leaders like Museveni is to continue with the war of development, or die in the war."

There you have it. War of a different kind.

And this just in: Robert Mugabe, who has run Zimbabwe for 28 years with sensitivity, courage and commitment, has just lost the country's 2008 election. Stay tuned for further coverage on how he now plans to leave graciously over the next 28. (Months later, Mugabe somehow "won.")

An American friend of mine, a pious and upright theology professor who hails from peaceful Minnesota, notes this: "We should pray for God to change his heart. Or stop it."

73 The charming monster

Kampala, Uganda
March 13 2007

Now that *The Last King of Scotland* has piled up its international awards and come full circle to show here, Ugandans can take a bow. Really. The film's success, including Forest Whitaker's Oscar, shows that Idi Amin may still be Uganda's best-known export, but the country itself has now had its own proverbial 15 minutes of fame, and on a world stage.

Outsiders can never really get enough of a crackpot like Amin, who had a rare capacity to be charming and comical and demonic all at once. It's not your average despot who calls himself Lord of All the Beasts of the Earth and Fishes of the Sea, while killing 300,000 of his countrymen, some personally with a sledgehammer.

But as Ugandans know too well, what is detached fascination from a distance is more personal and painful up close. This is why Ugandans can be proud. A difficult chapter in their history has been scratched open, again.

Two aspects of the film intrigued me. One is how small it's made the world. Director Kevin Macdonald said he loves to "bring audiences to new places they don't know," and this is what he did for millions of viewers abroad. But while we were watching at the Cineplex in Kampala, the world seemed so small we couldn't help but laugh at the absurdity of it: a film shot literally around the corner from our theatre seats, put together on the other side of the Atlantic and then sent back to where we now watch.

Look, on screen. That British journalist is really Dr. Dick Stockley, who runs The Surgery on Acacia Avenue. And, hey, there's Mulago Hospital. And now Amin is in the Sheraton's pool. And look, Rosie Button, a family friend from

Mukono who's sitting just a row away, is on the big screen as a hostage at Entebbe Airport.

My other note of interest is the criticism from some about this film's take on Amin. Apparently there's no issue with creating the fictitious character of Amin's personal doctor, Scotsman Nicholas Garrigan, but there's great offence with Amin, the beast, being portrayed as too human. As one *New Vision* respondent put it, "Amin was not funny."

Fair enough, considering the memories of loved ones lost in that terrible era. On the other hand, isn't this the nature of evil? Hitler, after all, could laugh easily with children, and over in North Korea Kim Jong-Nam loves Mickey Mouse.

Yes, darkness has this way of settling in any human heart, and evil certainly doesn't advertise itself by walking around with horns and a pitchfork. In this sense, the scriptwriters and Whitaker, who interviewed Amin's family extensively, got it spot-on.

This is all what gives this film a ring of truth. More so, it's authentic because it's about Uganda, with Ugandans in Uganda. Thank director Macdonald for bypassing more common shooting locations like Kenya and South Africa. Lack of film infrastructure here or not, he believed the story needed Uganda and was proved right.

And good for President Museveni for not just allowing shooting but giving producers carte blanche access to structures like parliament and the army. He didn't have to. After all, this all touches on what some might consider an embarrassing time, and this culture has certain views on shame and avoiding it.

Maybe that's the bigger thought to take away. There are certain benefits to telling the truth, even a Hollywood rendition of it. Yes, give truth a forum, stand back, and watch the good things that can unfold.

Forgiveness

74

Kampala, Uganda
January 20, 2007

Besides *I'm sorry*, the hardest words in any language have to be *I forgive you*. And never has the world needed them more.

The latest reminder comes from Somalia, a messy corner of Africa where a transitional government wants to move forward.

"We've passed through 15 years of civil war," President Abdullahi Yusuf said, closing 2006. "Now we need to forgive each other."

Somalia is a burial ground for untold thousands who've died brutally through political execution, clan warfare and plain starvation. How is such a place to know forgiveness? How is any place?

According to the annual listing of Canada's Project Ploughshares, there are now 32 armed conflicts worldwide – 13 in Africa – involving about one-third of the globe's population.

These clashes are part of history's fourth generation of warfare. It's a style of fighting no longer waged on battlefields, or with linear attacks, or even state-versus-state. Instead, wars now typically revolve around so-called "non-stable actors" – fighters with no capital to bomb or, sometimes, even uniforms to see. If they're not terrorists raising hell over ideology, they're resistance fighters or rebel-militias fighting civil wars over things like natural resources.

Innocent civilians get dragged in. They lose their economic means, their homes and their lives to what are often ambiguous forces. So while one of the greatest challenges in today's world is finding healing for entire populaces, the issues are increasingly complex. How, for example, do you handle fighters wanting to return to their homes?

In Somalia, many of the 80,000 militia, in 50 groups, now want to settle down. After 20 years of war in northern Uganda, peace with the rebel Lord's Resistance Army depends on their leaders' amnesty. But the UN wants them tried in The Hague.

South Africa's well-known Truth and Reconciliation Commission put that country on a new road. It gave amnesty to 849 of 7,112 apartheid criminals. Was that right? Today dozens of reconciliation tribunals are active worldwide, also trying to somehow weigh justice and mercy.

The secret, according to Nobel Peace Prize winner Archbishop Desmond Tutu, is "to strike a balance between Nuremburg on one hand, and amnesia on the other."

Arthur Kulah, a leader in Liberia's Truth and Reconciliation Commission, didn't wait for his former enemies to show any regret. He found the rebel commander who killed his father – a man who's now in Liberia's parliament – and forgave him unconditionally. That led the perpetrator to take responsibility, to apologize and to give information that, in turn, helped Kulah's healing.

"If you don't forgive, you'll carry that burden your whole life," says Kulah. They're noble words in a country where soldiers routinely decorated roadblocks with human intestines during a 1990-2003 war that killed 150,000 of three million Liberians.

Some will disagree. The West tends to tilt away from the mercy of amnesia toward the justice of Nuremburg. Its culture has been influenced by moral philosophers like Immanuel Kant, who reasoned that forgiveness should be granted only to the deserving. This, arguably, keeps the dignity of both victim and perpetrator intact.

But what if nobody is deserving? Could anyone ever atone enough for something as heinous as the Holocaust? Yet in one of history's most striking examples of reconciliation, Germany was rebuilt by former enemies.

During following decades, Germans responded with *Vergangenheitsbewaltigung*, a deep introspection dealing with the guilt and shame of their past. They dialogued, made apologies, built memorials. They transformed their identity.

There are other options. One is to do the daily dance of saving face, causing vicious cycles of retribution and counter-retribution, where, like in a Newtonian law, every atrocity must be answered with an equal and opposite atrocity. Look at the Middle East.

Even on a personal level, who among us has never been deeply hurt by someone? Still, it seems that the only thing harder than forgiveness is unforgiveness. Unforgiveness has its own price. It destroys the bridge over which anyone must cross.

Individually, this is really what Somalians, and others in the reconciliation process, are being led to consider. It's something for all of us to keep in mind. We can't, and shouldn't, ever really forget. But we do need to forgive.

Revenge may be sweet today, but, for our own sakes, mercy is sweeter for the long tomorrow.

If a tree falls in the forest... 75

Kampala, Uganda
April 28, 2007

If a tree falls deep in the heart of Africa, will anyone hear?

That's the question for the outside world, as the debate that often pits the environment against the economy has taken a chilling twist here in Uganda, with riots, murder and parliamentarians jailed.

While the dust is still settling, there's no resolution on the storm that involves the Ugandan government's proposed giveaway of 7,100 hectares of prime forest, known as the Mabira Forest, to clear it for large-scale sugar growing and processing.

Giving Mabira for clearing to the Mehta Group, a company run by successful Indian nationals in Uganda, is part of the government's goal of industrializing its developing economy. Processed goods feed your citizens and sell internationally for exponentially more than raw material does.

"It's much easier for us to grow forest, or allow them to regenerate, than to attract factories," Ugandan president Yoweri Museveni said recently. "Our people have gone without jobs long enough."

And Uganda, now the same size as Canada, will need plenty of jobs at the other end of its breathtaking growth rate. With an average of seven children per woman, that rate will give it 180 million people by 2050.

Like many Africans, most Ugandans – 90 per cent, in fact – use either wood or charcoal for cooking. It's no surprise, then, that scientists say Africa is losing its forests three times faster than the rest of the planet. You know the rest of the story: rivers dry up, drought hits, floods come, or there's general weird weather caused by the greenhouse effect – and God knows what else.

In this case, in a developing country without checks and balances, environmental issues have additional political components, namely shady backroom deals. When foreign investors get loans or tax breaks or other incentives – like a forest – while everyday folks starve with unpaid pensions, or in slums with high rent, or with poor public schools or horrible hospitals, things tend to brew and simmer.

Thus Uganda's recent firestorm. A public demonstration against the Mabira giveaway turned into a riot, an Indian national on the wrong street at the wrong time was beaten dead, and police then killed a few Ugandans in the crowd.

For their roles in leading the demonstration, several opposition MPs were jailed for a few days. While Asian businessmen closed their shops in fear, more hell then broke loose in protest of those MPs incarcerations. That was then quelled by stick-wielding Ugandan vigilantes dubbed the Kiboko Squad, apparently not even known by police.

President Museveni, meanwhile, who has generally had his way in Uganda for 22 years, may be facing the political fight of his life. Most government MPs, including his cabinet, are strongly opposed to the forest giveaway to Mehta.

Now it's reported that Mehta already received some 30 billion Ugandan shillings (about Can$19 million) from Museveni's government in recent years, apparently for losses during previous regimes when Asians in Uganda lost holdings and, under former dictator Idi Amin, were expelled by the thousands.

All this, and that first proverbial tree in the forest hasn't even gone down yet.

"If we just managed our own resources better, we'd have no need for foreign aid," a Ugandan journalist commented to me, regarding the government's money deals. I see everyday issues here and agree. There's a dearth of domestic leadership everywhere, and while there are plenty of foreign aid workers around, some new help should come in new forms.

The West is reneging on its current promises anyway. Africa's debts were cancelled after the 2005 G-8 summit, but aid has increased just two per cent since, hardly on course, as promised, to go from today's $25 billion to $50 billion by 2010.

That promised increase, by the way, is less than one-tenth of one per cent of the rich world's income. It's equivalent to what Wall Street Christmas bonuses are for one year.

Maybe someone should use it to buy a few million saplings. Really. And a whole lot of boots on the ground.

If that kind of aid came, some Africans might see some alternative economic profits – from replanting programs – at Mabira or anywhere else. And that might save some African lives, and futures, never mind trees.

One thing I've found in my travels on the world's bumpier roads, where the world's poor are juxtaposed against a well-to-do Westerner, is that I start holding everyday things a little closer to the heart.

A bicycle is no longer just a bicycle, but a way to connect with a more natural pace of life; a train is no longer just a train, but a way to explore that often unmapped territory inside of ourselves; and 16 days in Uganda is not just two weeks and two days of living, but a lens into the relationship we have with our global neighbours.

Such are the following selections.

One visit to a refugee camp in Congo, a large and troubled patch of earth, left a particular impact on me, and these first three pieces explore some observations from that country.

Concluding the section is a short piece on evolution, a particularly interesting issue because some folks around here believe that East Africa is humanity's cradle. It's a worthwhile issue to wrestle with because it deals with those pesky questions of where we come from, why we're here and where we're going.

Opposite page photo: *Children from Oicha, Congo, gather around a universal love: their bicycle.*

WINDOWS From the Heart

Congo 1: Don't forget the lights

76

LONDON, CANADA
September 15, 2003

One of the more interesting reactions over this summer's so-called great blackout came via the car radio when my wife and I were driving in the Muskokas, learning how the outside world was faring in the darkness.

One caller, a young woman, complained bitterly to the CBC, lamenting that she had to sit in the dark while just over Toronto's waterfront stood a sea of office buildings, fully lit. And empty.

Jean and I couldn't help but laugh, sadly, and see an all-too-apt metaphor of Earth's haves and have-nots, a picture of those who sit in towers of plenty and those who see them from across the water.

I wonder if the caller felt a little like Sarah Muwafaq, a young Iraqi woman who said she was actually "thrilled" the lights went out for 50 million North Americans. "We want them to know what hot means for us," she said. "We want them to feel it for one day."

Folks from other countries were more relaxed about the woes of so many Canadians and Americans, but they wondered what all the fuss was about. Unal Karatas, a pretzel vendor from Ankara, a city in a fairly progressive place like Turkey, summed it up for millions when he said, "Blackouts are part of our daily life."

My first experience with limited electricity actually unfolded earlier this spring when Jean and I were in Congo with some of that country's thousands of war refugees. Many are bright, articulate professionals, yet, with no homes, they are left with the most rudimentary of life's tools.

Their new homes are simple tarp and thatch structures. Food, a pasty millet, is cooked over an open fire. A rubber tire for a toy means a kid is lucky. Electricity, I'm afraid, isn't even on the map for most.

You can imagine the type of infections and sickness that visit. More enlightening was how these people gave us sincere and warm smiles. I doubt many North Americans could do the same.

Sure, Blackout 2003 led to some true experiences of community. But, really, our ice cream melted for a couple of days and now we think we have great stories of survival to tell our grandchildren.

Don't get me wrong. Some poorer countries live in darkness because of their own doing. Also, I very much enjoy the lights in my Ontario home. Even in our other home, in Yemen's capital, Sana'a, the power usually works. Our flat also has running water.

We even have a flush toilet. But did you know that three billion humans, half the world's populace, do not have such a pot to call their own? That's a perspective rich Westerners often don't have and, sometimes, don't want to have.

Take Congo's chaos. It's caused in part by outsiders mining its vast resources. Al-Qaida has been into Congo's $1-million-a-day blood diamond trade, selling to European merchants to bankroll terrorist hits. And North Americans also benefit from Congo's coltan, a key raw material in computer chips and cellphones.

That's not to say all Westerners are cruel robber barons who turn their backs on the orphans of the world. Historically, the West has also been a key provider of aid. But Blackout 2003 should be more than a wake-up call to improve Ontario's faulty power grids. It should be an alert to our culture about what's on the other side of the water.

Taking notice will not only help us turn off our lights. It will help us develop more simplicity and thanksgiving, things that, in the end, are more satisfying than amusing ourselves with today's flashy toys.

77 *Congo 2: The givers and takers*

Oicha, Congo
June 6, 2003

Dr. David Livingstone, celebrated explorer and missionary to Africa, was once asked by a group back in England, "Have you found a good road to where you are? We want to send others to join you."

"If you have men who will come only if they know there is a good road, I don't want them," he replied. "I want men who will come even if there is no road at all."

Livingstone, who was found in Congo in 1866 by *New York Herald* reporter Sir Henry Stanley and asked the well-known question "Dr. Livingstone, I presume?" was recently described in *The New Yorker* as "a morally righteous man of God and a man of science."

His comment about roads was vintage Livingstone. He didn't take life's easy street. Neither have doctors Philip and Nancy Wood, Aberdeen Avenue residents in Hamilton when home – which hasn't been much these past 30 years, as they have made Africa their main address. After landing in a single engine plane on a rough patch of earth, narrowly missing a goat, Jean and I spent

time with them recently at the Christian medical compound where they care for Congolese refugees.

One barely knows where to begin. Almost 150 years after Livingstone, there are still no roads linking most of immense Congo to its capital, Kinshasa. No national airline. Heck, often no phones. Little wonder the government can't handle out-of-control tribes.

Philip and Nancy got a taste of tribal violence when their long-time Congolese home of Nyakunde, population 18,000, was wiped off the map last fall. Dozens of patients and staff at Nyakunde mission hospital were hacked to death. Incredibly, hundreds of others escaped by walking through the forest for 10 days to Oicha.

Indeed, Congo makes a place like Yemen look like a five-star hotel. Months before Congo's most recent mass killings, 90,000 refugees had already poured into the greater region of Oicha, a town originally the size of Ancaster.

Many are professionals. Now they have thatched homes with simple blue tarps. Food is a pasty millet cooked on an open fire. A kid is lucky to have a rubber tire for a toy. Malaria, malnutrition and anemia visit often.

Philip and Nancy have a small, spartan, red brick house where Philip enjoys Brahm's symphonics over BBC satellite, often in the dark. When you generate your own electricity, it's rationed. And for US$200 a month, you can get e-mail. Just travel 27 kilometres to the nearest phone line.

I dryly call the place Camp Paradise. And yet these refugees, having lost everything, often have big smiles and friendly dispositions. Philip and Nancy also exude satisfaction all too rare in Canadian culture. "You put down tent pegs wherever the Lord puts you," says Nancy. That's perspective.

Congo's problems are caused in part by outsiders. African neighbours supply rebels with weapons. That makes it easier for foreigners to pilfer Congo's resources like timber and gold. Even al-Qaeda has been found to be involved with Congo's $1-million-a-day blood diamond trade, selling to European merchants to bankroll terrorist hits.

But ordinary North Americans also use Congo's resources, such as coltan, a key raw material needed for computer chips and cellphones. Congo may also have significant oil, and one international relief worker told me she believes evidence already shows North American interests are ready to exploit that, saying, "It's the same issues as in Sudan."

It's food for thought.

It's especially interesting considering that revisionist historians like to blame Christian figures like Livingstone for the evils of colonialism. Similarly, modern missionaries, like Philip and Nancy, are often wrongly accused of being narrowly Western-centric.

In truth, these brave souls are keeping desperate people in places like Congo from falling completely into disarray. They work under pressures from all directions, including from their home culture, one that promotes the silly notion that flashy things like diamonds last forever.

Sorry, only divine love lasts that long. And peace can only be found when we take our own road less travelled, as Philip and Nancy Wood have.

We still see doctors Philip and Nancy once in a while when they do their shopping. Unable to find supplies in all of Congo, they fly into Uganda's airport in Entebbe and then bus it to Kampala for certain goods before staying for a respite at our place.

Really, Wal-Mart could make a killing in Africa.

Love 101

78

KAMPALA, UGANDA
October 24, 2005

"We are all so much together, but we are all dying of loneliness."
Albert Schweitzer, missionary doctor to Congo, 1875-1965

In my brief and privileged time in the Third World, the most memorable image I've seen comes from Congo.

Walking through a refugee hospital one spring day in that traumatized country, I came across a figure that I can only describe as a human soul with skin stretched over it.

She lay on a bed, motionless, covered with just early-morning shadows and a thin sheet. She was barely identifiable as a woman. Her eye sockets were dark and hollow.

She seemed the embodiment of loneliness. And I, an intruder.

The scene reminds me of home, where I lived from kindergarten to when I left for post-secondary studies 15 years later. During that time, my family operated a rest home in our large Niagara house, where we cared for as many as a couple of dozen residents at once.

Like this African woman, some were frail. Others, less. Some had mental disease. Others, not. Some had loved ones visit. Others, never. Out of sight, out of mind: this was life for many of these discarded people, my extended family.

It comes to mind now, on the heels of World Mental Health Day and after yet another global natural disaster. Pakistan's massive earthquake has thrown thousands into an ocean of grief. Remember, Third World trauma survivors suffer more than those in rich countries. Most have no support during their loss.

Pakistan, for example, gives one per cent of its GDP to healthcare. Mental health gets one per cent of that. Meanwhile, in some sub-Sahara African countries, there's one psychiatrist for five million people. Such is the developing world.

Globally, about 450 million people suffer from mental illnesses such as depression, bipolar disease and schizophrenia. Include a broader range of brain disorders like developmental diseases, epilepsy and stroke, and the number is 1.5 billion.

Sparked by trauma or otherwise, a mental problem at some level will apparently hit one in four of us sometime. Yet nearly half of the world's countries have no mental health policy, and nearly one-third have no program for coping with rising needs.

Not surprisingly, suicide is rising. It now kills about one million a year. The World Health Organization says that's currently higher than annual deaths

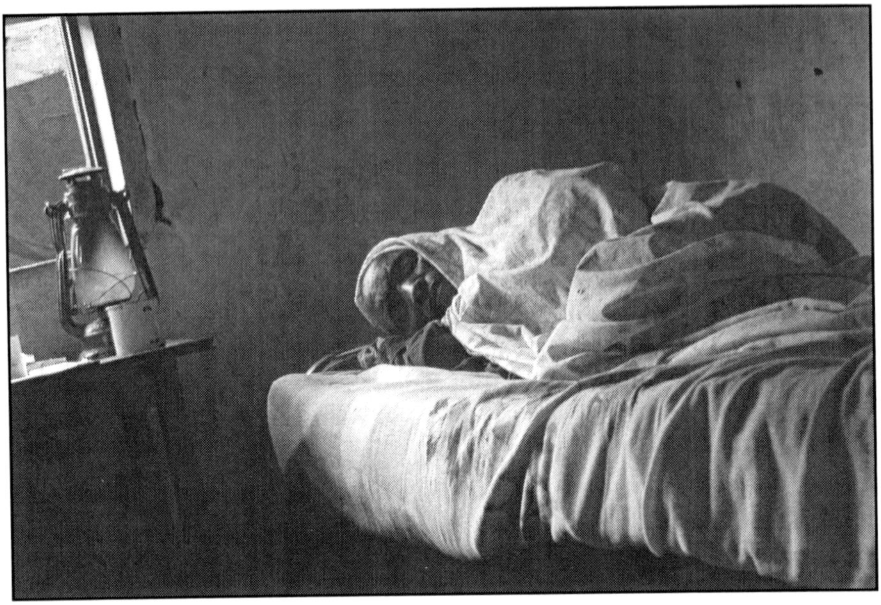

from global conflicts and homicides combined. You didn't suspect that because suicide's terrible stigma makes it hard to talk about. I know. My mother committed suicide.

Now consider that by 2020, clinical depression, which is exasperated by loneliness, is expected to be the second largest contributor to the world's burden of disease.

Loneliness.

Leo Buscaglia would say something about it all. Buscaglia was a world traveller and professor who talked incessantly about something as nebulous as love. In the 1970s he led a popular class at the University of Southern California called exactly that: "Love 1A."

Some of his lectures were later broadcast on PBS. I recall them well, because my fondest memory of home was gathering residents around the TV to watch and listen.

The warm professor would say how peculiar it is that in the West people are measured by what they have, not who they are. And he'd say other incredible things, like "Real love always creates. It never destroys."

One young woman told his class, it's funny how few people hesitate to touch a baby, or pat or hug a strange dog. "And here I sit," she said, "sometimes dying to have someone touch me. And nobody does." With this, she passed the students on all fours. And they met her need.

Dying for touch. Maybe that's how that woman in Congo felt.

Now, in Buscaglia's words, imagine if all people were naked and we closed our eyes. We'd see how the flower girl could be confused with the queen, the jester could pass as the king, and the president could be seen as the migrant worker. "Because there's no greater knowledge than this: that each person in the world, no matter how lowly or princely, is basically a human being."

I know the residents of my family home understood the good professor. The rest of us might still need to work at it, if we're going to brighten life in our own particular circles.

W

Other memories from my family's former business in Niagara, that is from Ye Olde Niagara Home, come easily, particularly on staff-resident power dynamics. The Jack Nicholson movie 'One Flew Over the Cuckoo's Nest' touches on some truths about this, and while I didn't see it until long after, I recall nurses at my family's home clucking like hens when it hit theatres when I was 10.

Of course, besides the smokes I hawked from the medicine cupboard, I was too young to appreciate much. The so-called patients were just old people. So when Big Mike pulled out his droopy penis to show off its length, or when Tom swallowed a brightly painted Easter egg – whole – or when Walter smeared his excrement all over his bedroom wall, I just thought, 'Hey, whatever. They're old.'

In fact, many residents were young but had suffered various abuses, including from themselves, not the least of which was a shot liver or two from too much drink. It all made for the odd scene that's not a lot different from something like on the drama ER.

Take Burt, a lanky 40-something, generally quiet man. He once threatened a nurse with a knife. It was a bit small and dull but dangerous enough to rope "the boss," my father, into a tussle where Dad Froese got his leg broken.

It was the seizures that really got Burt. He had them quite often. During one he thought he saw the flames of the end of the world. So he jumped through a glass door. During another, during my later-teens, he just died. There he is breathing his last soft breath. In my father's gentle arms. In the kitchen. In front of me.

W

I was particularly fond of one resident, Gerry, a truly gentle man who had been a very winning amateur boxer, losing his front teeth in the process, and later, before coming to us, losing other things while in and out of psychiatric care.

He often warned me about the ring, as it made him in his words "punch-drunk." "Thommy, promise me that you'll never get into boxing," he'd say, while he worked outside in our home's vegetable garden or inside Ye Olde Niagara Home, early to late.

He was often thanked in ways more becoming of Jack Nicholson's antagonist Nurse Ratched, a fair example of why some humans should never be left to care for others. Still, most days Gerry would go through it all with his gap-toothed grin, singing about his precious Saviour.

One might not think this would help a young reporter, but some years after these experiences while working in St. Thomas at the Times-Journal, a story unfolded down Highway 3 in Aylmer, Ontario. This sleepy burg of 5,000 got a little bigger when 33 residents from a Toronto rooming house some hours away were bused there in a way described as "Toronto dumping its trash in rural Ontario."

These less fortunate folks, who were not unlike those in my family's former home, were told they were just going on a day trip. Instead they landed at Aylmer's so-called Borden Home, a new facility where it was thought they would be out of the way.

The story exploded all over the press, often written by reporters who didn't (how could they?) have the foggiest about the needs of residents or caregivers. Some editors at the region's larger paper in London also didn't know what to do with a guest column of mine, a rather biting, esoteric piece referring to Gerry boxing his way out of certain difficult days.

Can't use that? Fine. I wrote more straightforwardly, asking why the suits in Ontario's legislature were so lax in responding to long-known needs of non-regulated homes, referring to the Lightman Report, a paper that followed a coroner's inquest into the previous death of an Ontario home resident. Of Ernie Lightman's 148 recommendations, how many had been implemented? One.

The response from a London editor to This Scribe's new piece? "I'm going to move heaven and earth to make sure this runs." And so it did.

Some months later, Borden's residents were taken back to Toronto. The Aylmer home closed. And the newshounds moved onto other things.

It was after I got my first motorcycle, sometime between my boyhood and manhood, when my friend Gerry died. It was of unexplained causes, at the Niagara home where he went to live after ours.

But it was not before I had taken the opportunity to start up the bike and visit him there one summer day, a day I saw him truly happy, still singing, smiling bigger than ever with those missing front teeth.

Such was the education and ride of my youth: Leo Buscaglia, Nurse Ratched and ER. Add the Robin Williams movie 'Awakenings,' a powerful view into these very human themes, with Robert De Niro trapped in that painful body, now on the floor, shaking uncontrollably, looking up at Williams – and you – saying, "L-l-l-l-e-le-le-lear-lear-lear-lear-learnnn."

We know this is something that will grow to become the elephant under the rug that nobody wants to talk about: this difficult issue of caring for the neglected, the sick, the old and the dying.

In Uganda, of course, there are no homes for these people. The needy are taken care of by family. "Home" usually means the village, which is just about any area outside the capital of Kampala, which is where everyone goes during times like formal holidays. The elderly, then, are cared for by whoever might still be in the village.

And if you have no such family? Ask the old of Europe, a place that's going out of business, or at least becoming Eurabia, because nobody is marrying and having kids. Germany is poised to lose the equivalent of the former East Germany's population by 2050. By then, half of Italians will have no brothers, no cousins and no aunts or uncles.

In the developed world you need a birth rate of about 2.1 children per woman to keep a population constant. France has 1.8, Britain 1.7, Germany 1.4, Italy and Spain 1.3. Canada is slightly better, while the United States is fairing best.

So while the Middle East and Africa are dealing with problems of the other extreme (women in both Uganda and Yemen have on average 6.9 children), one wonders who will care for the richer world's elderly. Their cats?

One more reason to take your time when checking out your local seniors' home.

First hell, then college 79

London, Canada
September 25, 2004

We're finishing another back-to-school month, a good time to ask why so many Canadians are underwhelmed with our education system.

It seems "Would you like fries with that?" is the clearest call for a growing number of students, particularly in Ontario, where increasing numbers aren't finishing a new high-school curriculum.

Almost 40 per cent of students didn't graduate on time last year. Half of those quit altogether. International reports show that even before that Canada's drop-out rate was significantly higher than most industrialized nations.

So why do some youth flower in the harshest of places while others wither in the best? Take Grace, a young Ugandan woman I've met. She first went to hell, then college.

Akallao (Grace) Grall was born in a simple village hut and as a young girl feared that, like most Ugandan women, she'd be destined to work the fields. So she was ecstatic when her absent father sent her to a convent high school, St. Mary's.

Her bliss ended on Uganda's Independence Day, in 1996. Fighters in the Lord's Resistance Army, Uganda's cult-like rebels, arrived at St. Mary's with

torches and machine guns and, on orders from fanatical LRA leader Joseph Kony, kidnapped 140 girls.

They led the girls into the muddy night before a persistent nun convinced the young thugs to release most. But they kept 30, including 15-year-old Grace, as their "angels." Girls from St. Mary's were known to be bright, and the LRA wanted clever offspring.

The LRA, which abducts more children than any army worldwide, has about 17,000 children into warfare since 1984. Grace gave up trying to escape after seeing a girl beaten to death. She was taken to nearby Sudan to fight.

The commanders, the girls' so-called husbands, provided nothing. Food came from raiding villages. Or from rats, leaves, roots or, in worst cases, soil. Water was miles from camp. Grace was so malnourished that she was given up for dead and buried alive in a shallow grave. She escaped that.

Six months on, Uganda's army crossed into Sudan and raided their base camp. Hundreds of Kony's young recruits were cut down. Somehow Grace escaped it all for the last time, leading eight other girls through various hostile turns, eventually on top of a tanker truck, to return to Uganda.

Seven months to the day after her abduction, she arrived in safety. It was Good Friday.

"I've seen heads smashed. I've seen people beaten until their sockets swallow their eyes. I've survived hunger. I've survived burial alive and assaults," Grace said. But since then, this young woman has continued to pursue all she ever wanted: an education. It was at Uganda Christian University, near Kampala, that I met her, working toward a career in journalism. Most recently she shared in schools across the United States, at Amnesty International in New York City and on *Oprah*.

Amazingly, Grace hasn't blamed her poverty, though she's poorer than most. She hasn't blamed her ethnicity, gender or social background, but they've all worked against her. She hasn't blamed her parents, who haven't always helped.

She hasn't blamed her abusers, but she's been violated in ways we can't imagine. She hasn't blamed her government, but its politics nearly killed her. Grace hasn't blamed any schools or teachers or high tuition costs. She's simply moved on.

How could all this be? Despite her hard times, or maybe because of them, this young woman somehow learned that decent schooling has as much to do with discovering one's calling – a purpose larger than one's self – as much as anything. As Kierkergaard said, "And now, with God's help, I will become myself."

Do our schools really nurture much of this? If so, why is it that most people live somewhere between a grudging acceptance and active dislike of their jobs?

It's not that our youth have it too easy. Or too hard. Many are simply too distracted to hear much of anything. Some might even get all As in class and still flunk life, becoming typical modern people who live with too much but for too little.

If we want to give them a shot at a real future, then, for starters, why not encourage students to discover, like Grace, that there may be such a thing as a Caller? Otherwise, there are no callings. Only work. And in all honesty, that's not a great reason for anyone to leave bed in the mornings, is it?.

Since this column, Grace has spoken on The Oprah Winfrey Show and to a U.S. Senate Committee about her experiences as an LRA child soldier. Now married with one child, she has continued her studies in the Boston, MA area, getting scholarships at Gordon College and Clark University, in Welman and Worcestor, MA. Her interest is conflict resolution and international development. She recently told me that when the time comes to return to Uganda, she will be careful in her career steps due to her profile.

"If I became a journalist, I don't think I'd be alive very long."

In Africa, the bicycle rules 80

Kampala, Uganda
May 7, 2005

I am not a cyclist. Not a real cyclist. My hands are not cyclist's hands. They're the hands of a writer. Sensitive. Not mechanically inclined. They've rarely held a torque wrench. Never bled when it's slipped. They're not calloused from hard rides. Not gnarled, or red from the cold.

The rest of me is equally non-cyclist. Get out the levelling plumb. I'm a half-bubble shy of straight. My bicycle frames are smaller than for other riders my height. But I need an extra long seat-post. Raise the handlebars and bring them closer, high but tight. That gets me by.

Yet, I am a cyclist. I easily recall learning to ride on that small backyard hill by myself. I can measure my life by bikes I've owned. I can feel myself crouching low, flying down Mountain Road like a pilot, every morning to school, for years. I'd later ride to the beach on Lake Erie to watch the sun rise. I've carried bikes up stairs to newsrooms in both Canada and Yemen. I'll soon bring my Yemen bike to Africa.

Yes, I am a cyclist. Because I know a bicycle is never just a bicycle. It's an extension of who we are. It's that big Christmas wish. It's why last summer I came home from Freewheel Cycle in Dundas to proudly tell my wife I just bought a "bad-ass bike."

"What is that?" Jean asked.

It's a bike that puts fire under your backside. Full suspension. Special geometry. Aluminum-carbon frame. Fire red. It's my Canadian bike, awaiting my return to go through the gears on the escarpment that makes Hamilton such a special bike place.

I am not African. Not a real African. In fact, I'm as un-African as imaginable. In grade school they called me Whitey. Hair. Eyebrows. Lashes. Everything. I'd be voted the kid least likely to ever live in Africa.

No, I am not African. I'll likely never know the loss of a loved one from AIDS or see the savagery of civil war. I'll never personally feel the cold grip of Third World poverty or the deadly hand of preventable disease. As a Westerner, alas Canadian, I feel more like a citizen of ancient Rome, going anywhere, anytime, with clout.

Yet, I am African. Because in Africa, the bicycle rules. It not only returns life to its natural pace, but the bicycle is the great leveller. This is the type of truth that hits like when the ground rushes up to meet you. Regardless of who you are or where you're from, when you're out there pedalling as hard as the guy, or gal, beside you, you're reminded how we all have the same need for, if nothing else, oxygen.

Yes, I'm African to the extent I can, in a small way, connect with Africans. Or their bikes, which are like our granddads' tall, single-geared uprights. They carry everything from bananas to beds, besides passengers (usually gals sitting sidesaddle). A new one costs 90,000 shillings. That's about 80 dollars, two months pay for the average Ugandan. With spare parts, it can last decades. And it saves gas, now $1.31 a litre in Uganda.

I am not a boy. Not a real boy. Father of Elizabeth-Katherine and a soon-to-be-born son, I turn 40 this bike season. Have had arthritis in my back for 20 years now. It's getting tiring. So for longer trips, despite Jean's worries, I'll have to get a motorcycle. Just picked out my machine from Kampala's motorcycle alley. It's for the rough stuff as much as anything. Same type I had as a teen. Soon it joins our growing family.

No, I am not a boy. Yet, I am a boy. The same one who used to rise early with the morning mist and, with that red Honda, explore Niagara. I wonder if it will be the same here along these red-dirt roads, in the lush countryside, on the equator. I wonder if I'll feel like the African kids I've seen who, with their own two-wheelers, look so bright-eyed and full of wonder.

If so, I think I'll be very happy. And free.

The lessons of the Lunatic Express

81

KAMPALA, UGANDA
March 20, 2006

Bring in the workers and bring up the rails.
We're going to lay down the tracks and tear up the trails.
Open her heart, let the life blood flow.
Gotta get on our way, 'cause we're moving too slow.
Gordon Lightfoot, "Canadian Railroad Trilogy"

It's not the Glacier Express climbing through the Swiss Alps. It's not Vietnam's Reunification Express winding into the more exotic jungles of the world. And it's certainly not the Orient Express, that legendary locomotive of opulence and intrigue immortalized by Agatha Christie.

It's the Lunatic Express, and it's Africa's own.

When the British East Africa Company announced in the late 19th century that it would cut through more than 1,000 kilometres of wilderness to lay track inland over the Great Rift Valley, across equatorial highlands and down Lake Victoria's shores into today's Uganda, people called it a lunatic line. Its train became the Lunatic Express, and the moniker stuck, even as the insane brilliance of the project came to light. A six-week trip was shortened to 24 hours, and East Africa opened to the world.

Today, for 14 hours and US$54, you can still ride the Lunatic Express between Kenya's port city Mombassa and its capital, Nairobi. That's longer than the two-hour flight but about 50 times cheaper than the Orient Express, London to Venice – the type of transport I've only had the means to once walk past.

Now, if concessionaires get their way, today's Lunatic Express – a cracked-china, apron-stained ride for which you'll want all your immunizations – will get new life. The South African firm Rift Valley Railway Consortium has won a bid to run all of Uganda's and Kenya's state-owned, debt-burdened railways for 25 years. It will spend $320 million to improve lines and rolling stock.

First, the final hurdles. One is that Uganda needs to compensate its national rail workers or Kenya will close the deal alone. And being shut out would be a blow to Uganda.

One obstacle to long-term development here and in Africa generally is the high cost of moving freight to and from ocean ports. Improved rail transport would get sluggish trucks off the roads and help Africa to market its untapped resources. If fairer global trade policies ever evolve, that's the type of infrastructure that would give Africans real hope instead of just Western handouts.

But this is about more than chasing progress. It's about helping a fragmented continent discover its spirit. If you've ever travelled significant distances by train, you know what I mean. Without the early construction of the Canadian Pacific Railway, for example, Canada's story would be different.

For at least some time it would have stayed, like Africa, a vast, disjointed collection of regions with different languages and cultures. Instead, we sense that, as Robertson Davies said, "Canada has a soul, and we should get to know it better."

A dozen summers ago, I discovered this myself when taking the train from Ontario to the Pacific and back. There was nothing to do but sit. Sit and see the many postcard scenes. Sit and understand that there's a certain art to living.

On this level, taking the train is about forgetting those trappings that make us huff and puff down the fast track to nowhere in particular. It's about forgoing television and reaching for a book. It's about walking past the car to take your bike. It's about leaving work early to see your kids.

Taking the train is understanding that we're each on a journey, unable to see where any one track may lead but believing through faith that there's a station at the end and it's a destination as worthwhile as the journey.

Taking the train is about a kind of fabled youthfulness, about leaving space for one's imagination, for the unexpected and for change.

It's about getting to know your soul.

Whether we live in Africa or Canada, or on the moon for that matter, this all points to living in the moment. And towards what we, with some divine help, might someday, somewhere become.

My long ride from Toronto to Vancouver on a buffed-chrome train dubbed 'The Canadian' unfolded just before Canadians took trains and planes and buses to Quebec to join the fight of Canada's life, the 1995 Quebec referendum on separation.

On the eve of the vote, a last-ditch unity rally was cobbled together and I found myself in the rush; stepping on a midnight bus, camera around neck, recorder in pocket, just gone.

In the morning, October 30, just past the historic CN station on Rue de la Gauchetiere, in Place du Canada, a square in downtown Montreal, some 100,000 Canadians asked Quebecers to think about it all, that maybe Robertson Davies was right: that Canada does have a soul, one that is deep and wide and full of passion. (The only other time I've been so overwhelmed by Canadian flags was while walking down the streets of Dieppe, France, where they still remember the Canadian boys who liberated them from the Nazis.)

Besides obligatory photos of Prime Minister Jean Chrétien and other earnest politicians, I remember getting a shot of a small sign that poked up through the sea of heads, a plain placard that simply read "St. Thomas, Ont., Loves Quebec."

Back on the bus on the highway, with an early version of a mobile phone, I sat on the toilet lid reporting details back to the St. Thomas newsroom. And as it was, the following day's tally was tipped in stunning fashion: 51 per cent of Quebecers voting to stay within Canada, 49 per cent wanting to go. Canadians, known for their soft-spoken politeness, decided to get bold, and it saved the country.

Quebec hasn't had a referendum since.

After stops for relatives en route, that summer trip on 'The Canadian' ended in Vancouver, where I hopped to the island and drove a rental north for some hours, through forests of Douglas firs bigger than many African homes, and eventually up to Tofino, a relaxed community of trekkers and artists and old VW vans with ugly curtains. I stayed just long enough to wade in the Pacific and sleep in a crowded hostel between some recreational drug users.

On the drive back down the island, several passengers joined me, including a world traveller from the UK who hadn't seen home in years and a young, very pregnant native woman about to deliver. Halfway through the return, she insisted I drop her off in an unknown burg where she thought she could find some kind of bed.

Such are the lives of Canadian aboriginals, a people group as desperate as they are misunderstood in a culture where they've never felt at home. Today, half live on reserves and half are younger than 25. Their level of disillusionment is anyone's guess.

Sometime before, I had learned something about this while reporting on a couple of St. Thomas grandparents and their half-native grandchildren.

The two children were born to a white mother and native father. Neither parent could care for them, so they were given to their mother's parents until foster care arrived. The children, however, bonded with their grandparents, who then applied to adopt.

When the local native reserve, the Oneida (or Onyata'aka), then also laid claim to the kids, the wormy can opened. Children's Aid told the grandparents to deliver the youngsters to their doorstep or they'd be thrown in jail.

The grandparents called me. The Times-Journal's presses rumbled. And the fight was on. The lawyers and psychologists and social workers prepared for the complex dance to determine where the children would fare best, particularly taking note of native self-identity and their stages of so-called wondering and wandering.

As the months dragged on, the children were allowed to stay with the grandparents. Then, in a twist, the snarly and costly legal wrangling was avoided, thanks to the grandparents' church. It stepped in to negotiate directly with the Onyata'aka. With a literal pass of the peace pipe, elders from the church and reserve met and struck a deal giving the grandparents official custody, recognizing the community's role with the kids. Interestingly, in native tradition, children such as these, born to both native and white parents, are recognized as bridges between cultures, unique agents of healing.

Of course, journalists love to give each other awards for putting their noses into these things. And since this mirrored a similar page in The Froese History Book, when I was the subject of a bitter children's custody battle, it was only more interesting.

So This Scribe was invited to Toronto for steak and wine and a hip party; a long night of back-patting; and awards given by Sun Media, a Canadian company birthed from the ashes of the Toronto Telegram, the paper that had covered my own family affair in Berlin 30 years earlier (See page 113 to 114). A big deal was made of it all and everyone left happy.

Today, the children's grandmother is still alive and stays in the picture of their lives. And the children? The boy has fared well, still at home and finishing high school. His slightly older sister, meanwhile, left home early and, like the young native I drove south on Vancouver Island, became a young single mom. Somehow wandering, somehow wondering.

The chrome-domed 'Canadian,' meanwhile, still runs cross-country.

Getting over yourself? Priceless

82

Kampala, Uganda
November 3, 2007

And now this, from Michael J. Fox.

"If you were to rush into this room and announce you'd struck a deal with God, that the 10 years since my diagnosis could be magically taken and traded for 10 more years as the person I was before, I'd tell you to take a hike. I'd never want that life again, a sheltered narrow existence fuelled by fear and made liveable by insulation, isolation and self-indulgence."

You'll recall that Fox, a Canadian, and one of Parkinson's disease's better-known voices, was Alex Keaton on the hit show *Family Ties,* a rather comical TV character who once told his parents that his biggest fantasy is to roll in bed, naked, with mounds of money.

And now? This candid quote from Fox, which I recently stumbled across during an office cleanup in my African home? Thud. It falls like reality. Fox now easily tells of his freedom, no longer "very driven and very ambitious and very consumed by outside things" but rather into "very inside things."

The price? Losing your health. Finding your soul? Priceless.

Days after I rediscovered Fox's quote, John Angle, a successful banker from Los Angeles, told me, "Coming to Africa reminds me to live with less. We don't need half of what we have."

The price? Foregoing a luxurious holiday elsewhere. Seeing everyday simplicity? Priceless.

Shortly afterwards, in a grass hut, an American friend told me of his desire to rescue Obvious, a Zimbabwean student struggling to get even one meal a day for his family in that disastrous country. The price? Taking a minute to hear of a stranger's need. Knowing I have food? Priceless.

A few days later, the cops stopped me for talking on my mobile while driving, during an emergency call from Alice, our house help, who was in hospital to deliver a child. "Tell the magistrate," said the officer, grabbing my phone, before telling me that Uganda's floods have dislocated his family. We entered into an all-too-common dance of police bribery.

The price? Twenty thousand shillings, about Can$13, or two days police wages. Being reminded of thousands of homeless Ugandans? Priceless.

The next day my gardener Richard approached me, shaking like a leaf like last Christmas when Emmanuel, his four-day-old son, died. He needed emergency medicine for his three-year-old daughter, Peace. She'd been vomiting all night with malaria, which now kills 70,000 Ugandans, mostly children, annually.

The price? Fifteen Canadian dollars. Knowing this maybe saved a little child's life? Priceless.

That night Alice phoned, screaming in horrific pain, from her cellphone to mine. "Mr. Thom, the baby's not coming out!" In a surreal 9/11 moment where anyone can now relay their own death via mobile, I knew Alice could be perishing in childbirth, just like 6,000 Ugandan women do every year.

She survived, and I soon held newborn Divine. "Mr. Thom, tell me a prophecy," Alice said. "Tell me she's going to 'America.'"

Noting that I'm not much of a prophet, I could only muster "Alice, with a name like Divine, she'll probably eventually go to heaven, a much better place."

The price of helping Alice? Besides her transport, and that police bribe? About 20 bucks Canadian for the gloves, buckets and cotton that Ugandan mothers supply at their own deliveries. And holding Divine? Priceless.

This has been the first 16 days of my family's recent return to Uganda. And life's beat will go on like this, interesting and disturbing, for the next eight months of our current tenure.

So am I impressed that some 53 heads of state, and the Queen – one of the most pampered persons on the planet – are about to arrive for Uganda's first-ever Commonwealth summit? Not really. Not when you see these other folks here.

Because it's been said that if you say just one prayer in your entire lifetime, "Thank you," that it would suffice. And here, unlike in the rich world's credit-card culture, where someone has somehow switched all the price tags, you can actually find the right headspace to do this.

It's called getting over yourself.

So to Divine and those others who are heroic and true survivors, thank you for helping me to at least whisper today, and if I'm fortunate tomorrow, that simple gratitude.

Gardeners are common in Uganda, especially here at the university where I live, a campus that sits on 80 acres of lush landscape with some areas needing more development and work than others. And it's natural to develop a friendship with one's gardener, such as I have with Richard.

So, few scenes have disturbed me as much as seeing Richard weeping hopelessly a couple of Christmases ago after his newborn son, Emmanuel, died, virtually on the day of Richard's own birthday.

With certain views of the spiritual realm, the first thing many Africans believe in this scenario is that they're being punished by God for something they've done. And so the first thing I told Richard was "Richard, you have to know that this not has not happened because of anything that you've done."

Darling Doctor Wife notes that little Emmanuel, (which means 'God with us'),

likely had an infection at birth, undetected due to poor testing at the clinics here, and, without treatment, it was no surprise he died shortly later.

And so the funerals, or burials as they're called here, continue. "I've gone to my friend's [brother's ... cousin's] burial today" is something still heard week-in, week-out, all too matter-of-factly, from Richard and other Ugandans in our circles. Like with little Emmanuel, much of the time nobody even knows the exact cause of death.

About this monkey business

83

Hamilton, Canada
July 12, 2007

Polls suggest that most Canadians take the middle ground on evolution, believing that life is created but also adapts to changing environmental needs.

The question remains, however: Do we believe we've evolved from an apelike being, as Darwin theorized? Or do we believe human adaptations have been less dramatic, and humans have always had a higher place among living things?

And how does this all affect how we see others in our human family? As someone who's worked extensively in other cultures – the Arab world and now Africa – I find this an interesting underlying aspect of the evolution debate.

At its worst, Darwin's theories have been exploited hideously. Hitler often used the German word for evolution, *entwicklung*, citing "lower human types," and often spoke of "monstrosities halfway between man and ape."

But even without such madmen, 20th century Social Darwinism brought its own harmful mentalities, often operating under the surface of daily life, arguably even now as global disparities deepen. Further, how does believing our ancestors were anything less than human affect how we see ourselves personally?

I, for one, would stay in bed with the drapes closed.

There are scientists who see reasonable evidence that intelligent beings with a purpose, like you, have originated from an intelligent source with a purpose. I buy that, because the alternative seems not only harmful to others but deflating personally.

This brief item originally ran as a letter to the editor at the tail end of a mid-summer debate folks in Hamilton decided to have on how we all got here anyway. Raised were names like Richard Dawkins, an evolutionist who is also known

for writing 'The God Delusion,' which notes that religion is not just wrong but terribly dangerous.

Richard, tell us something we don't know. Of course religious people are dangerous. Open the papers. And irreligious folks are pretty difficult too. Open the same papers.

When bright guys like Dawkins say that "opposition to evolution is laughable to anyone knowing even a fraction of the data," they're also creating an unfortunate zeitgeist that says if you don't buy into evolution then you're a boob. Not so. Some equally bright guys – Michael J. Behe, author of 'Darwin's Black Box,' for example – say that in light of new discoveries, like subatomic designs, Darwinism is, in fact, turning into a rather inadequate theory.

Or take British philosopher Antony Flew, a deep-thinking chap who for many years was the world's best-known atheist, but who now says that new intelligent design observations have led him to an unexpected belief in a Creator.

Or there's the eminent Phillip Johnson, author of 'Darwin on Trial,' among his penetrating books on this issue, a brainy fellow who This Scribe personally had the embarrassing chance to borrow a tie from on one day, on the Strand in London, while hobnobbing with a crowd that was asking how to bring more truth and hope into the public square.

My observation is that, like Dawkins and other evolutionists, these guys have personal beliefs that push them in their own direction, in this case to creationism or intelligent design. But they're also running a ramp of reason before taking any wild leaps of faith.

My other observation is that as we sit in the stands and watch all this, most laypeople aren't fully familiar with the issues, specifically that of adaptation to environmental changes.

Scientists of various stripes agree that my short-haired husky Rex and a long-haired wolf in Canada's arctic could have the same very-great-great granddaddy. In fact, this sort of modest change through natural selection within the same species can explain how humanity's so-called races, with their slight differences, could have originated from one created pair.

But some scientists, like Behe or Johnson, note it's very improbable that Rex evolved from, say, a cat. Likewise, they argue that an oceanic blob likely can't become a fish, can't become a mammal on all fours, can't become a monkey-like man, can't become, well, you, regardless of how much time has passed. They don't believe the data supports this type of cross-species, simple-to-complex, evolution.

As a lay spectator, I also can't help but wonder if evolutionists are not caught in a trap of their own making when they insist (Richard Lewontin first coined this phrase) that "We can't allow a Divine Foot in the door." Why not? Doesn't this just stack the deck? Is it not better to simply, as Socrates said, "Follow the evidence wherever it leads"?

As a traveller, I'm interested in how evolution theory at its worst (like religiosity at its worst) can lead us to treat each other in ways we'd rather not talk about.

Hitler manipulated a Europe that had immersed itself in Darwinism and its related racial and social theories in the late 19th century, before it bathed itself in blood in the 20th. The Jews were almost wiped off the map because Germans were systematically taught that some humans, namely Jews and blacks, are less evolved.

Before that kind of wonky teaching, there were still atrocities like the slave trade, when Africans were shackled in ships, piled on each another in the dark, in their own excrement, and fear, with freedom only in sickness and the resulting dump overboard.

But maybe the common denominator is that there's always big trouble when some human beings believe that they're more valuable than others. For a recent made-in Africa example, we have Rwanda.

This is not to say that such evil is taught on the blackboards of today's evolution classrooms – teachings which, by the way, permeate the West but don't exist in much of the world. Still, given our bloody track record, our propensity to butcher each other so easily, it seems to me that's it's a good idea to ask what kind of scientific – or religious – views help in our relations and which ones lead us down the garden path of animal-like behaviour.

Personally, believing that our great uncle's cousin (a few billion removed) might have been related to a chance-evolved monkey-man – rather than a created being with purpose – doesn't make me respect my global neighbour, including you, very much.

It doesn't make me feel so hot when looking in the mirror either.

I suspect the monkeys who run across our front yard in Africa would say the same.

These thoughts may not win me a popularity contest among some, but I'm still safer than academics who dare bring such debate into the college classroom. For a more stimulating look, I refer you to Ben Stein's thoughtful docudrama "Expelled: No Intelligence Allowed" (www.expelledthemovie.com), which takes a hard look at how academic freedom on this issue is threatened in today's schools of so-called higher learning, where, in Stein's words, science is expelling smart ideas from the classroom.

Historically among the most spiritually active continents on earth, Africa is no stranger to both the harm and wonder of religious belief.

In the case of East Africa, a modern Christian revival lasting from as early as the 1930s to as late as the 1980s – from Rwanda to Uganda and Kenya – has had lasting effects. After the dark days of Idi Amin, Uganda was particularly touched by the movement of the so-called 'Balokoles' or 'Saved Ones.'

This had theological roots in earlier Western revivals, but became an indigenous African phenomena. Some sectarianism followed, namely charismatics breaking from the Anglican Church, Uganda's dominant group, which was birthed from the Western mission movement of the 19th century. East Africa has thus been left a heavily Christianized culture, with Muslims a minority.

Ugandans, who are weary from a harsh preceding generation, have enjoyed benefits of this. Many argue that its exemplary performance in reducing its rate of AIDS, from as high as 30 per cent to as low as five per cent, is the result of this spiritual awakening. Still, this section takes a harder look at all this: some riddles and paradoxes.

With the exception of one other, these columns are the only ones in Ninety-Nine Windows that didn't previously fall on the opinion pages of mainstream newspapers. Instead, they were written for Christian Week, a national paper for Canada's Christian community. The last selection, "Freedom," ran in Uganda's national daily, the New Vision.

Africa's religious makeup will only loom larger as the world continues to flatten and shrink. Africa now has about 400 million Christians, about half of the continent's population. The Old World's missionized are becoming the New World's missionaries.

And so I hope my take on this growing global demographic is fair. And maybe, in the right spots, seasoned with just enough salt.

Opposite page photo: *A church in rural Congo, near the refugee community of Oicha.*

Riddles and Paradoxes

WINDOWS

Monday morning hunger 84

Kampala, Uganda
May 26, 2006

We're driving home with African radio on, and this is what we hear: Christian tunes. Nice.

Unlike in Canada, contemporary Christian music is mainstream here in Uganda. Yes, this is the so-called Global South, the part of the planet that, if you don't yet realize, is shaping 21st-century Christendom.

By 2025 South America is expected to have more than 600 million Christians, about double the number in North America. Asia will have 460 million, almost catching Europe. And the dynamic African Church will climb to 630 million.

Incredibly, 100 years ago, at the dawn of the modern Pentecostal movement, this continent had just 10 million believers. But these are the charismatic days of Afro-Evangelism. And they're staggering.

Visit the Redeemed Church of God in Lagos, Nigeria, and see an average crowd of 300,000. Folks meet in the open air to dance and shout and pray, sometimes all muggy night. The once evangelized Africans are now sending missionaries.

So on Kampala radio this evening, finishing the Top 7 at 7, there's a DJ doing her thing and singing the praises of a big miracle service that you can't miss. She's repetitive and hyper, and I wonder, since it's the holiday Easter Monday, if she's a fill-in.

Suddenly she thunders through my truck's poor speakers, "Jesus Christ! It's eight o'clock! My shift is over, and I've got to get out of here!"

Gulp. So long.

Now, I've heard God's holy name tossed around in this unholy fashion by other Christians in Uganda. Here, it's less a curse and more a casual expression of—well, I'm not sure. Annoyance? Still, there's a significant disconnect to the third commandment, the one about not misusing God's name.

So while Christianity is flowing here, it's often a mile wide and an inch deep. Is that stadium rally really revival, or emotionalism? Mass hysteria?

As put by a Canadian colleague, a counsellor here who has seen the issues, "Nobody knows what to do Monday morning. They're uninformed biblically." Just like the Church in, say, ancient Corinth.

Growing deep while wide has always been Christianity's challenge. And that's interesting, because the new Christendom of the Third World is just like the early Church. As then, signs and wonders and personal revelations dominate. There's neoorthodoxy and wonky spiritualism. Also, as then, there's an array of competing sects.

Another Western colleague here, a theology professor, tells me, "Something good eventually will come of it. But right now it's like mud-wrestling: a big free-for-all with no rules."

So yes, discipleship is needed.

Christian or not, many Africans also need deep inner healing. No surprise, considering so many have held hands with sexual brokenness and AIDS, with grinding poverty, with bloody civil war. What often lingers is a certain anger and denial, a failure to understand one's self and a heartbreaking inability to forgive. Rwanda, for example, was Christian during its hate-filled genocide.

The common image of Africa's needs is different. It's one-dimensional: a bony child with a bloated stomach and flies on the face. But spirituality, for better or worse, has always profoundly touched all of life here. The question is, what form is it taking?

Challenges of the Western Church revolve more around fighting secularism. Then there's the gulf between conservatives and liberals, mainline denominations now dying because, as one critic put it, they no longer appeal to people believing in God but to "Wiccan, vegetarians, sandal-wearers and people who play the recorder."

A very different set of issues is on the larger, global horizon. Come and look. Stay for a while if you can. Maybe you can help give a needy somebody a different kind of bread.

Doomsday diversions

85

Kampala, Uganda
July 7, 2006

After 20 years of terrorizing northern Ugandans, Joseph Kony and his hoods in the Lord's Resistance Army have made it to the big time. Their story, and that of the thousands of children they've killed or made into child soldiers, has made *Oprah*.

The UN and Washington are also, finally, showing more interest in this motley crew of East African guerrilla fighters, a cult that wants to see Uganda's constitution replaced by the Ten Commandments. Apparently they've somehow missed "Thou shalt not kill."

Uganda actually has a history of false prophets, self-styled leaders who seemingly wake up one day to declare they've heard God's voice, before they con innocent seekers and give bad names to those who truly do know the Divine's thoughts.

Kony's cousin, self-proclaimed prophetess Alice Lakwana, previously led the so-called Holy Spirit Movement. She sent hundreds to their deaths after telling them her special body oil would protect them against government bullets and her stones would turn to bombs.

Then there are Uganda's doomsday cults. About 600 followers died in one mass suicide at the turn of the millennium.

Affecting more folks here, though, are the everyday quacks pushing doctrines of blessings and curses to grow their congregations, sometimes into the thousands. Big churches, big cars and big miracles are all good for a certain segment of the so-called "Born-Agains" or "Balokoles," Christians who have bought into the American Dream, African-style.

Unlike traditional charismatics, Catholics or Anglicans, they wield authority because they recognize and fight old African customs like ancestral worship and witchcraft. Leaders attract money from members who simply want freedom from such fears.

What hasn't really caught on in this corner of the planet, though, is this type of thing: *Beyond Armageddon*, a Western-made End Times documentary I recently spotted while in a Kampala supermarket.

Watching the video at home, I wasn't surprised to see it full of premillennial dispensationalist theory, that view of Christian eschatology that links the birth of modern Israel to the end of our age and the imminent second coming of Christ. The world is coming to an end. Now.

Originally popularized by English minister John Darby, the theory has roared to life in 100 or so years, growing huge with blockbusters like Hal Lindsey's *The Late Great Planet Earth* and, more recently, Tim LaHaye and

Jerry Jenkins' Left Behind novels, which have sold more than 50 million copies.

It has some problems. One is pernicious date-setting, something that really doesn't help the Church's credibility. Lindsey, for example, predicted Christ's return by 1988. And when theory is presented as fact, ask yourself how the Church, especially in the powerful West, approaches, say, justice in the Middle East, specifically the Arab world, where I've lived and seen things rather closely.

The truth is that dispensationalism is one interpretation of mysterious biblical prophecies, and in time it may or may not be proven right. Justice for the marginalized, on the other hand, is something the Bible speaks about rather clearly.

In a Third World context, promises of the prosperity gospel are like bounty to the starving, which is, maybe, the most interesting aspect about false prophecy. Whether in Africa or the other side of the ocean, it takes a guise that's most relevant to its culture.

If you're physically comfortable, you have the luxury of wondering about that age-old question of how big a bang, or how helpless a whimper, the world will end with. If you're homeless and hungry, your theology will be dominated by more material ideas.

Too bad the former can become such a preoccupation and the latter a fixation, meaningless diversions and hollow purchases and so far off the path of real life.

For Joseph Kony it appears the end of the world, or at least his war, is imminent. The core of the LRA, believed to running from Sudan to Central African Republic, is still being accused of carrying out child abductions. Kony's lawyers in The Hague say the allegations are nonsense.

What is known is that Kony has knocked off at least one of his deputies recently and, so the African papers say, now another. The only question is if he ate his most recent victim in an elaborate demonic ceremony, as claimed by Uganda's more spicy tabloid, the Red Pepper. Meanwhile, tens of thousands of formerly displaced Ugandans have been able to move back to their homes in war-ravaged northern Uganda.

Rabbit City 86

Kampala, Uganda
March 15, 2007

Good grief. Just when you thought you knew the rules around here, where it's a given that cultural change is painfully slow, along comes a curveball that really makes your head spin.

The latest loopy news comes from Jinja. This Ugandan burg near my home,

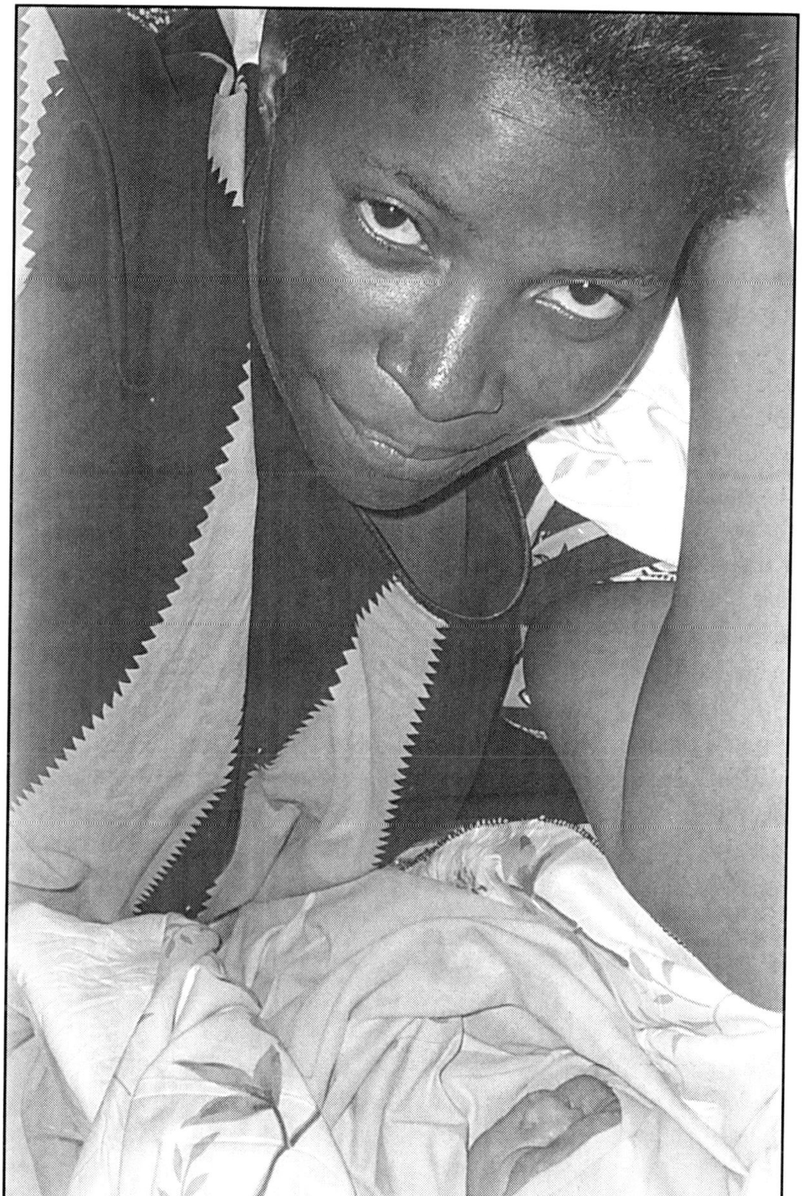

known to tourists as the source of the Nile River, is apparently to be nick-named Rabbit City.

This, after a Chinese health company visited with its sex-enhancing drugs, which led to Jinja's mayor telling residents to reproduce "like rabbits" in order for Jinja to triple its size to 500,000 and acquire formal city status.

You may find this strange, considering that – unlike Western countries like

Canada facing a birth dearth – many African nations already have a crushing number of youth. In Uganda, almost three in five folks are under 18, and Ugandan women still have, on average, seven kids.

Even though President Yoweri Museveni wants Uganda to emulate China in its rising economy, he likes his country's sky-high growth rate. Uganda currently has a population of 25 million, which is set become 180 million by 2050.

Gulp. Apparently the obvious questions about food and education and health care and employment aren't coming to mind. Nor, apparently, does anyone seem too concerned about whether proliferating like rabbits will leave enough water to drink, never mind worrying about irrigation, hydro or the family car.

In fact, 10 countries along the 6,000 km Nile River basin – nations expected to double in size in 20 years – are facing a water crisis. One cause is deforestation (all that wood is used for cooking), which hinders rain cycles and causes drought.

Yemen, where I lived previously, is another country among the world's fastest growing, and driest. That's strange, seeing as a country like Yemen is thoroughly Muslim while Uganda and much of East Africa is strongly Christian.

So guidance on all of this is not coming from the world's two largest faiths. Why not?

Muslims have traditionally believed that spreading Islam is dependant on having large families. Have more kids, spread the faith faster. At the same time, raise your personal value and family honour within the community.

Meanwhile, some Christians, certainly in Africa, have rather wonky ideas about birth control. Take a recent Christian marriage seminar I attended. One Ugandan participant said since no form of birth control is "safe," none should be practiced. Period.

To which my wife, an obstetrician and the mother of our two children, replied, "Life isn't safe." (Neither, by the way, is pregnancy, especially in the developing world.)

Of course life isn't meant to be safe. It's meant to be an adventure where we make decisions with a sense of stewardship and partnership with our Creator, not with blind or fearful obedience to out-of-context commands. Remember, Genesis' "*Be fruitful and multiply*" was given to specific people, in a specific time, for a specific reason. It's about as applicable to us as "Go forth to the mountain and sacrifice your only son."

True, as the Psalmist says, children are a gift from God, a very beautiful gift that Westerners can easily miss when distracted by cultural trappings of so-called success. Planning for children is not only a personal issue, to be worked-out privately and thoughtfully within the home; it's also one that's deeply spiritual.

But if gluttony can come from the gift of food and if drunkenness can come from the gift of wine, then overpopulation and the suffering it brings much of our planet can come from overindulging in children. Children are simply not meant to satisfy our deepest longings. God is.

This issue won't go away. The planet is on pace to grow to nine billion souls by 2050. Expect various wars over limited resources like water. In places like Africa, expect these conflicts to exacerbate politico-religious strife – not to mention poverty, disease and, ironically, the death of innocent children first.

Canada, which has one-fifth of the world's fresh water, will likely just be a spectator. And a rather comfortable one at that. But it can always export its Living Water. That, after all, is what's really needed around here. Or anywhere.

See no evil 87

KAMPALA, UGANDA
April 13, 2007

Evil is never easy to look in the eye. So it's no surprise *The Last King of Scotland* is getting mixed reactions in this corner of the world, where the story – both its real and Hollywood version – unfolds.

The film – which won an Oscar for Forest Whitaker's powerful performance as megalomaniac ruler Idi Amin Dada – recently opened here in Kampala. It's been quite a splash.

Keep in mind that Uganda, a country of 25 million, has just two small Cineplexes. But Whitaker showed up for the première gala, as did director Kevin Macdonald. The red carpets came out, and President Yoweri Museveni and his wife joined the entourage.

The movie, after all, was shot in Uganda, a place that has as much film infrastructure as a frozen waffle. Hollywood never comes here. If producers even reach Africa, which they are lately (*Hotel Rwanda, Shooting Dogs, The Constant Gardener, Blood Diamond*), they'll shoot in South Africa or Kenya.

Still, Ugandans can take a bow for their proverbial 15 minutes of fame. Several cast were Ugandan. More so, the film showed plenty of local sites just minutes from your theatre seat.

Which is where the pain comes in. When you see a familiar Kampala landmark, it's that much easier to connect the dots to that distant loved one who may have died in Amin's horrible era, when 300,000 Ugandans were killed or simply "disappeared."

Yes, Amin was a monster. So one criticism from some Ugandans is that the often charming, even comical, man portrayed by Whitaker was not real. "Amin was not funny," is how one viewer put it. Then again, evil rarely runs around with a pitchfork and horns.

At the other extreme, some have literally laughed, as if watching a comedy.

A newspaper headline noted "Amin taught us to laugh at tragedy."

Strange thing. Even here at the Ugandan Christian university where I live, during a recent Sunday message, when they were challenged to live pure lives and avoid consequences like AIDS, plenty of students laughed. It's one way to push one's pain to a deep and comfortable place of denial. Of course, anyone can build that kind of unreal world, such castles in the sky. The problem comes when we try to live in them.

I wonder if that same inability to face evil is what some Christians struggle with when a disturbing movie like this comes along. One North American Christian film website calls it "extremely morally offensive," and a reviewer warns, "My advice is to stay far away."

Sure, the movie was offensive. The real Amin, after all, would kill folks personally with a sledgehammer. Then there's the obligatory Hollywood sex. During this, President's Museveni's wife, an outspoken Christian, even covered her eyes.

Then again, the whores and thieves that hung around Jesus weren't really the epitome of clean living. And wouldn't the lives of several Old Testament greats be rated R, too? Isn't this – seeing evil and its consequences – the exact point of it all? Isn't this why these Bible stories are left for us?

Evil, by nature, will always be offensive. Christians, by nature, are meant to expose it. Some may have to cover our eyes in the process, but Christians are never called to pretend we don't live in the fallen and broken world that we do.

In this sense, *The Last King of Scotland* is a fine character study and an honest look at how darkness can settle in any human heart. It's also a reminder of one of the great truths that Jesus taught: life is hard.

Even by African standards, Ugandans know this well. After Amin's bloody reign of terror, another 400,000 Ugandans died in civil war. Soon after, AIDS arrived. The ensuing road to recovery still hasn't been easy.

Some might feel a need to laugh at all that. Others might run screaming in the opposite direction. But to engage culture and the broader world, thinking believers are called to something better.

88 *'God is not a black woman.' Is She?*

Kampala, Uganda
October 15, 2007

Okay, here's a question. What is the Gospel?

No, really. I'm not being facetious. What *is* the Gospel?

I ask because summer reading during my recent tenure in Canada was different than usual, especially after sitting on the side of my bed one late, warm night, reminded anew that we are more sinful than we know and more loved than we imagine.

I relearned these truths, which are as old as Eden, while reading the book *The Shack.*

At the time I was simply journeying quietly through William P. Young's allegory, learning about Mack and his Great Sadness after the brutal loss of his young daughter. As a father of a little girl, I felt a twist in my own stomach about it all.

And so I read about Mack's grief. And his anger. And eventually his unabashed judgment of others, including God. And I read about Mack's broader human frailties, particularly our propensity to do things our own way, seeking security in the wrong places, then blaming everyone else when things go awry.

And as I realized I was actually reading about myself, I grew in my own understanding of my God, our God, the One who loves us more than we realize, the Almighty God who wants to bring us, like Mack, past our pains and fears into wholeness and peace and joy.

Then I discovered that this hugely popular novel, with sales now somewhere past a million, has caused a tempest in our Christian community. And it's left me wondering, is it just me, or is something fundamentally and horribly amiss in our courtyard?

It was at Canada's largest Christian writers' gathering, in Guelph, where an American book-agent, a gatekeeper of the Christian publishing world, told me that he had earlier rejected Young's manuscript because, in his words, "I feared judgment."

Oh?

And it was at Canada's largest Christian retreat centre, visited in Muskoka by thousands, where a bookstore clerk told me the store didn't carry *The Shack* because "it's not biblical."

Really?

"It's just fiction," she said, as we stood amidst shelves of historical romances and End Time thrillers and other fluffy, and certainly fictitious, yarns. Then came her real concern, exactly what the book-agent told me earlier, that "God is not a big black woman."

So is the problem that this allegory has God the Father incarnated as a black? Or as a woman?

Now understand, working in Africa most of the year, I see more black women than most Canadians. But would anyone be troubled if the Divine was an allegorical figure like, say, a lion named Aslan? What about an old, white man with a long beard, stretching his outstretched hand from the heavens? Visit me in Uganda, and see how offensive that old Western image is.

Jesus, of course, loved fresh stories and images, and used metaphor often to keep us from falling into narrow presuppositions. When He called Himself a good shepherd, for example, He knew very well that shepherds of His time were people of ill repute, respected even less than say, today's large black women.

So why aren't we beyond this ignorance? Don't we know our own Scripture, that in Christ, as Paul aptly notes, there is no gender or race?

Apparently not.

And I wonder if this is, in part, because Christian subculture, in our fast and easy times, has made the entire Gospel too small: a message reduced to a series of steps to enter eternity with some kind of ticket, a partial view that's void of God's largeness and diversity and mystery, a clock marking time rather than a compass giving meaning and direction to every day.

When something outside its tidy box comes along, the subculture, illiterate to its own heritage, then rejects it. Meanwhile, other everyday folks who are hungry and thirsty for understanding are finding it, in this case by bypassing our community on their way to Chapters.

At its heart, the Gospel is Christ saying to those who would listen, "Wake up. God's kingdom is here." We can get distracted with other, more insular messages, and be irrelevant to today's broader culture. Or, as Christ's ambassadors, we can do what we need to: wake up.

Freedom

89

Kampala, Uganda
April 4, 2007

Gwyne Dyer's commentary in the *New Vision* of March 27, page 10, arguing that religion promotes bad behaviour while secularism promotes good, has more holes in it than a house of Swiss cheese.

Sadly, some religious people do behave in unbecoming ways. There's a saying that "with or without religion, good people do good and bad people do evil, but for good people to do evil, that takes religion." That has an unfortunate blunt truth. From ancient Aztec human sacrifices, to Christianity's mediaeval Inquisition, to Islamic extremism, history writes it with blood.

But the alternatives – humanism, agnosticism, atheism – aren't lily white either, and they're no alternatives at all. Especially considering the evils of evolution, a pet theory of secular humanists that's now trumpeted by Dyer.

Quoting religion researcher Gregory Paul, Dyer tells us that social ills, like murder and sexual diseases and marital weakness, are worse in the "anti-evolution" regions of the south and Midwestern United States than in America's northeast, "where societal conditions, secularism and acceptance of evolution approach European norms."

European norms? Give us a break. A couple of generations ago such so-called norms birthed a madman named Hitler who twisted Europe's fascination with evolution into a holocaust and global war that killed over 75 million men, women and children.

Closer to home, let's remember Rwanda, another atrocity branching from the demonic theory that some humans are worth less than others. At best, human evolution in its extreme forms is an unproven theory that continues to be riddled with contradictions.

The other note to keep in mind (besides the need to scrutinize Paul's data and methods) is that some of the planet's most significant social transformations have come from people driven by deep religious faith. History's greatest strides in science, medicine, education and social welfare, in fact, often have Christian roots.

Take the abolition of slavery. In its 200th anniversary, this turning point in world history is now being remembered across Africa and beyond. Abolition, in fact, was championed by British parliamentarian William Wilberforce, a rather weak-looking man who burned bright with a great passion for Jesus Christ, the force that helped him work tirelessly for decades on a new law that eventually freed millions of Africans.

Interestingly, Wilberforce's opponents included members of the established church, people who enjoyed the various profits and securities brought by the slave trade.

Which brings us to the real issue, one that unwittingly the skeptics are half-right about: dead religion is a poor counterfeit for living faith.

Yes, it is true. Dead religion does lead to questionable behaviour. But the answer is not to discard religious conviction but to, like Wilberforce, renew it.

This is especially relevant in a culture like in Uganda, a place where mainstream religion, Christianity in this case, is easily expressed but where following the rules often seems more important than understanding their context. Jesus, after all, was basically an irreligious man and the Bible an irreligious book.

This is worth repeating. Jesus was an irreligious man. He constantly challenged religious leaders by desecrating their cherished icons and tearing down their self-righteous walls. Over and over he broke rules of tradition, tribalism and territory.

Why? He knew that empty religiosity intimidated and burdened the masses, who, above all, craved freedom.

Freedom. Deep, liberating, cleansing and forgiving freedom. It's something that the secular humanists and other critics don't quite understand, because, apparently, they have not experienced it. Yet.

For those of us who have, the daily challenge is obvious. Preach the good news. And when necessary, use words.

Ever on the lookout for life's quirks and otherwise unintended cracks in the china, I might have a few gems in what follows. These may not be the deepest commentaries in the well, but they were fun to write. Really, I do hope they're fun at your end too. You've made it this far. You really do deserve a break.

And if they're not all that funny, well, have a great day anyway.

Opposite page photo: *A customer in front of a burger outlet in Belo Horizonte, Brazil.*

A Few More Light Ones

Bum Day, Hum Day or Sum Day? 90

Kampala, Uganda
September 26, 2005

> *"If you knew time as well as I do, you wouldn't be talking about wasting it."*
>
> The Mad Hatter in Lewis Carroll's *Alice in Wonderland*

We need a new holiday and, to get things rolling, I'm taking today off. I might simply be jet-lagged. Having arrived here just yesterday to start my new life as a Canadian in Uganda, I do feel a little spent. But it also seems to me that September's other holiday, Labour Day, has some serious problems. For one, early September is too nice a time to wind down summer. Secondly, isn't celebrating labour a little like celebrating root canals?

Meanwhile, today, the first Monday after Earth has reached fall equinox, goes totally unnoticed as summer's official end. Nobody stops to say, as my two-year-old likes to, "Bye-bye, sun."

Of course in Africa, summer never travels far away. September 26 could be December 26 or any other lazy, hazy day. Nonetheless, let's all think hard about this. Because a new September holiday, with just the right name, could have some major global appeal.

Sum Day is one option. Unlike Sunday, which is for shopping and football, or someday, which I'll get to soon, Sum Day is to take stock, or a "sum," of our work lives. How are our bodies, minds and spirits dealing with it all?

This name might appease some labour types. But it's too much like a foreign money exchanger, flipping and counting his bills, flipping and counting, never quite sure if he's accurate or if he has enough.

Bum Day is better. And it's closer to our real dilemma, that annoying relationship between time and money. You've likely noticed you want both, but the more you have of one, the less you have of the other. Why? Bum Day is to figure that out.

I personally practise unofficial Bum Days as often as possible. Back in Hamilton, Jean and I recently celebrated the birth of Jonathan Thomas, plus Elizabeth's second birthday, plus my fortieth, plus our wedding anniversary. They're fine days to ponder. And I need to ponder, because my job is to simply follow my wife around and then write from wherever I wake up.

In my travels I've noticed that unlike Westerners, who, sadly, never have much time, folks in the developing world tend to practice Bum Days quite well. In parts of Africa, where the sunsets are stunning, some folks even develop a relationship with their wooden stools. In Ghana, for example, stools are carried around. Nobody dares sit on another's stool.

The unfortunate thing about Bum Day is that dwelling on even the good things in life is like driving around a cul-de-sac. It's a pleasant view of the neighbourhood, but you still finish back where you started: with yourself.

Plus, take too many Bum Days and nothing gets done. That's a big issue in the developing world. Yes, the completion of my family's little house in Uganda's countryside has been well behind schedule.

In Yemen, where we lived until recently, this is typically called *inshallah,* or "if God wills." Sure, things will get finished. Someday. Don't like that timing? Blame the Big Guy.

Sum Day and Bum Day, then, may not be the most encouraging holiday names. Which leaves Hum Day. Because, while I doubt the Almighty appreciates being blamed for any culture's mishandling of time, He still has a way of whispering into our daily affairs.

I was reminded of this recently by a *Spectator* senior editor, a cancer survivor, who told me of a new awareness – a certain "hum," as he calls it – that he and a colleague, another cancer survivor, now live with. It's the simple knowledge that despite our best-laid plans, for anyone, anywhere, eternity can be as close as tomorrow.

"I'm living in a kind of limbo," he said. "I don't know exactly where to go, but I know I don't want to go back to where I was before."

Sounds like a mysterious place, one not found every day. But it seems to me that this so-called "hum" is short for *humility*. And that's a good place to find meaning in our holidays. Not to mention our work. Whatever the season.

The happy barber 91

Kampala, Uganda
November 21, 2005

The Beatles never made it to Africa. Which might explain some things about haircuts around here.

Not that I personally run around looking like Rip van Winkle or those woolly fellows from ZZ Top. One's haircut is a statement to the world. No sense making folks think you need dog tags around your neck. Nonetheless, after my first haircut in Uganda, I'm a little worried about styles, or lack of, in this corner of the planet.

I recently visited an establishment known as a salon. Most men have a problem with this sort of name, and I'm no exception. I grew up in a town of Italians where barbershops were named Nick's or Tony's or Umberto's, places with men's magazines and a steady stream of guy-talk.

But I guessed Africa's salons might be cousins to such old-time barbershops, where any journalist could get a good quote. And Anglo names are common in Africa. So I was curious. Could one of these salon barbers be a Floyd? Might he even have one of those big old chairs?

Remember those? Ahh, the original La-Z-Boy. They were monstrous thrones, complete with headrest and footrest for a quick nap. Usually red leather, they weighed three million pounds. When I was a kid, we actually had one in our home. I loved working that hand pump.

So I entered a local salon and bartered my price to a mere 1,500 shillings. That's $1, or 10 per cent of the rate downtown in a shop for *Muzungos*, or whites. Disappointingly, though, I discovered this shop had no Floyd. No special chair. No soothing hot lather. Not even a quick scalp rub.

I think my barber, a rookie, found it hard too. All he said was "Oh" when I removed my Team Canada hat to reveal my neglected blonde mop.

He had hair. Which is good, because I've always believed getting a haircut from a bald man is a little like getting financial advice from someone who's gone bankrupt.

More so, this young fellow had electric clippers. And this is my concern.

Because after asking the obligatory "How do you want it?" he quickly pulled them out.

"No!" I said. "I want you to use scissors."

"Scissors?" he said.

"Yes, scissors."

Then, slowly – so very slowly – he cut my hair. With scissors. Dry. So went my first African haircut.

Later, upon reflection, I realized every African man I've seen has short hair. Very short. In fact, they're all buzzed worse than Samson.

It wasn't always so. Hair historians say Europeans first contacting Africans in the 15th century saw plenty of hairstyles. That carried over to American slave culture. Most slaves could do with their hair as they pleased. During their early freedom and an oppressive racial atmosphere, Afro-Americans toned down self-expression.

But the 20th century saw free hair return. And the wonder of straightening was perfected by Madame C. J. Walker. Black scholar Henry Gates Jr. notes "It's a wonder we [Americans] don't have a national holiday for her rather than Dr. [Martin Luther] King."

By the time the Beatles arrived and seriously maligned barbers everywhere, the politics of black hair grew big. Wearing an Afro often meant supporting Black nationalism. But you could still go tall or small.

Styles still evolve, even on the face. I've personally sported everything from full beard to short goatee to Fu Manchu moustache before shaving clean so I don't scare my kids.

Thankfully, up top, the mullet (otherwise known as hockey hair) is now passé everywhere but at the small-town fair. Walk down any street and see locks, braids, shaved sides, the flattop, the ponytail, the messy look, you name it. Today, anything is in. Just not here.

Women will always have their mud facials and manicures. Here, virtually nothing can break a marathon date that a Ugandan woman has to braid her hair. I suppose by getting buzzed African men think they're keeping their own gender identity. But half-bald customers don't get haircuts at half price. So it seems me that more than anything, these guys are simply keeping their barbers in business.

Of course, there's nothing wrong with a happy barber. I'll just keep my two-year-old daughter away.

I know, you're sorry

92

Kampala, Uganda
November 7, 2005

It's a midweek night, and I'm on a cold metal chair in a dingy local police station. Sitting nearby under a dim light, a cop asks me questions.

"Sorry," he says, hearing of my loss. He writes slowly. Too slowly. I lose confidence early during this, my first Ugandan robbery report, file number 72.19.10.2005.

It could be worse. I could be dead. Or I could be the poor guy behind me, with passport, cash and credit cards all stolen. Still, the relative bad news is that my pricey work camera has been ripped off.

My family's vehicle – a 10-year-old Land Cruiser – was burglarized. In broad daylight. Near a large store entrance. Thieves smashed a back window to steal the vehicle's electronic door panels, apparently hot on Uganda's black market. A Roots Canada bag, with said camera, was likely just a bonus.

Thud went my heart when I saw the mess.

I called over parking security, three scrawny boy-men. Carrying old wooden guns, they might as well have played cops and robbers with hockey sticks underarm. They didn't have much to say. Two hours later police, with AK-47s, arrived. That was after I walked to the above-mentioned station to get them myself.

"Sorry," an officer said, scanning the damage. Another hour and the parking security manager arrived. "Sorry," he echoed.

Later, trying to understand why a competent investigation was going nowhere fast, I learned about Ugandan justice. Surveys show that less than half of Uganda's thefts are even reported. Victims simply have no hope of recovering their property. Just one-quarter of Ugandans are satisfied with their police. To compare, North America's rate is as high as 74 per cent.

No, cops here aren't society's top guns. In fact, broken relationships and rotten living conditions contribute to their high HIV-AIDS rate of 13 per cent, double the national average.

And they get no respect. None. A hydro company recently turned off the lights at precincts across the country, over unpaid bills. Such is police funding. A starting constable now earns 150,000 shillings, about $100, a month. No wonder Joseph, my investigating officer, had to borrow my mobile phone.

No wonder he had me pay for our taxi to get to the crime scene, a beater van with about 15 passengers crammed inside.

"You're the police," I protested, not yet aware of how Uganda's finest live.

The next day, while driving Joe and another vehicle-less detective to Kampala's police headquarters, we arrived to see officers running down the street, chasing a suspect who apparently just snuck out of HQ's front door. It was slapstick at its worst.

Joe, a veteran of 26 years, turned to me and said, "Things can happen here. That's the fun of life."

Yes sir. Yeehaw.

Of course he's right. Along with Latin America, Africa has the world's highest burglary and theft rates. One survey shows 41 per cent of Uganda's vehicle owners have experienced theft from their vehicles. Nobody is safe. Years ago, in traffic, one brazen thief reached in an open window of my wife's car, unlocked a back door and snatched a purse.

Don't get caught though. Two local construction workers recently convicted of stealing five bags of cement got two years in jail. And the state can't afford much. So Uganda's jails aren't the Hilton. They're also filled with folks who can't read or write, oblivious to their rights.

Back to police headquarters. Joe, his detective colleague and I drove there – in my messed-up vehicle – to photograph the damage for police records. In this saga's best comment yet, another detective greeting us said, "Cameras are pretty hard to find here [at headquarters]."

You don't say. I've even heard of Ugandan university students studying photography without cameras. That's the picture of my loss.

I'm hoping Joe can help get me some compensation. But I can't reach him these days. Seems his mobile isn't working.

"Sorry. But don't let this taint your view of the country," an expatriate friend later told me.

Heavens, no. Don't worry. Our vehicle is fixed. It's now loaded with an alarm that can wake the dead. I'll somehow get another camera. And I know most Ugandans are very fine people. But I'll still have to write about it all.

Sorry.

W

Along with this column, I filed a photo of Constable Joe in a Kampala precinct, taken clandestinely with My Royal Babe's camera, a little guy that fits in one's pocket.

I then quietly took some extra photos of the nearby brig, but was discovered, hauled before the captain, and had this second camera taken by police. It was later returned, minus the brig photos. Police were never aware of the shots of Constable Joe.

The original stolen camera was never found.

W

Police often don't get the respect they deserve in a place like Canada either. Ask Mike Irwin, son of Mike Irwin Sr., a Toronto cop slain in the line of duty

some 35 years ago. After following in his father's steps, Mike Jr. suffered an injury while he himself was in the line of duty with the Ontario Provincial Police.

Later, while a firearms instructor at the Ontario Police College, Mike's condition put him in a wheelchair. But having a cop in a wheelchair isn't great for the morale of young trainees. And when the college balked at his requests for a new job or building modifications, the fight was on. In came the doctors and insurers and suits from Workers' Compensation and arbitrators and others from Ontario's government, all trying to resolve this case of a cop as stubborn as he was brave, who wanted only what was fair.

I saw the painful affair unfold some years ago, when I wrote it up for the Times-Journal. And I kept up with Mike at his hobby farm in Aylmer, where from a distance he enjoyed, ironically, his horses.

Eventually the coverage prompted Ontario's solicitor general to personally intervene and fast-track the case, leading to an apology, a new police college job and a fair settlement for Mike.

And while This Scribe doesn't think journalists have the influence that we tend to believe, this experience did verify that you shouldn't pick a fight with a guy who has a bucket of ink. Or his friend.

Mike and I have still kept in touch.

Do you like my new face? 93

"Why, thank you. Oh, and please, call me Jak. I mean Thommy. No, no; Boris, please."

SAO PAULO, BRAZIL
January 9, 2006

So it's a new year, time for everyone to eat less, exercise more and finally start yoga. I've decided that a better way to a new me, however, is to visit a plastic surgeon and get a new face.

My current face was never really big with the girls. But now my two-year-old daughter is pointing toward my nose and a fresh zit and asking, "What's that on your face, Daddy?"

Now, faces are interesting things. Too pretty and you can't trust friends. Too ugly and you can't find work. Faces need to be just right, like Baby Bear's bed.

And thanks to modern face technology from France and a glut of plastic on the world market from Pamela Anderson's last mammoplasty, that's now possible. Cheaper plastic surgery is driving supply, while longer lifespans push demand. This is so mod.

In Rome, with all those parties and wars, folks died shortly past grade school. In the plague-filled Middle Ages, things weren't much better.

But now, thanks to inventions like hand soap and bran flakes, we can keep chugging until the queen writes to say we're 100. A new face will become just another way to keep up. Yeah, baby.

My pick from the pool of options is the brand-Euro metro face. It's square-jawed and hard-powered but still sensitive. For me, born in Berlin, it's perfect. Strangers around the civilized world, and even in New York City, have already told me years ago that I resemble former German tennis star Boris Becker.

Of course, a new face needs a new name. Stay true to yourself here. For example, I can use Boris. Or Thommy, my designer name from kindergarten. Or Jak, for J.A.K., not to mimic the mystique of J.F.K. but an acronym for my Arab pen name, Jamil Abdul Karim.

I won't use Mr. Chamberlain, my wife's maiden name. Strangers phoning our Hamilton home call me this, and it kind of bothers me. Unless it's the bank.

To find that special face and name, you'll want to travel. Or if you already have them, travel to show them off. I suggest Brazil, a place already well known for its perfectly shaped butts. They're called – and I'm not making this up – bum-bums.

A Mecca of cosmetic surgery, Brazil also has 700,000 Avon ladies, an

Amazon force larger than its army, placing Brazil second in world Avon sales, behind only the much larger and richer United States.

Yes, Brazilians take faces seriously. I've been in their voluptuous country, through Miami in a kind of vanity warm-up, to speak at a university about things like truth in journalism. But, between you and me, now I'll visit a plastic surgeon in the bush who'll call my daughter to say he's fixed everything.

Now, there are dangers to this. First, be careful where you show off your new look. Visiting the wrong places, like really dirt-poor parts of the world, is like tossing your pearls into the latrine. In my experience, many folks in developing countries, lacking basic skin care, simply don't understand things like image.

You know whom I mean: people with weathered, leathery skin, looking twice as old as they are, having faces with character if not integrity.

Facial crevices and folds are okay, I guess, if they hide zits. But if you're really serious about a new you, don't get confused with the pursuit of something as out of fashion and tenuous as character.

The other thing is, whatever you do, be careful at airports. I'm already envisioning security at my return flight to Canada. "Yes, Mr. Froese? I see you're using your German passport today. Your nose is smaller than in this photo."

"Why, thank you. Oh, and please, call me Jak. I mean Thommy. No, no; Boris, please."

"Is this not your passport, sir?"

"Well, it's for the old me."

"Then it's not for the present you, the one wanting to board this plane?"

See the potential complications?

But don't worry too much about this. The style of your response is more important than its substance. Just be cool. Relax. And show everyone that you love the skin you're in. Whatever it might be made of.

W

In Brazil I met one Elben Cesar: a white-haired publisher who got in the business sometime in the Pelé era, still enjoying the grind, running the publication he founded, Ultimato, and curious to interview This Scribe while I was in his woods. My university talk on 'Journalism in our Time' – that is, our postmodern and broken times – is what interested him, and so the Portugese magazine ran my profile.

This energetic grandfather later sent me a copy of it, along with a letter he gave his grandkids, one that mentioned me and how happy he would be if they took up the craft in which Elben had served so faithfully over the decades.

The readership of Ultimato magazine? About 100,000. The readership of the letter? About five. The more meaningful to me? Those five young lives.

Seeing a faithful scribe like Elben is a reminder that some folks can keep their eyes on the ball longer than others can. A couple of laps (20 years) into this business, I now try to approach it all like the young man in Donald E. Demaray's 'Joy and Healing,' a journalist who's getting criticism from his father for not getting ahead faster in his career. The son replied that he had intentions, and they were as follows: At 30 he would be a great newspaper reporter; at 40 he would be a great editor; at 50 he would be a great story writer; at 60 he would be a great fiction writer; at 70 he would be a great grandfather; at 80 he would be a great admirer of beautiful women; and at 90 he would be a great loss to the community.

This trip to Brazil was, in fact, almost cancelled when I couldn't get an entry visa into the South American country. Flying from Uganda with just days in Canada – over the Christmas break – before my departure for Sao Paulo, there was not enough time for the paperwork.

The dark-haired Brazilian behind the counter at the embassy in Toronto just looked at my Canadian passport and shook her head. "No, they won't let you in without a visa. I'm sorry."

Then she looked inside my passport again. "You were born in Berlin?"

"Yes."

"So you're German?"

"I'm Canadian, with a German passport also."

"You have a German passport with you?"

"Yes."

"Oh, well, sir, you don't need an entry visa. Members of the EU can travel to Brazil without a visa."

And the Euro-face thing continues. Since writing the above column, my mug has also been confused with that of Ottawa Senators' captain Daniel Alfredsson, a Swede.

This is a Canadian phenomena. It never happens when I'm in Africa. This is because in grade school I would have been voted the kid least likely to ever move to Africa. Yes, I was known as "Whitey." Hair. Eyebrows. Eyelashes. Everything.

So now I find Alfredsson, the captain of the team representing Canada's cold capital, apparently looks like I do, or vice-versa, like each other's doppelganger. It's something I discovered one summer day while on break from Africa, enjoying Niagara-on-the-Lake, a touristy place just north of the Snowy

49th Parallel that, in pre-Confederation days, happened to be the capital of Upper Canada.

On this day, a fine visitor – a hockey fan and an astute observer of grace and athleticism – approached My Royal Babe while Jean was waiting for me outside of one of those trendy shops. "Excuse me," she said. "Is that your husband in there?

"Yes," said My Royal Babe.

"Is he Daniel Alfredsson?"

"Well, I can see why you would come to that conclusion," continued Jean. "I mean, my husband really is a jock. He could easily score tons of goals in the National Hockey League with his right hand tied to his left skate. And certainly earning millions a year is well within his abilities, which really, quite honestly, is why I married him. Oh, and yes, those looks. Ohh, I just melt in my shoes."

At least I think that's what she said. Or, maybe it was, "No, he's not." The responses are so similar, you know? And when she told me about it later, I was so taken aback, I may have lost some of the exact words in my notes.

Fear Factor with Obama - Osama and Sarah Palin 94

Kampala, Uganda
September 23, 2008

Recently travelling from Canada back to Uganda through London, England – capital of history's most influential empire – I got some renewed perspective on global leadership and change and how, in politics, there's nothing like old-fashioned fear to move things along.

Like others, the Brits are distracted by the US presidential election, a vote that can only get more interesting before the Yanks chose their 44th president on November 4 and move the world along its wobbly trajectory. All we can do is hang on and wonder what will happen next to scare the life out of us in this strange political version of the US TV show *Fear Factor*.

The clever but inexperienced Barrack Obama, who, arguably, has as much charisma as anyone since JFK, has as much chance of being assassinated by some American crackpot who won't tolerate a black in the White House.

Meanwhile, old Republican warhorse John McCain, whose age puts into question his own ability to finish a full term, would potentially pass the presidential torch to a woman who's likeable-enough, but only a few years past being mayor of an Alaskan town about the size of Seeta in Mukono.

I'm just waiting for the next surprise, like Osama bin Laden, to join the fray.

Of course, there's political fear; and there's political fear. Africans know it intimately. We need not look further than this summer's "vote" in Zimbabwe. As an astute American cleric where I work at Ugandan Christian University said to me, "We should pray for God to change Robert Mugabe's heart. Or stop it."

But back to Osama bin Laden. Imagine how he could inject some real fear into things. Yes, if Obama were to take Osama as his new vice-presidential running mate, the Democrats could have a truly unstoppable ticket.

Think about it. The Republicans have pulled even in the polls because they've stolen Obama's mantra of change. Combined with her values that harness America's evangelical Christian vote, Sarah Palin's message to shake up Washington has already shaken things up.

The Democrats now need to fight fire with real fire. And who better to shake up Washington than the unpredictable bin Laden? You want fear? Even two Republican mavericks wouldn't get more trepidation than an Obama-Osama ticket.

Now, for several years, I lived in Yemen, where bin Laden has roots and where I reported on things like threats and bombings of extremists who called themselves "Friends of bin Laden." It was routine. And this may have some bearing on my views on these things. But, opening the British papers in London, you'd be interested to know that being close to the Big O is not as dangerous as it used to be.

In fact, an Asian lawyer was just awarded 600,000 British pounds after filing a suit that she was wrongly suspended for joking to a court security guard, just two weeks after the 9/11 attacks on America, that she was a "friend of bin Laden."

The payout to the 47-year-old Halima Aziz, a crown prosecutor from West Yorkshire who is also Muslim, is about 10 times the amount given to victims of the July 2005 London terror attacks and their bereaved relatives.

Hmm.

So it seems to me that we all do need to move on: a little less fearful of some things, and a little more fearful of others. And just enjoy the show. It's all too entertaining to miss.

It's been only by chance that this book generally frames the timeline of George W. Bush's difficult and flawed presidency. But, humour aside, the preceding column – a last-minute addition – points to needed changes in Washington as world challenges only mount. He's no guarantee, but two weeks before the vote, my hopes stay with Obama.

These final commentaries are among the most disturbing, and important, in this collection. There is no way to soft-pedal dying mothers.

I've had the privilege of partnering with Darling Doctor Wife in her work to help bring this neglected issue into the conscience of Canadians and, in time, others around the world. This section is a sampling of my published reflections.

The final piece includes the story of one African mother, Charity, an excerpt from the book 'Where Have All the Mothers Gone?,' an appropriate way to honour the tireless efforts of the author, that same darling.

This section's opening commentary is an old file from the vault, about the death of my own mother.

The pieces between then touch on Save the Mothers. In the three short years since its birth, this Ugandan-Canadian partnership has received growing attention. Advocates are being awakened.

Perhaps this might all prod you to also become an advocate for some unknown mother and her vulnerable children. You may save a life. You may save several.

And a future generation may look back and mark our frail efforts as a significant turning point in this bloody, age-old war.

For more information on how to help, or to order a copy of 'Where Have All the Mothers Gone?' please visit www.savethemothers.org.

Opposite page photo: *A mother and child from a refugee hospital in Oicha, Congo, show the haunting look that typifies motherhood in Africa.*

Remember the Mothers

WINDOWS

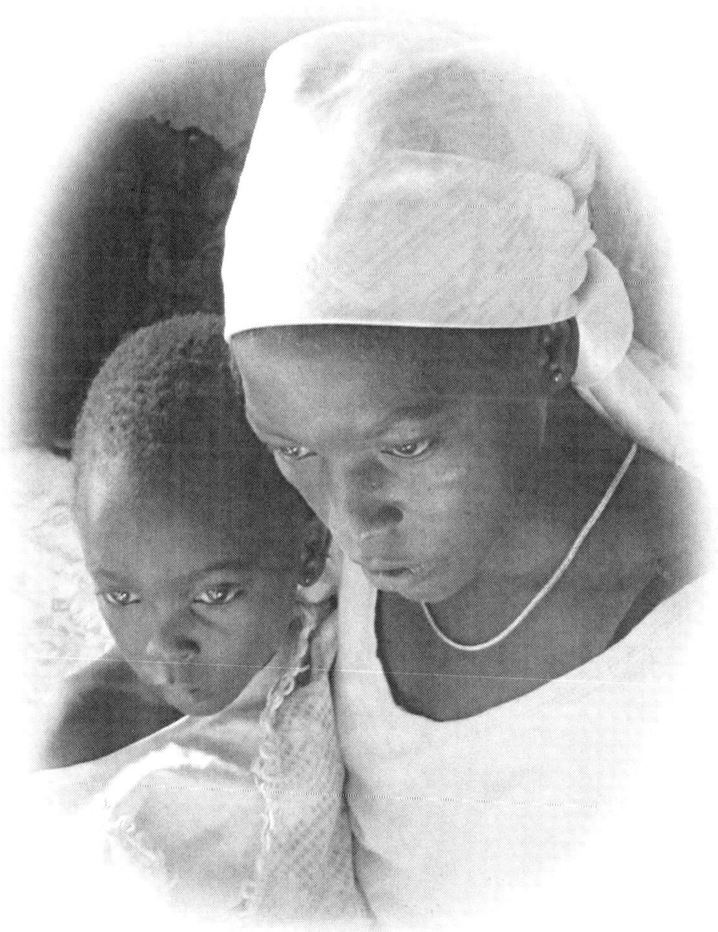

A thorny red rose

95

St. Thomas, Canada
May 10, 1997

> *"We are one, after all, you and I. Together we suffer. Together we exist. And forever will recreate each other."*
> Pierre Teilhard de Chardin, 20th century French philosopher

Tomorrow is Mother's Day, the one day of the year I'm vividly reminded that I have never held my mother, looked into her eyes and told her I love her. I have never offered a soft kiss on her cheek. I have never even given her flowers.

My mom killed herself before I ever had the chance.

Every year at this time I'm reminded that a little boy, too young to understand the complexities life can dump on us, was left behind, with his sister and daddy, by a beautiful woman he barely knew.

There's no easy way to describe such a loss. It's even harder when there are few memories to fall back on. It's a loss of someone who was never really there.

My mother had severe mental illness. I understand she had deep paranoia and hallucinations (she believed people, or "things," were chasing her, among other fears). She was eventually given the label of schizophrenic.

Then one day my mom, an experienced nurse, having already lost her children, took her own life in her Berlin apartment by injecting into her veins a solution she knew would poison her blood. She left notes to her loved ones, expressing her sorrow for hurting them and her desire for true peace.

So, my mother's world ended not with a bang but with a whimper, alone, on the floor of a small room on the other side of the ocean, one day in 1970.

Her absence is still felt.

Her death falls into the relatively small category of those caused by mental disease. Schizophrenics have the highest rate of suicide among the mentally sick. One in 10 eventually kill themselves.

Historically it has been common to have simplistic explanations or warped fascination for such things. The superstition that demons possess the mentally sick still hovers over us like a dismal mist. A few centuries ago the public would even pay to see "lunatics" displayed at their local mental hospital. It was fashionable.

And now? Will closing London's regional psychiatric hospitals bring madness to our own streets?

To find the answer we should know that mental disorder does not reflect any fundamental personal deficiency. It is not shameful. Science shows every one of us shares the potential for becoming disordered.

We should know that more serious mental disease is brought on when particular stresses are put on someone with a genetic predisposition to it. We should understand that mental illness does not necessarily make people more dangerous than otherwise. We should see that the days of "Oh, it's because of bad upbringing" are disappearing for more biological-based studies.

Most importantly, we need to know that hope is what the mentally diseased need most.

We all need trusting relationships, a sense of being appreciated and valued, of being loved unconditionally. Language is powerful, and the words we choose can give hope. So can listening to the life story of the man or woman who may sit down beside us. Or using humour.

"Recovery" for the mentally ill may not mean their suffering has disappeared and symptoms removed. Rather, it means they will have strength to move on despite their condition.

Sickness, particularly severe disease, reminds us that our earthly home is out of sync. As part of such a fallen world, we too can easily lose the harmony and flow of our existence, especially when we are jolted through seasons that are not easy. But Jesus said He would be with us in these storms of life, as our refuge and strength.

I was reminded of this several years ago when, overseas, standing at my mom's tombstone one summer day, I placed a thorny red rose and said goodbye. But even God chose His son to be a wounded healer and spared Him neither pain nor humiliating death. In this paradox is the deeper essence of hope, a gift given to us.

It's like the final crossing of the chasm between humanity and the divine. Whether we drink Socrates' poison hemlock or pass away in more natural ways, we will all face the same pit. In the end, no death is really natural. Some diseases just take longer to run their course.

We will all be left helpless. We will all have to be carried.

The above is a shortened version of my first freelanced column. Pre-dating all writing in this book, it ran in the London Free Press. And while it entails such a tragic and personal subject, I couldn't think of a more suitable way to start my journey as a columnist.

There are, I believe, very few things in life that are so sanctimonious that they need to be hidden, at least if uncovering them can touch, if not comfort, others.

Telling each other our stories, even the hard ones, is one way to do that, one way to bring healing in the broken times – the deaths, the divorces, the disappointments – that are around each of us.

(For more on the author's personal background, see Windows 27, 51, 62, 78 and their addendums.)

An intolerable terror

96

Sana'a, Yemen
May 8, 2004

Tomorrow is Mother's Day. Most of us will likely say thanks to our moms in some fashion.

Good thing. A mother's job is not easy.

It's a good time to also think about mothers in the developing world.

Some 525,000 die in childbirth every year. That's 1,450 every day, more than one dead mother every minute. It really is a global terror.

It's also an intolerable terror, because most can be saved.

One in four simply bleed to death. A medication costing less than a cup of coffee could stop that. But often neither properly stocked clinics nor properly trained medics are within reach.

Cultural ways and familial attitudes can also block proper medical care. Can you imagine two strong-armed men holding a woman upside down to move a breech baby? When ignorance rules, such things happen.

Few people know these issues better than my wife, Jean, an obstetrician who has worked with some of the world's poorest women in places such as Yemen and various African countries. In response, she recently launched a new Canadian-based charity, Save the Mothers International (savethemothers.org). Its aim is to create new infrastructures in developing countries by targeting professionals and teaching them public health leadership skills.

Starting in Uganda in 2005, the program will enrol professionals in health care, government, law, media and education in a university master's program near Uganda's capital, Kampala. With a goal of 20 annual graduates, in five years 100 key leaders throughout the country will help champion mothers' rights in practical ways.

Jean, who trained in obstetrics at the University of Western Ontario and occasionally lives in London, notes, "The solution is not just more medical people in hospitals or clinics. It's a multi-disciplinary approach where everybody in society becomes involved in women's health."

This past century, we beat polio and smallpox. Space was explored. Genetic codes giving clues to life itself were cracked. And maternal death rates in the developing world are no worse than what the West saw 100 years ago. Most can be prevented with the same proven formula: better access to proper care and resources.

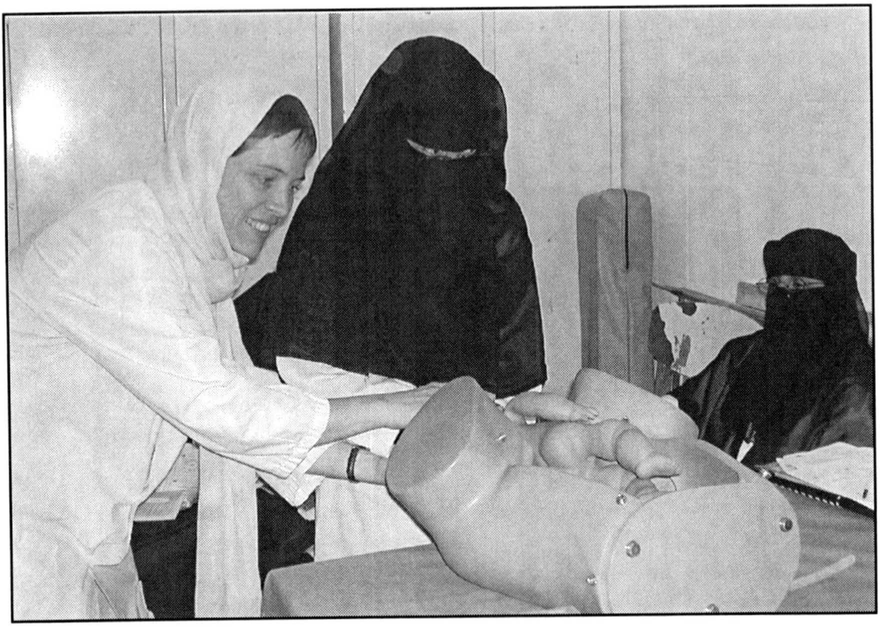

The question is, how much do illiterate village women really count on the global agenda? The U.S. recently cut funding to UN safe maternity programs. Other rich countries, such as Canada, have not done better. In 1987, they met in Nairobi, pledging to halve maternal deaths by 2000. Instead, rates increased. Cheap midwifery training was offered, but nobody would pay to get mothers clean blood, other supplies and, most critically, better access to decent obstetrical services in the neediest rural areas.

We have political commitments for peacekeepers in Afghanistan. There's now easy money for AIDS clinics in much of Africa. Some folks happily send clothes and toys to impoverished children around the world.

Not that these aren't all worthy. But I do wonder, is a faceless mother in some Third World backwater who is trying to bring new life to the world not sexy enough an issue to compete?

Here's where, believe it or not, others can help. In time, donors will learn about Save the Mothers. In fact, it's now getting attention in a national media awareness campaign. No doubt, this type of organization can make a lasting impact.

And, as it launches, one item now in its war chest is a new book by Jean, *Where Have All The Mothers Gone?* Based on her Third World experiences, it's a powerful collection of stories of mothers showing uncommon courage during childbirth. It's like a few loaves and fishes, really – in need of being multiplied in the right hands.

Average Canadians, common foot soldiers in a sense, can join this under-reported global battle by buying a copy and educating themselves. A full 100 per cent of the $10-plus-delivery price goes to Save the Mothers.

Of course, the value of this kind of book goes beyond dollar price. Canadians could be part of something great, not the least of which is saving somebody's mother.

In the end, how meaningful is that? Well, think of your own mom.

The forest and the trees 97

Kampala, Uganda
February 27, 2007

Following up on some recent commentaries in the *New Vision* fearing abortion is going to be legalized in Uganda, maybe the only thing left to say is that it's not happening. Uganda is not close to changing its law. Nothing is happening. Zero. Zilch. Negative. No action.

"There's no bill before government, and I can't see one anytime soon. Not even in the next 10 years," is how Mityana district MP Sylvia Namabidde Ssinabulya said it to me. Indeed, hell might freeze solid before Uganda's top leaders compromise their own convictions on the issue. It just won't happen.

With this said, Uganda's penal code, which carries a 14-year jail term for anyone causing an abortion, isn't stopping 300,000 annual abortions apparently performed in Uganda already. Neither is the constitution, which prohibits abortion unless "authorised by law," that is, a doctor seeking judge approval.

Law or not, abortion appears here to stay. It's unfortunate but true. And this now is enough about this non-story. Except to say that it arose at the recent African Union gathering in Ethiopia, where, again, top Ugandans made assurances that abortion is absolutely not being legalized.

And except to add that even the term *legalizing* can be unclear, because globally abortion laws vary widely. Of 193 countries, 64 now allow abortion on demand or for socio-economic reasons, 59 to save the mother, 122 to protect her health, 83 in cases of rape or incest, and 76 to remove an unhealthy child. Officially, three countries – Malta, El Salvador and the Vatican City – ban abortion outright.

For Ugandans, the real story is this: dead mothers. Shaking and convulsing, crying in horrible, blood-splattered agony, mothers are dying terrible deaths while doing something as natural and loving as giving birth. This is the real story that needs to be told repeatedly until nobody can stand it any more.

In Uganda, 6,000 women now die annually in childbirth. Three in five are females between 13 and 24, girls who have barely left the playground. For every dead mom, three infants die, four other children are left behind, and 35 other mothers who survive childbirth are disabled.

Uganda's government is beginning to understand this, the real story. This is why MP Ssinabulya recently moved the government to at least start monitoring maternal deaths and boost obstetrical services to the extent possible in Uganda's meagre health system, where just four per cent of rural health units have emergency obstetrical care.

True, Ssinabulya's recent motion included unsafe abortion as a cause of maternal deaths. To ignore this would be to put one's head in the sand. But that's not any movement to legalize abortion. It's just a fact.

Uganda is not alone in all this. Maternal mortality has been called "the last unreached frontier of modern medicine." In the developing world, 1,450 women die in childbirth every day. Last century, more women died from childbirth than soldiers killed in either world war, and from 1980 to 2000, childbirth claimed more women than AIDS. Nonetheless, there are people who believe that this country can be a leader in this fight, just like it's been a beacon of hope in reducing AIDS.

So we need to let the government continue what it's started with health workers, and encourage other sectors – educators and lawyers and social scientists and others – to join the team.

If we distract them from keeping their eye on the real ball, that is, saving mothers, we're just missing the forest for the trees.

98 *No voice, no face, just death*

Kampala, Uganda
December 22, 2007

A pregnant woman here in Uganda's capital was recently beheaded by her husband. Maurine Ampire, 38, was a mother getting close to delivering number six.

It's one picture of life here and a comparable image to the lack of voice that pregnant women have worldwide. No voice. No choice. Just death, and often violently.

Some 525,000 mothers now die annually in childbirth, 99 per cent in the developing world. That's 1,450 a day or one every minute. One in four simply bleed to death. Millions of children then also perish.

Some of these moms are just girls with underdeveloped bodies, married young or defiled. Others are forced to have so many children without child-spacing that they're just digging their own graves.

Uganda is among 13 countries with 70 per cent of all maternal deaths. In Africa, others are Tanzania, Kenya, DR Congo, Ethiopia, Nigeria and Angola. Outside, add Pakistan, Indonesia, China, India, Bangladesh and Afghanistan.

Incredibly, these deaths are virtually all preventable. But they continue, due to lack of skilled birth attendants and emergency care at delivery, often fuelled by cultural myths and patriarchal attitudes.

It's among the planet's biggest stories. But you likely haven't heard much about it; haven't heard that from 1980 to 2000 more women – about 12 million – died in childbirth than of AIDS; haven't heard that other crises, like, say, Darfur, pale in comparison.

In an information-soaked era, why not?

There's plenty of talk about human rights and mutual respect and gender equity these days. Much came from world leaders at the recent Commonwealth Summit in Kampala, just days before Maureen's head was taken off. But we remain miles from even old maternal death targets, like the Safe Motherhood Initiative of 1987 to cut deaths by half by 2000.

While other global health indicators improve, the world's poorest mothers just keep dying quietly. Hollywood icons and rock stars don't campaign for them. Cheering for motherhood isn't popular among Western feminists either, so they're silent. So are religious groups. And governments. It's all quite deafening.

I was just reminded of this after photographing Sarah Brown, wife of British

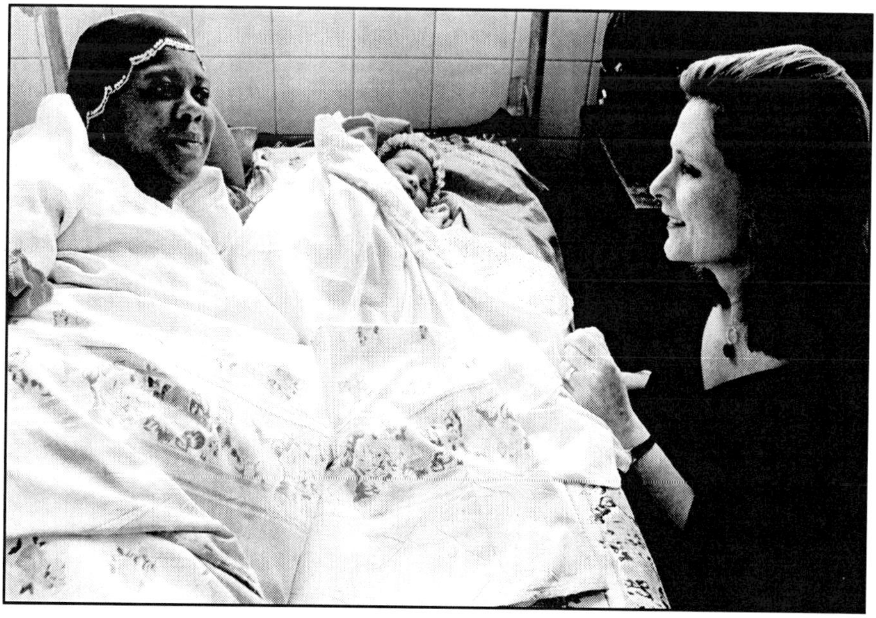

prime minister Gordon Brown, during the Commonwealth Summit. In a breath of fresh air, she went beyond the rhetoric and social luncheons and visited Mulago Hospital, Uganda's main birthing centre. Then her personal aid forbade me from releasing the ensuing photos, strangely fearing Brown's image would somehow be tarnished in the UK.

Regardless, I released one for worldwide distribution through Reuters news, a little wiser of the silly challenges that confuse the real issues. Here's another example.

Many Hamiltonians know the work of my wife, Dr. Jean Chamberlain Froese, a McMaster University obstetrician who's founding executive director of Save the Mothers, a ground-breaking program based in Uganda. In just two years, it's seeing results, because it trains a range of societal leaders. Four Ugandan MPs are among its current class of 55.

As a result, maternal health is now on Uganda's national budget for the first time. One of the four MPs, Sylvia Ssinabulya, visited parliamentarians in Ottawa this summer. Too bad five requests for a Canadian official to visit this unique program, just 45 minutes from the Commonwealth Summit venue, failed. The prime minister's office didn't even bother with a courtesy reply to its two invitations.

By the way, Canada spreads about $4 billion in annual foreign aid to some 161 countries, including 46 in Africa, in tiny allotments that, according to a Senate report, give no results anywhere. Ottawa is rightly streamlining the system. One wonders, though, if it will ever learn to pinpoint aid to core issues, like maternal care, which, when stable, secure a country's entire health system.

Few Westerners would say it's acceptable that so many African women are dying on dirt floors in mud huts, alone, in bloody agony, any more than it was acceptable for African slaves to be chained to ships and carried over the Atlantic. But, like during abolition, fundamental thinking needs to change. The broader public needs an awakening. And since dying mothers can't, others need to speak for them.

As 2008 marks the 60th anniversary of the Universal Declaration of Human Rights, now is a good time.

A few weeks after this was published, Darling Doctor Wife did get the ear of the Canadian government, in Yemen, where we were visiting for the first time in several years.

Due to various fears, Canadian officials usually don't tread in such a place. But as part of a Middle East visit, and on the invite of Yemen's ambassador to Canada, Abdullah Nasher, some senators came to lunch, right, as it happened, in our hotel in Aden.

And so while a few senators took a dip in the Gulf of Aden, we chatted with others, including the very encouraging Speaker of the Senate, Noel Kinsella.

W

Since you want to know, Yemen is always warm but not unbearable like Dubai.

Where we live now, near Uganda's capital, it's always a balmy 25C or so. We're almost sitting on the equator, but Kampala is moderate due to its elevation. There are no seasons. Unless you consider the rainy season. Which is nothing as miserable as Vancouver or London.

W

And here's the fuller story on Sarah Brown, wife of the UK's PM Gordon Brown, with the names changed to protect the innocent, namely This Scribe.

I was asked to photograph the lovely Sarah by one Nervous Doc from the UK's Royal College of Obstetricians, which was trying to stoke a relationship with Downing Street. He suggested, to keep the photo-shoot efficient, that I be the lone official photographer, and the local Ugandan papers could then get photos from me. I asked to have photos of my choosing for my own use, and we all smiled in agreement.

So I put on a tie, pulled out my camera and did the job. (I noticed that the usual scenes of pregnant mothers strewn all over the lobby and floors of Mulago Hospital, sometimes delivering on the dirty spot, were cleaned up for Sarah's visit.) And I was particularly happy with the shot attached to this column, which I set up by taking Sarah to this particular mom's bedside.

Sarah, who has been a great supporter in the cause to save the world's neediest mothers, was happy at the end and gave me a parting smile and wave as she was whisked away in the back of a BMW. Which is when her personal handler, a Big Bear kind of guy, approached me and, like a poke in the ribs, said gruffly, "I don't want you to release any of these for public use."

Excuse me?

Here's an abridged version of my following conversations with these two gentlemen.

W

This Scribe: "There are half a million women dying in childbirth every year. Getting this photo of Sarah at a mom's bedside out would help draw attention to it. It's a story that needs telling, and this puts a face on it."

Big Bear: "I don't want it released."

This Scribe: "I'm a journalist. This is what I do. Sarah is a public figure."

Nervous Doc: "I didn't know you were a journalist. I thought you were just a photographer."

This Scribe: "I'm going to release it. I have a moral responsibility to do so."

Big Bear: "I don't want it released. It will harm Sarah's image."
This Scribe: "How? It makes her look rather sensitive."
Big Bear: "Just trust me. I don't want it released."
Nervous Doc: "I didn't know you were a journalist."
This Scribe: "Okay, I won't release it if Sarah tells me. I'll respect her wishes. Have her call me."
Big Bear: "Sarah call you? Who do you think you are?"
This Scribe: "The guy who bothered to take her photos."
Nervous Doc: "Are photographers journalists?"
This Scribe: "There's a timeline on this. The news marches on. If I don't hear from Sarah in 12 hours, I'll assume she's fine with it, and I'll release it."
Big Bear: "That's blackmail."
This Scribe: "No, it's giving Sarah an opportunity to state her own wishes."
Nervous Doc: "You should listen to [Big Bear]. We just don't want to upset Sarah."
This Scribe: "Can you explain why she'd be upset? I think you're afraid of a boogeyman."

And so the circles went. I never heard from Sarah. I sent the Royal College and Downing Street their 50 or so photos from the day, and released the one to Reuters for distribution to papers worldwide. I was told that Big Bear, who I never heard from again, was "livid."

Nervous Doc, though, later rejoiced over his additional package of "great photos." He told me that Sarah was very happy with her visit, and "all's well that ends well."

I never heard which papers around the planet may have picked up the photo via Reuters. But weeks later, a UN official from Geneva was at our Ugandan dinner table and mentioned that he just received a Christmas card from Sarah, a card showing ... wait for it ... a touching scene with Sarah at the bedside of an African mother and newborn.

Apparently Downing Street thought such a thing might be good for PM Gordon Brown – sinking terribly in the polls – after all.

Then, months later, when back in my Canadian home, in the mail came a copy of New Statesman, Britain's popular current affairs weekly, with a cover story about the world's poorest women, written by Sarah, complete with ... wait for it again ... my photo of her in Mulago Hospital, splashed good and big inside.

Oh, and the photographer's credit? Somehow forgotten.

First Ladies in developing nations, while much more accessible than their counterparts in the West, also have security issues. Consider Janet Museveni, who, on Jean's invitation, just spoke at Uganda Christian University about safe motherhood. (Janet is not only wife to long-time prez. Yoweri Museveni but a Ugandan MP herself.)

The day before the big address, all media, even the staff I coordinate at the Standard, that is, Young Campus Paper, had to bring their cameras to the State House in Kampala for overnight keep and then fetch them the next day from the First Lady's security team after they arrived on our campus.

One more confirmation that a camera is a dangerous thing.

Where have all the mothers gone? 99

Kampala, Uganda
April 2008

For men, there really is no knowing what motherhood is all about. I've twice watched my wife Jean labour in childbirth. In awe. In fear. And, as a journalist who has lived in the developing world for seven years, I've had some experiences that only add to those feelings, especially the fear.

Recently, here in Uganda, a friend of ours, Alice, was delivering. Jean was out

of the country, ironically at an international conference on maternal mortality. Still, I felt good after ensuring that Alice had arrived at a clinic safely, with the gloves, buckets and cotton batting that Ugandan mothers are required to bring.

But later, Alice called me. "Mr. Thom," she screamed, in horrific pain, from her mobile phone into mine. "The baby's not coming out." In a surreal 9/11 moment where anyone can now relay his or her own death via mobile telephone, I knew Alice could be perishing in childbirth, just as 6,000 Ugandan women do every year.

She survived, as did Baby Divine. And we're thankful. But in the developing world, such is everyday experience – always somewhere on the fine line that separates life and death.

Here's another all-too typical story about another African woman, Charity, told by Jean.

> *Charity hoped for a quiet delivery, with just her mother and sister beside her in her small African hut. She would hear the roosters crowing and the dogs barking in the distance, just as she always had. The 18-year-old tried to imagine what giving birth was like, but that was difficult. People told her different things. Some women said that the discomfort was mild and the sense of fulfillment was wonderful. Others told her hair-raising tales that sent cold shudders racing down her back. Whom should she believe? There was not much time to decide. She would soon be in labour.*
>
> *The sun was setting, the crickets were chirping, and the fires around the little hut were shimmering with heat as she began to feel the early pains. No rest tonight; it would be a "night of labour." Charity called for her mother, who was overjoyed by the news. This would be her first grandchild. The generations were starting to multiply, thanks be to God!*
>
> *Her mother quickly shooed away the men and then waited patiently for labour to start in earnest. She knelt beside her daughter and laid her hand on her abdomen. "These are good tightenings, my dear child," she said. "You must be strong and deliver this baby with courage." She kissed the perspiring brow of her young daughter.*
>
> *Midnight came and went, and the contractions intensified. But the baby was not coming out. "Mother, what is the matter? I am trying to be brave. What more can I do?" Charity cried.*
>
> *"I fear your baby may be coming out buttocks first. Remember, the midwife warned about this at your last visit. She said we should go to the hospital for your delivery. I did not think that it was necessary then. The hospital will want money, and even the transportation is more money than we have."*

Charity grimaced at the next contraction, then asked, "Mother, is it too late? Can we still go to the hospital?"

"Remember your sister. The doctor said that she needed a Caesarean birth. I will never forget my last sight of her, wheeled on the stretcher towards the operating theatre through the large white swinging doors. They told me later that she died from the needle in her back that was meant to give her pain relief. I never knew if I should believe their story. The one thing I know for sure is that I brought in a living daughter and carried out a dead one. I fear the hospital and all who work there."

Still, she reluctantly placed her labouring daughter on the back of a neighbour's motorbike. The ride to the hospital, three miles away, was rough, but she braced her daughter between the driver and herself. Three silhouettes without helmets sped through the night in the direction of the small government hospital. The night watchman met them at the gate and said he would tell the midwife that they were there. The doctor's shift had ended at 5:00 p.m.

The hospital was mostly dark, and silence hung like a sheet as they hobbled to the labour area. The midwife found Charity a bed and confirmed the earlier midwife's diagnosis and her mother's fear: the baby was indeed a breech. However, it seemed to the midwife that Charity was doing okay so far. Her cervix was two centimetres dilated, with eight more to go.

Her frail mother sank into the cold steel chair just outside the room. She would not be able to deliver her grandchild herself, but perhaps this hospital visit would not be tragic, like the last one. Two more hours passed. Water from the birth sac continued to flood everywhere. Surely, Charity would deliver soon.

The new day awoke. No baby, no new life, just ongoing pain. Worse, the contractions seemed to be lessening. A new crew of midwives took charge of the labour and delivery ward. Charity was re-examined. Not much change was noted. She was only three centimetres dilated. This was not good.

The labour and delivery ward was busy. Women came and went, delivering their babies and then leaving. It was now three days since Charity had presented in early labour. She did not move much now. Her water had been broken during this entire time, which meant that she was dangerously exposed to bacterial infection, and a fever had started.

The midwife seemed relieved that Charity's labour picked up on the fourth day, and it was not long before she was nine centimetres dilated. Despite the many examinations, very little had been written on the chart that hung still at the end of her bed. Another change of shift, and another examination. She was so close to delivery, why not get the process started?

The midwife told her to start the pushing motion. She puffed up her face and gave the mightiest blow she could muster. "That's not hard enough," the midwife snapped. "Give it all you've got and then a little more."

After an hour and a half of the strongest effort Charity could muster, she delivered her newborn son's buttocks and legs. A look of panic appeared on the midwife's face. It reminded Charity of her mother's look a few days before. What was the matter? The baby was nearly out – she would give all she could to get his precious little head out.

Despite her valiant effort, the head wouldn't budge. For a long time, the dangling little body struggled, as if to wiggle out. But after four hours of partial delivery, no life was left in him. The midwife continued to pull and tug on the body. It was like a key stuck in the lock. For Charity, it was a nightmare she could not awaken from: a lifeless body trapped between her legs.

Charity was exhausted. And her heart was broken. Was there no one who could help her? The midwife was paralyzed with fear. Why didn't the doctor come?

The midwife announced, "I have made arrangements for you to be transferred to another hospital. It is a mission hospital just 10 miles away. There is a doctor there who specializes in maternity. He is called an 'obstetrician.' I will send for the ambulance."

The cloud of dust behind the old ambulance was the only thing Charity remembered from the glum ride. The twinkling stars seemed to taunt her. They drove through the whitewashed gate and entered the hospital compound. This time, things seemed a bit better. Lights flickered in the maternity ward. A midwife from the labour and delivery ward greeted them at the door and assured them that the doctor would be coming soon.

By now, Charity's mind was wandering. The face of her mother was blurred and horribly distorted. She wondered where her sister was. Shouldn't she be here? A plump Muzungu (meaning "white") doctor with glasses and white coat appeared. Charity could not understand his quiet words, but he seemed gentle and caring.

The baby's legs still lay motionless between the young mother's legs. After giving her some medication to dull the pain, he delivered the baby's head with instruments that looked like large metal spoons.

But by now, she hardly noticed what was happening. Intravenous fluids and antibiotics were pumped through the young girl's veins. But delirium was overtaking her, and she attempted to pull out the lifeline. Apart from that, she was too weak to even lift her head. Her mother, who slept on the floor on a wool blanket, began to worry that she would slip into eternal rest. She knew by the frequent visits from the nurse that things were not looking good. She dared not ask what was happening. She could only sit and pray that the night would not steal yet another life from her family.

Once again, the doctor returned. Charity was strangely still. Beads of sweat lay on her brow. The intravenous fluid continued to flow from the suspended jar. He approached the bedside and laid his hand upon Charity's chest. He waited and hoped. He reached into his pocket and withdrew his stethoscope. He laid it over young Charity's heart. Then he gently placed his instrument back into his pocket, and his hand moved slowly towards Charity's mother. He rested it on her head-covering.

Words were not needed. His eyes told her. Her daughter's life was over. Charity's mother had done all she could. She did not understand the medical term for the cause of her daughter's death: overwhelming sepsis, or infection. Perhaps she did not clearly realize that the mismanaged care at the first hospital had contributed to her death. What she did know was that safe motherhood was not a priority in her country. She had two dead daughters to prove that.

She started for her village that night. There was no telephone, so she could not call to tell her husband and son-in-law the terrible news in advance. She wondered whether they would even believe her. Charity had been working in the field just a few days ago. Well, they would have to believe her, because they would have to go and collect her body. Of one thing she was certain: intense wailing and tears would soon shatter the African night.

Of course, Charity's story – told in Jean's book *Where Have All the Mothers Gone?* – is just one of many. Most are never told.

Consider also that in a typical Canadian city, one mother dies for every 4,000 births. In the developing world, the rate can be 150 times more.

Often it's nearly impossible for women to reach a clinic. Sometimes families refuse medical care because of the cost or cultural misconceptions. One in four of these mothers simply bleed to death.

So where *have* all the mothers gone? In the 20th century, why, in fact, did more women die in childbirth than soldiers killed in either world war? Why, in the information-saturated West, haven't we heard this? Why aren't more of us outraged, especially since so many are teens?

One reason is, unlike other global tragedies such as AIDS or child hunger, this issue hasn't been given a personal face. Cheering "Rah, rah motherhood!" in fact, might be rather unpopular, cutting against pos-modern Western values of independence and freedom.

There are good news stories, too. Consider Hon. Sylvia Ssinabulya. Two of her four deliveries were breech, one with the baby's umbilical cord wrapped dangerously around its neck. "But I had a doctor for one and a midwife for the other. If not," she told me, "I could have lost my life."

Sylvia knows that the largest single issue is lack of a skilled attendant. But in places where life hangs by a thread, even that is no guarantee of a successful delivery.

She tells of her own sister-in-law. "She said she was hungry, and then she complained of stomach pain. Thirty minutes later, the midwife checked in on her and she was dead."

Sylvia, an influential MP in Uganda, is now a champion for maternal rights in her country. Recently, she was able to get maternal health into Uganda's national budget for the first time. She's also mobilized three dozen other MPs to focus on finding solutions for their country's mothers.

In the summer of 2007, Sylvia also travelled to Canada to speak with Ottawa's parliamentarians. Then she was in the UK to attend Women Deliver, the same international conference Jean was attending during that frightening delivery of our friend Alice.

How has this happened? Sylvia – and this is the good news story – has enrolled in a program in Uganda known as Save the Mothers, a groundbreaking multidisciplinary program that's open to both medical and non-medical professionals.

Students such as Sylvia represent the revolution that's possible. Indigenous leaders, such as politicians, educators, lawyers, journalists and social services professionals, learn why their women are dying and then go back into their spheres of influence to initiate broader societal change.

Jean founded Save the Mothers on this model because her experience convinced her that his was the best way to bring grassroots change. International debates often just verify problems rather than implement new solutions.

Of the program's 68 current students, four are Ugandan MPs. Another, a teacher, educates teens about the importance of avoiding pregnancy. A national newspaper journalist informs readers. Others use their vocations in radio, vital in a country with high illiteracy.

"We in the West don't have all the answers, but people in their own cultures can make it happen if they want to," notes Jean. "Even in the West, there's been change. Three generations ago, our rate of maternal death during childbirth was many times higher than now."

Save the Mothers is now planning to duplicate this approach in neighbouring countries, making the Ugandan location an international training centre.

It all may seem like a drop in the ocean. But on the long journey to create safety for the world's mothers, torchbearers like Sylvia, and supporters who give them resources, are giving hope.

I'll never forget, shortly after I got to know Jean, seeing her weep for women whom she'd never met. In fact, Jean's parents tell me she was just a little girl when she first announced her desire to "be a doctor for poor people far away." That would have been about the time my own mother died.

Today, others are being moved. One Canadian business leader supporting the work equates the human rights violations of these mothers to the slavery confronted by William Wilberforce, the British parliamentarian who, after decades of struggle, saw abolition become reality 200 years ago.

"I see Save the Mothers as a 'Wilberforcian' moment in time, and I want to be part of it," he told me.

Having observed men in developing nations, I don't think most intend to hurt or kill their wives, or sisters or daughters. Most simply don't realize how big a difference their attitudes can make. Concurrently, too many Westerners assume little can be done, because "it's just the way things are."

So, like Charity, more mothers will perish agonizingly and needlessly. But with these new voices, something new is stirring: something that we can only hope grows deep and wide, into a great force.

If so, we'll realize that even mothers on the other side of the ocean are our neighbours. And learn to take care of them as our own.

"You and I will meet again, when we're least expecting it.
One day in some far off place, I will recognize your face.
I won't say goodbye my friend, for you and I will meet again."

Tom Petty, American singer

Notes and credits

These 99 commentaries have been selected from a larger volume of published columns by the author. Most originally appeared in the *Hamilton Spectator* or the *London Free Press*. Several were first published in the national edition of *Christian Week*. The *Waterloo Region Record*, the *Yemen Times* and the *New Vision* in Uganda have also published some of them, or similar versions.

Almost all 99 are republished here as they originally appeared, but a few were merged or slightly edited, including Windows 2, 4, 15, 30, 43, 68, 88, 95 and 97. There is similar phraseology in a few columns because the same theme was written about for different publications. Window 99 is a shortened version of a piece the author originally co-wrote for the Canadian writers' anthology *Hot Apple Cider* (ISBN - 9780978496302). Window 99 also has an excerpt from *Where Have All the Mothers Gone?*, by Dr. Jean Chamberlain Froese, (ISBN - 9781553067627).

Canadian Press (CP) is the editing guide in *Ninety-Nine Windows*, including in the author's addendums. None of these addendums were previously published, except for the newspaper excerpts [*Toronto Telegram*, July, 1968] that follow Window 27.

The author changed most of the 99 title headlines from their newspaper originals.

He shot most of the photographs, including on pages 32, 39, 44, 47, 55, 80, 104, 106, 133, 137, 142, 145, 150, 157, 163, 175, 179, 187, 191, 196, 203, 211, 216, 221, 223, 229, 234, 242, 247, 257, 261, 264, 273, 283, 289, 297, 301, 321, 325, one in p. 21 grouping and three in p. 107 grouping. Most were published previously with the author's newspaper columns.

The author gratefully acknowledges other photo contributors: Dr. Jean Chamberlain Froese (p. 5, 93, 97, 115, 313, one in p. 107 grouping, two in p. 21 grouping); Gerald Chamberlain (p. 100); Peter Willems (p. 60, 69); Marcos Puig (p. 65); Reuters (p. 109, 121, 167); the *Yemen Times* (p. 128); Catherine Power (p. 182); the (Ugandan) *Monitor* (p. 239); the (Ugandan) *New Vision* (p. 254, 286); Eric Miller (p. 268), Dwight Bull (p. 306), and Charles Jones (p. 333).

Essence Publishing, in Belleville, ON, designed *Ninety-Nine Windows*.

To see more Thomas Froese photography, visit his website at www.thomasfroese.com and go to the link '99 photos.'

Thomas Froese was born in Berlin, Germany, and grew up in Canada's Niagara Region. He was a reporter at the *St. Thomas Times-Journal* before becoming an international freelance columnist. While in Sana'a, Yemen, he was a senior editor at the *Yemen Times*.

His travels have led him to write from five continents and his work has garnered numerous journalism awards. It has appeared in the *Hamilton Spectator* often, and in other publications including the *London Free Press*, *Toronto Star*, *Waterloo Region Record*, and *New Vision* in Uganda.

Froese lives with his wife, Jean, and their two children, Elizabeth and Jonathan, in Uganda most of the year. When not in Africa, the family makes its Canadian home in Hamilton, Ontario.

Front cover photos of Yemeni girl in window and young boy from Congo are by Thomas Froese. Photos of American soldier in Iraq and young Muslim student are courtesy of Reuters.

Back cover photo of woman and donkey in Kokobon, Yemen, is by Thomas Froese. Above photo of the author is by Dr. Jean Chamberlain Froese.

LaVergne, TN USA
28 September 2010
198778LV00004B/9/P

9 781554 523092